# CORPORATE INNOVATION

# CORPORATE INNOVATION:
## Marketing and Strategy

## Gordon R. Foxall

ST. MARTIN'S PRESS
New York

658.57
F 794

© Gordon Foxall 1984

First published in the United States of America in 1984

Library of Congress Cataloging in Publication Data

Foxall, G.R.
    Corporate innovation, marketing and strategy.

    Bibliography: p.
    Includes index.
    1. New products—Management.    2. Product management.
I. Title.
HD69.N4F68  1984    658.5'75    83-40096
ISBN 0-312-16995-7

# CONTENTS

# TABLES

# FIGURES

For CAMPUS

# PREFACE

Innovation is a wide-ranging subject. Its formal study cannot be confined within the bounds of a single discipline, embracing as it does aspects of economics, design, engineering, corporate policy, politics, sociology, buyer behaviour and marketing. Doubtless there are others. In concentrating upon the role of customer-oriented business strategy in the process of new product development this book touches upon a number of these perspectives but its relevance derives principally from considerations of marketing strategy. The theme which unifies its chapters is the uncertainty which pervades the development and commercialisation of new products and services in consumer and industrial markets. Much of this uncertainty reflects unavoidable ignorance of the vicissitudes of the market place, the partly unknowable strategies of innovation planned and pursued by competitors and purchasers. The investigation of corporate innovation leads to the conclusion that much uncertainty is ineradicable: despite enormous advances in the development and refinement of analytical and predictive techniques, far more new products fail than succeed.

But the book is not pessimistic. The rewards of new product success are considerable and critical study of the innovative process is likely to result in a more accurate conception of the difficulties involved and the appropriate managerial response in each case. No matter how desirable innovation may be — socially, economically, politically — new product development is first and foremost a decision for individual companies, a decision that must be taken and implemented within the context of those firms' separate and diverse opportunities, capabilities and strategic responses. The book is concerned, therefore, with the strategic need to innovate and the role of marketing-oriented management in the creation and delivery of profitable new products. From this perspective, it goes on to assess current knowledge of the other half of the innovative process, the behaviour of innovative buyers upon whom the diffusion of new products and the effectiveness of corporate innovation ultimately depend. Thereafter, the book examines the new product development process as a means of reducing uncertainty with respect to the management of innovation.

The conclusions of this analysis are uncomplicated, though their implications for marketing thought and practice could be far-reaching.

The need to accommodate the new product development process at each stage to the strategic mode of the enterprise can be expressed in terms of a simple model of strategic response to the external environment and the firm's capacity to match its innovative efforts to that environment. As a result of achieving the required accommodation, the firm ought to develop those innovations which are strategically necessary to the attainment of its overall economic objectives, though this will not necessarily lead to the radical innovation which is generally understood to be required for the achievement of the ends of macro-economic and social policies. An important question raised by the analysis is whether innovation produced in response to firms' *immediate* strategic needs is likely to fulfil even their long-term requirements. This involves consideration of the role of marketing-oriented management in the attainment of strategic accommodation; this role may well be changing in ways which have important consequences for the identification and location of the entrepreneurial function in the large-scale enterprises which currently dominate industrial economies. The later chapters which examine new product development in some detail draw closely upon the analysis contained in earlier parts, even though the themes of these earlier sections — innovation in its corporate strategic context and innovative buying — are dealt with comprehensively in their own right. Most chapters have long concluding sections which obviate the need for a repetitive restatement of the dominant conclusions in the final chapter; a little repetition in earlier chapters has been tolerated in order that the main threads of the argument are not lost as the discourse covers several subjects and themes. The concluding chapter examines anew the far-reaching relationships of corporate strategy and marketing orientation, innovation and entrepreneurship, and suggests priorities for further research.

I would like to thank two colleagues from the University of Birmingham: Professor A.L. Minkes for interesting me in the question of the locus of entrepreneurship and Dr P. Hanson for discussions of innovation in general. I am also grateful to Mrs M.A. Sheridan for typing the manuscript so well. The usual disclaimers apply.

# CORPORATE INNOVATION

# PART ONE

# EFFECTIVE INNOVATION

# 1 INTRODUCTION TO PART ONE

It is sometimes said that marketing is not and cannot be an academic subject in the same sense as the physical, natural and social sciences. Marketing's practical roots, according to this view, render any attempts at theorisation and generalisation more likely to result in useless intellectualisation rather than applicable conclusions. There is something in this. Some of the most prestigious academic journals display a preoccupation with academic matters almost to the point of excluding genuine managerial concerns. And some of the research and teaching which is conducted under the marketing banner proceeds at a level of abstraction which precludes and perhaps even discourages application.

However, the idea that marketing education must be concerned with the unadorned description of practice and that more formal research and teaching inevitably go beyond the needs of managers is too far-reaching. Indeed, the suggestion that to try to systematise marketing knowledge and to conceptualise practice in ways other than those used by managers themselves cannot be helpful is somewhat disingenuous. To speak or write about marketing at all, even to describe a single case, is to abstract from observation and experience. To describe two or more cases can hardly fail to involve systematisation and some of the elements of theorisation. Language itself is, after all, a model of reality.

Academic work of the right kind can, moreover, provide a useful foundation for practice. If nine per cent of new bridges collapsed, civil engineers would, among other things, return to the intellectual basis of their profession in order to discover reasons. In marketing, where up to ninety per cent of new products fail in the market place, precious little such foundation exists. Academic research is unlikely of itself to solve this problem — not all facets of management are currently susceptible to systematic understanding, anyway — but the absence of a body of critical knowledge of new product development must be reckoned more a disadvantage rather than an advantage.

There is, of course, no shortage of checklists for the better managment of innovation, nor of books and booklets, texts and tomes which purport to show the most appropriate ways to organise and administer the new product development process. The tendency of these writings is to offer, from a distillation of knowledge and experience, the one systematic approach to corporate innovation which guarantees success.

It would be misleading to claim that none of this work has borne commercial fruit during the last quarter century but the latest accounts of the effectiveness of the innovative process do not suggest that widespread gains are being made. Rockwell and Particelli[1] report the results of an extensive investigation of American new product marketing in the 1970s. They conclude:

> The mythical Sisyphus was condemned to push a large boulder up a mountain, only to find himself at the bottom again after almost reaching the summit. New product managers have faced a similar frustration over the past 25 years . . . Improvement in the new products management process has only helped us stay even in performance. On average we have seen no appreciable change in new product success rates during the past 25 years. Like Sisyphus, new product managers are still at the bottom of the mountain striving for the summit. Only the boulder seems to be getting larger and the mountain steeper.

These authors are speaking in terms of averages. They identify successful companies whose effectiveness in new product development improved during the last quarter century and describe in general terms the organisational and managerial differences between successful and less successful innovators. But, in the circumstances they describe, there is little point in producing yet another textbook on the marketing of new products. The current need is not for more managerial prescriptions but to understand better the innovative process. No single publication can develop full understanding of this highly-complex procedure. Innovation is a huge subject studied by economists, marketing specialists, engineers, designers, historians, and many more besides. This book concentrates, therefore, upon a small number of selected themes and issues.

There is an urgent need in studies of innovation to perceive and conceptualise the innovative process in its entirety, even though academic and managerial divisions of labour naturally make it necessary from time to time to concentrate upon a subset of the overall process. It is valuable, for instance, to remind oneself that innovation is not only a managerial activity but a facet also of customer behaviour. The effectiveness of the former is, moreover, dependent upon the latter. Only by understanding the dynamics of innovative buying in the market place is it possible to plan corporate new product development and to manage the innovative process over time by anticipating and responding to customers' changing requirements. Related to this is the very nature of innovation. Many writers on this subject habitually think in terms of large scale, radical innovations based upon major technological breakthroughs. Important as such innovation is, however, the vast majority of new product launches comprise product modifications and improvements which accommodate the basic product concept more and more closely to the wants of the market. Viewing the innovative process from an industry-wide perspective, it is clear that over time the most radical of innovations provide numerous small scale, incrementally-different new products as the plasticity of demand becomes increasingly apparent. This realisation is of importance to those individuals and groups who have explored the value of industrial innovation in the stimulation of economic growth. Innovation is so highly desired that numerous commentators and politicians now advocate that the innovative process be stimulated by means which modify or supersede the market. But established efficient companies will not produce and market new products unless it is clearly within their strategic interests to do so, unless the innovative opportunities open to them are appropriate to their strengths and requirements. Sometimes, perhaps most frequently, the strategic interests of firms are such that incremental innovation rather than radical breakthrough serve them most appropriately.

A particular issue raised by this consideration is the place of marketing-oriented management in entrepreneurship and in the formulation and implementation of corporate strategy as a whole. Marketing, innovation and strategy all involve the new product development process of the firm. This book concentrates upon that process as a series of procedures designed to gather, analyse and interpret information in order to reduce the uncertainties and risks of corporate innovation. Information is required in order that efficient and effective decisions can be made throughout the process with respect to the allocation of resources among competing projects. The formidable array of new analytical tools and decision techniques could easily give the impression that much is knowable. The reverse is true. A recurring theme, particularly in the later chapters, is that much remains unknown even at the point of launch and beyond it. Indeed, so much is unknowable that the management of innovation is essentially an art rather than a science, to which managerial judgement and entrepreneurial alertness at the level of the individual company will long continue to make essential and unique contributions.

## Note

1. Rockwell, J.R. and Particelli, M.C. 'New Product Strategy: How the Pros do it', *Industrial Marketing* (1982) p. 49. The survey covered over 13,000 new product launches by over 700 companies. Industrial product-markets comprised sixty per cent of the sample and included information technology, machinery, chemicals and textiles. The consumer goods which made up the remainder of the sample were equally-divided between durables and non-durables. The study replicates the well known investigation, *The Management of New Products* (New York: Booz, Allen and Hamilton, 1965 and 1968).

# 2  INNOVATION IN PERSPECTIVE

## The Value of Innovation

Innovation and change are highly-valued components of modern industrial societies. Often they are desired simply of themselves for the intrinsic variety and interest they afford, and thereby for their capacity to enhance the quality of life. But industrial innovation is generally valued not so much as an end in itself as for its perceived consequences. Economic innovation is frequently acknowledged in these societies as a means by which many of the benefits promised by politicians and expected by voters can be delivered. Such benefits as economic growth, full employment, consumer satisfactions, international trade surpluses and the reduction of inflation have all been attributed to increases in the quantity and quality of applied scientific knowledge in industry. Moreover, one of the most entrenched values in industrial societies is the belief that further progress in living standards, national prestige and security is guaranteed by the continued pursuit of industrial innovation. Cairncross[1] expresses thus the value of innovation:

> Perhaps we ought to remind ourselves more often that income levels have risen fourfold here and in other industrial countries in less than half a century . . . It is not because we work harder or longer that we are better off than our forefathers: hours of work are much shorter and the physical effort involved is generally a great deal less. We are better off because of the enhancement of productivity that rapid technological change has made possible.

In the same vein, Freeman[2] has argued that

> innovation is of importance not only for increasing the wealth of nations in the narrow sense of increased prosperity, but also in the more fundamental sense of enabling men to do things which have never before been done at all . . . It can mean not merely more of the same goods but a pattern of goods and services which have not previously existed except in the imagination.

That industrial innovation is a source of the benefits attributed to it is

17

not the result of commonsense observation alone. Several empirical investigations have clearly linked the exploitation of technical progress with the rate of growth of output per employee and with other indicators of economic and social wellbeing.[3] Technological advance is a wider concept than industrial innovation, of course, but it is innovation in the industrial sector which is most widely perceived as the means to highly-prized ends. While such innovation is sometimes associated with increases in structural unemployment, a case may be made for its being ultimately causative of increases in real incomes, demand for specific goods and services and higher levels of aggregate demand as a result of increases in investment, all of which stimulate economic expansion and employment.[4]

## Intervention for Innovation

So highly-valued are the goals of social and macroeconomic policies and so widespread the view that they can be quickly attained through industrial innovation that there are often calls for state intervention to increase the rate of development of new products and processes, particularly where unaided private industry is deemed to have failed. The argument that innovation can and should be so fostered is put especially strongly in those societies which have experienced relatively low rates of economic growth, relatively high unemployment and inflation and/or international payments deficits. In the United Kingdom, for instance, where one or another of these symptoms has been chronically suffered for a generation or more, there is a tendency to attribute industrial decline to falling levels of innovation and to look to governments to intervene in industry in order to reverse this trend.[5] The Advisory Council for Applied Research and Development (ACARD) which advises ministers on the use of technology has stated unequivocally that 'innovation must be at the heart of any improvement in the performance of British manufacturing industry' and has proposed that government should incorporate greater practical encouragement to innovators. National industrial strategy should, it argues, include the provision of tax incentives for investment in new industrial equipment, more support for industrial research and training and the provision of loans to small, technologically-advanced companies.[6] Similar conclusions have been reached by ACARD's counterparts in the USA, Sweden, Japan and Canada[7] and by the OECD's Committee for Scientific and Technological Policy.[8]

Such concern is certainly understandable in the cases of the UK and North America. In terms of the measures of innovative activity frequently employed in international comparisons, Britain, Canada and the USA are outperformed by countries whose macroeconomic performance has, over the years, been judged superior – Japan and West Germany, for instance.[9] The former group show a notable decline during the 1970s in research and development (R&D) expenditure as a proportion of GNP; in Japan and West Germany, that proportion increased. While the number of R&D scientists per 10,000 of the labour force increased during that decade in the UK, West Germany and Japan, it declined significantly before stabilising in the USA. Patent applications are also frequently used as indicators of underlying innovative activity: relative to those of the UK, Canada and the USA, the performance of Japan and West Germany in this respect during the 1970s suggest considerably greater innovative propensities. The North American economies are, moreover, increasingly dependent upon imported technology and this is reflected in their trade figures as technological transfer is manifested in royalty payments and licensing fees. The view is often heard that innovative activity in the UK and North America consists primarily of minor, incremental product modifications rather than the radical application of fundamental scientific advances, and that this is indicative of poorer quality.[10]

Relatively poor industrial performance appears to be both a cause and an effect of declining innovative activity: failure to innovate leads to reductions in sales levels, profits and market shares which act in turn as disincentives to investment in technical and marketing research, novel technology and new product development. Some commentators have found in this state of affairs 'a classic argument for state intervention'[11] and, while the issue of intervention is not central to later chapters, it is of interest to understand further the grounds of the interventionists' arguments for what they reveal about how corporate innovation and the process of new product development are increasingly viewed by commentators.

## Styles of Intervention

The precise form in which government assistance is appropriate remains, however, the subject of considerable uncertainty and dispute. Generally, the case for intervention in relatively decentralised economic systems is founded upon the argument that markets have failed to encourage and nurture sufficient innovation or have operated to develop products and processes which are unsuitable for the attainment of the wider social and political ends mentioned above. Interventionists differ among themselves over the extent to which they believe 'market failure' to inhibit socially-desirable innovation and over the alleged capacity of 'amended' markets to correct previous misallocations and/or prevent their recurrence. At one polar extreme are those who would retain the market system and are optimistic about the ability of the state or its agents to render markets more effective without replacing them. Carter[12] describes as 'marginalists' those among whom 'a market economy [is] seen as having many different decision-makers, reacting to situations in different ways and creating a competition of ideas; therefore government action should recognise this decentralisation of responsibility, and not seek to impose uniformity'. At the other pole are those who deny to markets any ability to foster sufficient, appropriate innovation and argue for their supersession by administrative bodies. Carter speaks of those for whom the replacement of the market system is axiomatic as 'structuralists' whose approach 'involves a plan of action, in which particular industries or technological developments are selected for preferential treatment, for instance by subsidy, by special access to finance, by government action in R&D or training, or by the establishment of new state industries'.

The case for intervention rests frequently upon a widely-accepted body of economic doctrine. Although neo-classical economic thinking which underlies so many approaches to state action celebrates the unfettered operation of competitive markets where this is consistent with the production of desired outcomes, it urges central intervention (i) to establish a general framework which encourages such operation, (ii) to supersede the market mechanism where it is unlikely to have socially-desirable consequences, and/or (iii) to provide modifications to market behaviour which do not replace markets but increase their efficacy.[13] This line of economic thinking is of general significance in establishing an intellectual foundation for 'mixed' economic systems but it enjoys specific prominence in the context of arguments for government intervention in the process of industrial innovation. Rothwell and Zegveld[14] admit that intervention runs the risk of ignoring costs and market realities but claim that it 'would be illusory to conclude that trust can always be put in the market, or that government need finance only basic research and the development of skills'. Central action may be necessary they argue for one or more of three reasons: to overcome market imperfections caused by monopoly power, entry barriers and the lengthening lead times of industrial projects; to nurture nascent industries in the face of international competition (they cite the US Government's encouragement of more general industrial innovation by means of subsidies to military and aerospatial developments); and to facilitate adjustments by firms and employees to the economic and social changes required for appropriate responses to technological progress.

Another strong line of argument is based upon estimates of substantial differences between social and private rates of return on innovative investments: private returns, it is claimed, are often insufficient to encourage new product development on a scale which would permit society as a whole to reap such rewards as high levels of employment.[15] As a result of low private rates of return on new projects, financial institutions are likely to be unwilling to lend funds and shoulder the risks involved in the development of novel ventures. At the same time, businessmen are unlikely, given the prevailing complexities of commercial life, to obtain from the market mechanism sufficient information to justify their undertaking further innovation.

Styles of actual and proposed intervention are numerous. Governments might limit their innovative policies to the training of technologists through subsidies to higher education and to the pursuit of advanced research in the universities and public sector research establishments. Rather less arms-length intervention might take the form of reductions in interest rates, extensions of patent protection, corporate tax reductions and increases in tax relief for investment in new equipment and for R&D expenditures.[16] Some authors draw attention to the inevitability of some state intervention in the economy for the foreseeable future and state agencies might, they argue, attempt to improve the quality of innovation by means of highly-selective procurement practices.[17] Governments are also inevitably in close touch with businessmen and might take this opportunity to disseminate information — about energy-saving innovations, for instance — in order to speed up the process in which new products are diffused through markets. A successful precedent for such action is available in the encouragement which governments have given to farmers to adopt new agricultural practices.[18] All of these interventions fall short of central control of industry, the administrative replacement of markets and entrepreneurial businessmen.

To summarise, the pervasiveness of arguments for state intervention, whether founded upon marginalist or structuralist reasoning, indicates the value which is attached to innovation in industrial societies. Yet these arguments are not so ubiquitous that no alternative is heard. Individuals and groups who argue for minimal state involvement in economic affairs are also intimately concerned with the establishment and maintenance of conditions which favour the flourishing of industrial entrepreneurship and innovation and their case is in fact increasingly put. Their work contains quite distinct emphases and prescriptions for the making and implementation of social and macroeconomic policy. These prescriptions do not provide for businessmen who have discretion to make decisions about innovation and investment only 'at the margin'. Rather they cast the role of the businessman in the process as unique, a *sine qua non* of economic development. As will be shown in greater detail in a later chapter, such writers as Kirzner[19] who is a member of the 'Austrian' school of economists, argue that entrepreneurial behaviour begins with an individual's discernment of an opportunity for personal gain. It follows that governments cannot guarantee to deliver effective innovation for they are far removed from the dynamics of markets and have no incentive to be as alert to opportunities for innovation as those whose livelihoods and ambitions depend upon such alertness. Governments and their members lack the possibility of direct personal gain from entrepreneurship and innovation. They are unlikely to possess the information which would enable them to select the requisite nascent industries for subsidised development; thus, since their members are not fitted to exercise entrepreneurial alertness in innovative situations, the role of governments in the process of new product development must necessarily be small.

The neoclassical approach to economic policy, with its reliance upon the competitive model of market behaviour, actually obviates the need for entrepreneurship of this kind by assuming that the decision-maker has complete knowledge of a static market situation.[20] Judged by the criteria of neoclassicism, actual markets are bound to evince imperfections and 'failures' simply because the information required for the full co-ordination of producers' and consumers' plans and actions is generally unavailable. While interventionists assume that governments are capable of succeeding where markets — and the interested individuals who compose them — have 'failed', Austrian economists stress that uncertainty and unco-ordination are endemic to markets. So-called 'market failure' is an inevitable consequence of an economic system founded upon exchange, but such failure (e.g. an overlooked opportunity to produce a new industrial process) should be temporary since new entrepreneurs with new information may come forth at any time. In any case, market failures are unlikely to be overcome by disinterested governments, lacking as they do the appropriate awareness and knowledge.[21] It is not so much that governments *should* not intervene: rather that they cannot hope to do so effectively given the nature of the innovative process and the uncertainties which surround it.[22]

**Innovation as a Corporate Activity**

The Austrian approach is closer than the neoclassical to the level of analysis undertaken by marketing research workers in that it has a definite place for the manager and begins to see the world from his point of view. But, for purposes of both macroeconomic policy and the improvement of business practice, there is a clear need to understand still more accurately the nature of the process of industrial innovation. In particular, it is desirable that the role of the individual company be better understood since any attempt at increasing the quantity and/or quality of innovative activity must be grounded upon knowledge of the causes as well as the effects of new product development. The reasons why companies undertake innovative projects, the prerequisites of effective innovation at the levels of industry and company, and the complex nature of the entire innovative process are all too easily over-looked by those writers whose perspective is innovation policy at the macroeconomic level. The adoption of so general a viewpoint also leads one to focus excessively upon the financial assistance which governments are able to provide and to overlook the non-economic aspects of successful new product development and the complex social as well as economic processes of adoption and diffusion.

There may, moreover, be good strategic reasons why firms fail to fulfil the expectations of social and economic planners and administrators who look to the private sector to produce radical innovations as a means to more diverse ends. These reasons may have little to do with the constraints of macroeconomic and social policies but much to do with the perspectives, expectations and capacities of industrial managers operating at the level of and reacting to the market place. Central innovation policies can be no more effective than micro-economic constraints and the limitations posed by their accompanying interpersonal social processes permit. The fact that industrial innovation has become so central a social value does not mean that the innovative process can be activated at will by the construction of government policies and the provision of state capital. Furthermore, not all new industrial development constitutes effective innovation − that which fulfils the needs and goals of the enterprise by fulfilling profitably the needs and goals of buyers − and industrial innovation can make no wider social contribution unless it achieves these fulfilments.

More than ever it is necessary to understand the components of the innovative process at the level of the innovators, those who produce new products and processes and those involved in accepting and using them. While the architects of macro-policies generally ignore the detailed analysis of these components of the innovative process, they remain crucially important in the analysis of strategic management and marketing and it is to these disciplines that we must turn in order to understand that process. Having done so, it may be possible to make more informed judgements of the appropriateness of particular policy objectives and strategies and to assess more precisely the effects and effectiveness of intervention. But these are not our primary concerns in the pages which follow. They are concerned with the fact that effective innovation is highly valued within the industrial system itself both by producers and consumers — and for rather different reasons from those which have thus far been considered.

## The Process of Innovation

The process of innovation links inextricably the behaviours of producers and their customers; each of those patterns of behaviour can be conceptualised as a subsystem and studied in its own right and, indeed, many who have investigated the innovative process have concentrated upon one or other of its principal parts. While this reflects a realistic and necessary division of labour, however, it can easily obscure the significance of the overall innovative system. To focus upon the development of new products within the firm may be to take the demands of the market place as given and to ignore the necessity of accommodating new product development at every point to the wants and purposes of purchasers and users. At its extreme, this perspective is embedded in the orthodox economic analysis of the firm in which what is produced equates with what is sold and bought; this simplifying assumption is legitimate in the theoretical context to which it belongs but it obscures the realities to which policy-making should be addressed when it strays into that area. Similarly, to stress the diffusion of new products through the market edits one's conception of the overall process by ignoring the managerial orientations and the strategic needs and purposes of those who develop and market innovations. Both viewpoints are prone to undue emphasis of the physical product or the service which is produced and consumed and each de-emphasises the non-product elements of the marketing mix such as marketer-dominated communications and channels of distribution.

The weakness of an edited view of the innovative process is primarily manifest in the accompanying tendency to ignore the interdependencies of producer innovators and customer innovators as well as those which link both of these groups with later buyers and users. To speak of and interpret the behaviour of any one of these groups is to make far-reaching assumptions about the behaviours of the others. Producer innovation is vitally dependent for its effectiveness upon an entire subprocess of buyer behaviour which is open to an indeterminate amount of producer influence but which is also shaped by numerous forces outside the corporate domain. Without the appropriate purchase and consumption behaviour on the part of the earliest adopters of a new product, the socio-economic procedures by which the majority of innovations are communicated to the later adopters who form the mass market would not be inaugurated and the diffusion pattern which is crucial to corporate effectiveness would not occur. For, although buyer innovators are (almost by definition) willing to purchase entirely novel items, the vast majority of the population are willing to make even a trial purchase only after the product has been extensively-used and thereby socially-legitimated by the first adopters. This social process is more obvious in the case of certain innovations than others and is perhaps more obvious of consumer products; but the adoption and diffusion of industrial products and services often follows a similar pattern. Understanding the transmission of product acceptance from one member of a social system to others is therefore a pre-requisite of comprehending the subprocess of corporate innovation and of gauging its effectiveness.

Unfortunately, the same word is employed both for the new product development process which is the responsibility of the producer organisation and for the process in which new products are accepted by customers and users: *innovation*. Similarly, the use of the term *innovator* to refer to the producers and new products *and* the earliest adopters of recently-launched products *and* the installers of new capital equipment in industry is confusing. One official definition of innovation[23] shows some recognition of the vast scope of the word:

> At one extreme, innovation can imply simple investment in new manufacturing equipment or any technical measures to improve methods of product; at the other it might mean the whole sequence of scientific research, market research, invention, development, design, tooling, first productions and marketing of a new product.

Yet even this is not sufficiently broad enough to embrace the innovative process in its entirety as does the definition provided by

Schott[24] who speaks of innovation as

> a process which is distinctive in each case and hence really defies adequate definition. It covers all that goes on from the beginning of an idea, to an invention, through to the marketing of a new product and the use of a new process. Innovation, in fact, continues until the new product or process has been completely introduced into the economy, along with any modifications and improvements. It could be said that innovation begins with an idea and ends with the widespread use of a new product and widespread new process diffusion.

## Continuity of Innovation

Attempts at defining innovation face the problem of representing with a single word a range of types of product and practice which alter over time. Innovations are not homogeneous. Some 'new' products are no more than repackaged brands; others present the customer with minor improvements or modifications to the product itself; and a few are based upon radical changes and previously-unknown benefits. Of the 13,311 new products investigated by Rockwell and Particelli[25] ten per cent were 'new to the world', 19 per cent 'new product lines', 26 per cent 'additions to existing product lines', 26 per cent 'revisions or improvements', seven per cent 'cost reductions' and 11 per cent the result of repositioning. Thus 29 per cent were new to the organisation, and approximately seventy per cent represented modifications to existing items. Although quantitative classification of degrees of innovation is probably impossible, useful categorisation of new products is not. Robertson[26] has provided a terminology for the various types of new product in terms of their differential effects upon consumption behaviour. Such new products as fluouride toothpaste, menthol cigarettes, improved craft technologies and enhanced chemical fertilisers, all of which involve relatively minor product changes and have negligible or slightly disruptive effects upon purchase and consumption behaviours, are termed *continuous* innovations. Rather more disrupted behaviour is the result of buying and using *dynamically-continuous* innovations such as electrically-powered lawn mowers, computer-aided design methods, and the substitution of agricultural tractors by rough-terrain forklift trucks. Finally, the level of disruption involved in the adoption of television and computers, video recorders and combine harvesters qualifies them as *discontinuous* innovations.

Although these categories permit only qualitative measurement, they are valuable for relating innovation to the behaviour patterns of customers rather than the perceptions of industrial managers. Relative continuity or discontinuity is inferred from changes in behaviour such as customers' verbal descriptions of their experiences with the product, observed or reported changes in their purchase, consumption and general behaviours. The categorisation of innovations in this way can lead to the more effective planning of new product management especially during the crucial introductory phase of the life cycle. For instance, the greater the degree of discontinuity perceived and experienced by users, the greater is the uncertainty which precedes initial purchase and product trial, and the greater tbe risk involved in brand switching.[27]

## Patterns of Innovation Over Time

The diversity of interdependent roles in the overall process of innovation and the differing nature of innovations over time (notably the progression from discontinuous to continuous innovations as manufacturing capabilities advance and customer tastes become more apparent) are components of a model of the innovative process which synthesises studies of product diffusion, customer decision-making and the management of the product life cycle. Abernathy and Utterback[28] observe that radical innovation (that which is discontinuous for both firms and their customers) is usually fostered by small, technically-progressive productive units (firms, plants or groups of either). At this initial stage of the process, the new project is surrounded by uncertainty since the precise requirements of the market, if any, are unknown, perhaps unknowable, and the novel technology upon which such product development is usually firmly based is largely unexplored, its full capabilities unknown and its full potential unknowable. Subsequent development of the innovation depends upon a succession of incremental changes rather than further radical breakthroughs, small product modifications which increasingly exploit the underlying technology and cater to the subtleties of demand by segmenting markets on the basis of variations in customers' requirements. As the fundamental technical and market uncertainties are gradually reduced, the incremental development of new products makes possible rapid increases in productivity and gains in general material wellbeing.[29]

The transition from the small, highly-technological, entrepreneurial unit to the established, high-volume productive unit represents a key pivotal point in the innovative process and occurs when a dominant product design becomes available. This dominant design may incorporate several previously-tried inventions and innovations in a novel configuration which delivers the benefits demanded by the mass market. Abernathy and Utterback exemplify this transition by reference to the DC-3 aeroplane which represented 'a cumulation of prior inventions. It was not the largest or fastest, or longest-range aircraft; it was the most economical large fast plane able to fly long distances. All the features which made this design so completely successful had been introduced and proven in prior aircraft.' The evolution of a dominant design for the industry enforces standardisation and permits high-volume production based upon scale economies in production (and frequently in distribution too). Whereas the productive unit responsible for the inauguration of the new product may well have been reluctant to commit its principal R&D resources, it and other units usually become willing after the emergence of the dominant industry design to assign R&D funds on a comparatively large scale in order to achieve the product changes which fulfil precisely the requirements of customers. In the case of industrial innovations, new *products* devised by small, technologically-progressive firms in the initial phase of the innovative process often become the *process* innovations adopted by large high-volume manufacturers. These authors cite numerous examples including light bulbs, transistors, motor cars, frozen vegetables, dry pet foods and canned foodstuffs which conform to the general pattern of innovation through time which they postulate: in every case the industrial or consumer innovation

came first from individuals and small organisations where research was in progress or which relied heavily upon information from users. As each project won acceptance, its productive unit increased in size and concentrated its innovation on improving manufacturing, marketing, and distribution methods which extended rather than replaced the basic technologies. The major source of the latter ideas is now each firm's own research and development organisation.

In the course of the innovative process, therefore, products and productive units undergo considerable changes. Abernathy and Utterback discuss the major productive and organisational changes experienced by the enterprise during the course of product evolution which lead eventually to its successful product-market leadership. As these corporate changes occur, accommodating the successful enterprise more and more to the technical and marketing imperatives of effective innovation, so customer behaviour alters in line with the demands of the innovative process. Howard and Moore[30] argue that when a radical innovation (i.e. a new brand in an entirely new product class) is introduced, most customers can be said to engage in 'extended problem solving', the essence of which is the comparison of the new item with products which are as similar as possible to it. In this comparatively lengthy process, which occurs during the introduction and growth stages of the product life cycle, the buyer comes to categorise and evaluate the brand according to its perceived benefits and remains rather insensitive to price. This is consistent with the typical profile of the innovative customer who is often inner-directed, relatively well-off and venturesome. During the growth stage of the product class life cycle, consumers who have already formed a strong idea of the brands in that class find it much easier to obtain the information by reference to which a comparison of brands can take place: the introduction of further, incrementally-innovative brands at this stage is therefore somewhat easier. Any benefits to be gained by switching brands can be computed by consumers.[31] At this stage, price becomes a much more important variable in the marketing mix and again this is consistent with what is known of the behaviour of non-innovators or later adopters. When a specific product design comes to dominate the industry as a result of technological refinement and the alignment of production and marketing with detailed knowledge of customers' requirements, brands become more standardised. As a result of this, customer segments based upon willingness to pay for brands of varying qualities emerge: some customers will pay more for the provision of greater benefits, while others demand a basic product at a relatively low price. In the mature phase of the product life cycle, new brands are rarely launched; consequently buyers can be expected to know all of the available brands at least sufficiently to be able to compare and evaluate them. In other words, according to Howard and Moore's argument, their decision-making is characterised by 'routinised response behaviour' based upon well-informed comparisons of brand attributes and benefits. The most important sources of different benefit are now price and availability; customers' choice processes are, accordingly, the outcome of deliberation and comparison based upon these restricted dimensions. As manufacturers use price increasingly as a competitive means of overcoming product standardisation, so customers evince little, if any, brand loyalty.[32]

The management of the enterprise requires considerable strategic awareness as the innovative process unfolds. The capacity to appreciate the need for and to implement organisational change is crucial. The appropriate organisation for the entrepreneurial production unit which is responsible for radical technological innovation is (generally) structured organically, with flexibility of interaction among members of creative teams; but the development procedures for brands which differ only slightly from their immediate predecessors are likely to become routinised and evolutionary. These conditions are classically those in which bureaucratised organisational structures develop and, as Abernathy and Utterback conclude,

> Major new products do not seem to be consistent with this pattern of incremental change. New products which require reorientation of corporate goals or production facilities tend to originate outside organisations devoted to a 'specific' production system; or, if originated within, to be rejected by them.

**New Product Development**

Clear understanding of the present stage of development of the innovative process in the requisite industry is thus of substantial strategic importance in new product development. It is much easier to detect this stage than it is, for instance, to identify the nature of the life cycle of a given brand or make; these are simply the three broadly-defined stages of (i) flexibility, when new technological developments and products based upon them are coming on stream; (ii) the emergence of the dominant product design and (iii) the proliferation of incremental innovations. New product development is a notoriously complex process, fraught with uncertainties and risks, which has been cast as essentially a series of procedures concerned with information-gathering and analysis.

*Most New Products Fail*

Although estimates of the rate at which new products fail vary considerably, depending to some extent upon what they are attempting to measure and how they go about doing so, all are high. As noted earlier, Rockwell and Particelli found that taking consumer and industrial products together, 'the success rate remains at two out of three commercialised products'. More surveys of product failure refer to consumer products than industrial goods and it is commonly accepted that up to ninety per cent of new consumer products are unsuccessful, though there are notable variations from product-market to product-market.[33] The criterion of success/failure employed in studies of innovative effectiveness is whether the product performed as well as expected by corporate management. As many as one in two products which survive test marketing subsequently prove unsuccessful. A principal of the Linsey Dale advertising agency which has been involved in numerous new consumer product launches goes further than this, declaring recently that only 25 of every 500 new product concepts prove worthy of test, one third of tested brands are nationally launched, and after ten years only *one* is likely to remain profitable.[34] Urban and Hauser[35] summarise several surveys of fact-moving consumer innovations in both the USA and UK and conclude that from 45 to 65 per cent of test marketed products fail while in test and that between 10 and 20 per cent of those which survive test marketing fail at national level. As expected, figures on failure vary considerably depending upon circumstances, but a director of Unilever[36] has stated unequivocally that 70 per cent of new food products fail at the stage of consumer reaction.

A survey of grocery product launches in Britain and the USA which was published in 1967 concluded that the number of major grocery products effectively *launched* annually was six or seven in America and two or three in Britain. The author, William Ramsay[37] who is Development Director of General Foods International, defined a major brand as one which achieved a turnover of $10m. in the USA or £1m. in Britain, arguing that the figures were comparable in the face of population differences and exchange rates. A replicative study based upon data for the 1970s and published in 1982, concluded that while the annual average number of major brand successes for the two countries as a whole was between three and seven in the 1960s, that number had become four or five during the second decade.[38] In the second survey a major brand was one with 1980 retail sales of £4m. or $30m. (Line extensions were omitted in both cases.) Ramsay's figures for the 1970s are partially summarised in Table 2.1. The most salient results are that the 43 successful major brands launched in the UK during the decade constituted 23 per cent of all grocery brands earning a turnover in excess of £4m. per annum by the end of the decade. Only 26 of the categories surveyed had product successes and 16 of these had only one success. The companies which launched three or more successful brands were also responsible for more than fifty per cent of all new products included; these five companies were 'all substantial and amongst the top

12 in Great Britain'. Twenty-five per cent of the new grocery store products launched during the decade succeeded and half were food products.[39] Comparative studies of industrial product failure are not available but several estimates suggest that three out of four such products are unsuccessful. The unpublished results from Cooper's 'New Prod' investigation of factors in industrial product success and failure suggest a more optimistic trend: 'for every 100 industrial products developed, 21.9 per cent are killed prior to introduction; 18.7 per cent fail in the market; and over 59.4 per cent are commercial (financial) successes'.[40]

Table 2.1: Major Grocery Brand Successes, 1971-80

|  | Great Britain | USA |
|---|---|---|
| Number of product classes surveyed | 84 | 62 |
| Annual average of new product launches of 'major' brand status | 4 | 5 |
| Total number of new major brands over decade | 43 | 49 |
| New launches as percentage of all major brands | 23 | *c* 25 |
| Number of product classes surveyed having no major new brand during decade | 58 | 35 |
| Number of product classes showing only one major success | 16 | 13 |

Source: Derived from Ramsay, W., 'The New Product Dilemma', *Marketing Trends* (A.C. Nielsen Co.), no. 1, (1982), pp. 4-6.

*Trends in New Product Launches*

The tendency for many companies to concentrate upon relatively safe product modifications rather than high-risk innovation based upon fundamental technological breakthroughs was noted earlier. An article in Business Week[41] observes that, while American technology is still unsurpassed,

lately there is frightening evidence that the ability of US industry to innovate — to convert ideas to commercial products and processes — is slipping. Even while potent new technology such as genetic engineering waits in the wings, the flood of new products is dwindling, and there is fear that the US may be reaching the bottom of its technological cornucopia.

The article quotes Allen H. Skaggs, director of research at the Aerospace Industries Association of America as saying that 'It is abundantly evident that US technological innovation and productivity are on the decline.' Similar statements have been made for so long about British industry that they have become commonplace. Pavitt[42] argues, for example

that, for a very long time, British industry's performance in technical innovation has on the whole been unsatisfactory in comparison with nearly all its major competitors, and that there are few signs of improvement. For Britain's economic performance and living standards to improve relative to those of other OECD countries will require — among other things — a deliberate policy to deal directly with British deficiencies in technical innovation.

Nor is the unwillingness or inability to innovate confined to high-technology industrial products. The figures presented in Table 2.2 which are based upon an examination by the Nielsen Company of recent new product launches indicate that the introduction of fast-moving consumer goods in the UK slowed down during the recessionary years between 1979 and 1981. Although food product launches continued to represent rather more than one third of the new launches surveyed, their absolute number declined from 261 in 1979 to 239 in 1981, perhaps an indication only of the peculiar economic circumstances of the period making innovation temporarily less attractive, but perhaps of a longer-term tendency of many companies to pursue much more cautious strategies of innovation. Certain companies have been criticised by retail buyers for failing to innovate more rigorously, others for producing products which lack distinctiveness.[43] At the same time retailers are making more consumer-oriented judgements of the value of new products and are refusing to stock those which offer no advantages over existing brands or which are perceived to be located in declining markets.[44]

## The Uncertainties of Innovation

In spite of the exhortation from those concerned with macroeconomic policy analyses to innovate radically, companies face an extremely complex situation where new product development is concerned. While competitive and intra-channel pressures suggest that no company can

Table 2.2: The Trend of New Product Launches

| 1979 % | 1980 % | 1981 % | Category | 1979 | 1980 | 1981 |
|---|---|---|---|---|---|---|
| 36.3 | 36.0 | 36.0 | Food products | 261 | 238 | 239 |
| 22.2 | 18.9 | 16.9 | Toiletries (inc. cosmetics) | 160 | 125 | 112 |
| 8.8 | 16.6 | 14.3 | Confectionery | 63 | 110 | 95 |
| 8.6 | 7.8 | 10.5 | Liquor | 62 | 52 | 70 |
| 7.9 | 6.6 | 7.5 | Other | 57 | 44 | 50 |
| 6.5 | 6.3 | 6.5 | Medicinal Products | 57 | 42 | 43 |
| 7.8 | 4.4 | 5.0 | Household Products | 56 | 29 | 33 |
| 0.7 | 2.3 | 2.3 | Pet Products | 5 | 15 | 15 |
| 1.1 | 1.1 | 1.0 | Tobacco Goods | 8 | 7 | 7 |

Source: A.C. Nielsen Company, 'New Products in 1981', *Nielsen Research*, no. 1 (1982), p. 11. Used by permission.

afford not to innovate, the problems of doing so successfully are increasing. If companies appear reluctant or unable to pursue major innovation, it is in part because of the risks and uncertainties they face in attempting to make decisions with respect to innovation. It is important to emphasise how far-removed is this strategic decision-making from the activity of the so-called entrepreneur in the traditional economic theory of the firm. In microeconomic analysis, the businessman is depicted as operating within a world of perfect knowledge; his need to make genuine decisions is obviated by the simplicity of the profit maximising objective attributed to him and the total predictability of the productive and sales procedures of his firm. His managerial competence is limited to the capacity to monitor costs and equate marginal quantities of each. Like the routes to the optimisation of managerial decision processes offered by contemporary 'management science', neoclassical microeconomic theory generally assumes more knowledge to be available than is the case in strategic management, the essence of which is that while rationality may be intended, it is bounded in practice by the lack of information. As Simon[45] puts it, managers are forced to *satisfice* 'because they have not the wits to *maximise*'.

Strategy involves decision-making under conditions of partial ignorance or uncertainty. The extent to which strategic planning can contribute to the stable and effective relationship between the firm and its environment depends increasingly upon the nature and dynamics of the general social and economic context within which it operates. Substantial changes are apparent in this framework over the last two decades or so. While fundamental change in the economic climate is associated with the fourfold increase in oil prices which occurred late in 1973, profound changes in the world economic order preceded the OPEC crisis. Since the 1960s the profit rates in several industrial economies have declined; inflation increased dramatically during the 1970s increasing significantly the costs of raw material and other inputs to the productive system; the exchange rate system that governed international currency transactions since 1945 was modified in the early 1970s and more countries pursue floating exchange rate policies: all have added to the hazards of business forecasting and planning.[46] In the context of corporate strategic planning, Shah and LaPlaca[47] note particularly the slower rate of economic growth, greater intensity of competition for sales, market share and profits, more complicated and unpredictable patterns of government intervention in the economy and the general difficulty of predicting the future.

These authors discuss six sources of uncertainty and areas of high risk which impinge upon strategic planning and management: marketing, competition, finance, business portfolio composition, technology and regulation, six interdependent factors which help translate the pattern of general change in the economic climate into direct corporate concerns. *Marketing-related* uncertainty derives from three problems. The first is that of adequately and accurately defining target markets since segmentation criteria are seldom foolproof. The importance of market definition lies in the need to assess market growth rates and market shares (primary inputs to portfolio analysis); market definitions ought therefore to reflect customers' perceptions of substitutable brands (i.e. brands which offer similar benefits), but producers' perceptions of industries and markets tend to predominate in practice.[48] The uncertainty which surrounds market definition contributes to the second problem of marketing-related uncertainty, that of determining the minimum level of market share required for business viability. The work of the Boston Consulting Group has led to the conclusion that most industries tend towards oligopoly in which only three or four major companies compete; firms whose market share falls below the critical threshold level of 25 per cent are thus in danger of becoming marginal. The third problem stems from unfamiliarity with markets. The further the firm proceeds along either or both of the dimensions of Ansoff's familiar growth vector[49] (leaving the safety of market penetration to seek the relatively risk-prone ends of product development, market development or diversification), the greater is the probability of failure. The need for market familiarity once more raises the demand for accurate market definition, this time in order that *relevant* strengths, weaknesses, opportunities and threats may be identified and appraised. As Shah and LaPlaca point out, Campbell, the well-known manufacturer of canned liquid soups, a field in which it possessed considerable knowledge and expertise, failed to enter the dried packaged soup market successfully despite being the first company to attempt to do so.

Uncertainties and risks which are related to *competitive* threats also present three main types of difficulty. The high growth/high technology industries which are most attractive also present strong competitive risks to new and prospective entrants because of the capacity of established manufacturers to employ price reductions as short-term tactical weapons as a result of their relatively high-volume/low cost production and marketing operations. Furthermore, such established producers are in a favourable position with regard to non-price competition based upon their experience in understanding and anticipating customers' requirements. Lastly, there is the difficulty of estimating the current phase of the product-market life cycle in order that productive capacity may be accurately planned in line with competitors' capacity and strengths. *Financial* uncertainty results from the inability to know precisely when new capacity should be brought into use: if it is employed as soon as it becomes available, the result may well be over-supply which so often brings in its wake price-cutting, margin reductions, reduced cash flows and smaller than expected profit levels. With special reference to the financing of innovation-related research and new product commercialisation there is the problem of ensuring that the company's *product/business portfolio* contains sufficient cash flows to generate the required funds. This, as will be seen, is but one of the difficulties arising from product portfolio management and its attendant uncertainties and risks. Concentration upon a single, successful product line is a common fault of small but growing and medium sized companies. An undiversified approach to the product mix offers no hedge against competitive pressures which cause margin-cutting and thus reduce revenue and profits.

Rapid *technological change* poses the constant threat of product obsolescence and the need for the firm to invest frequently in new capital equipment in order to maintain its national and international competitive positions. This has had direct consequences for companies' strategies with respect to product innovation and their capacity to act as effective innovative buyers. Finally, *government regulation*, especially product liability and other forms of consumerism, environmental pollution and the use of the promotional and pricing elements of the market mix, encroaches increasingly upon current and proposed product strategies. It is reported, for instance, that when the upper capacity of motor cycles which may be ridden under a UK provisional driving licence is reduced from 250 to 125cc, there will be a considerable swing in demand from the former capacity motor cycle which is predicted to lead to the demise of the product-market it currently serves and a corresponding increase in the popularity of smaller motor cycles and mopeds.[50]

## Conclusion

Increasing knowledge is obviously the key to reducing uncertainty; knowledge can also help reduce risk by enabling the firm to choose among available innovative options in order that those new product ideas are developed which are most compatible with the strategic position of the enterprise. Information is specifically required with respect to the identification and measurement of customers' requirements and the technological, marketing and distributive means of fulfilling them and this aspect of the innovative process within the company is dealt with more fully in Part Three which is concerned with the efficiency of the new product development process as a means of obtaining decision-related information. However, this is not the only area in which the management of innovation may be appraised and suggestions made for its improvement. The intervening chapters therefore examine corporate innovation in its strategic context and the quest to understand better innovative buyer behaviour.

## Notes

1. Cairncross, Sir Alex, 'Government and Innovation' in Worswick, G.D.N. (ed.), *Uses of Economics* (Oxford: Blackwell, 1972), p. 3.

2. Freeman, C., *The Economics of Industrial Innovation* (London: Penguin, 1974), pp. 15-16. See also the second edition published by Frances Pinter, London, 1982.

3. E.g. Schmookler, J., 'The Changing Efficiency of the American Economy', *Review of Economics and Statistics*, vol. 34, no. 3 (1952), pp. 214-31; *Invention and Economic Growth* (Cambridge, Mass.: Harvard University Press, 1966); Solow, R.M., 'Technical Change and the Aggregate Consumption Function', *Review of Economics and Statistics*, vol. 39, no. 4 (1957), pp. 312-20; Denison, E.G., *The Sources of Economic Growth in the US* (New York: Committee for Economic Development, 1960). See also: Baker, M.J., *Marketing New Industrial Products* (London: Macmillan, 1975), pp. 5-11; Gold, B., *Productivity, Technology and Capital* (Lexington, Mass.: D.C. Heath, 1979), *passim*; Mansfield, E., *The Economics of Technological Change* (London: Longmans, 1968); Parker, J.E.S., *Industrial Innovation* (London: Longmans, 1979); Pavitt, K. (ed.), *Technological Innovation and British Economic Performance* (London: Macmillan, 1980), Chapters 3 and 18; Rothwell, R. and Zegveld, W., *Industrial Innovation and Public Policy* (London: Frances Pinter, 1981), Chapters 2, 3 and 4; Schott, K., *Industrial Innovation in the United Kingdom, Canada and the United States*, (London: British-North American Committee, 1981), Chapter 2; Thurlow, L.C., 'Technological Progress and Economic Growth', *Technology Review* (March 1971), p. 45; Haeffner, E.A., 'Innovation Strategies for Industrial Corporations and for Satisfying National Needs' in Baker, M.J. (ed.), *Industrial Innovation* (London: Macmillan, 1979), pp. 125-32; Mansfield, E., 'Research and Development, Productivity and Inflation', *Science*, no. 209 (1980), pp. 1091-3.

4. Thirlwall, A.P., 'Deindustrialisation in the United Kingdom', *Lloyds Bank Review*, no. 144 (1982), pp. 22-37.

5. Knight, Sir Arthur, 'A Strategy for R&D', *Guardian*, 26 May 1981 p. 17.

6. ACARD, *Industrial Innovation* (London: HMSO, 1978); *Technological Change: Threats and Opportunities for the United Kingdom* (London: HMSO, 1979). See also ACARD, *The Applications of Semiconductor Technology*

(London: HMSO. 1978); *Joining and Assembly: The Impact of Robots and Automation* (London: HMSO, 1979); *Information Technology* (London: HMSO, 1980); *Computer Aided Design and Manufacturer* (London: HMSO, 1980); *R&D for Public Purchasing* (London: HMSO, 1980).

7. See Rothwell and Zegveld, *Industrial Innovation and Public Policy*, Chapter 5.

8. *Innovation in Small and Medium Firms* (Paris: OECD, 1982).

9. The following conclusions are based upon the figures and discussion provided by Schott in *Industrial Innovation in the United Kingdom, Canada and the United States*, Chapter 1.

10. Hayes, R.H. and Abernathy, 'Managing our Way to Economic Decline', *Harvard Business Review*, vol. 58, no. 4 (1980).

11. *Guardian*, 27 July 1981, p. 10 (Editorial: 'Not Nearly Enough for R&D').

12. Carter, C. (ed.), *Industrial Policy and Innovation* (London: Heinemann, 1981), pp. 225-33.

13. Meade, J.F., *The Intelligent Radical's Guide to Economic Policy* (London: Allen and Unwin, 1975), pp. 13-16.

14. Rothwell and Zegveld, *Industrial Innovation and Public Policy*, pp. 93-5.

15. Mansfield, E., 'Measuring the Social and Private Rates of Return or Innovation' in *Economic Effects of Space and Other Advanced Technologies* (Strasbourg: Council of Europe, 1980); Shonfield, A., 'Innovation: Does Government Have a Role?' in Carter (ed.), *Industrial Policy and Innovation*, pp. 4-20

16. Schott, K., 'The Relation Between Industrial Research and Development and Factor Demand', *Economic Journal*, vol. 88, no. 349 (1978), pp. 85-106.

17. Rothwell and Zegveld, *Industrial Innovation and Public Policy*, pp. 97-115.

18. E.g. Rogers, E.M. and Shoemaker, F.F., *Communication of Innovation* (New York: Free Press, 1971).

19. Kirzner, I.M., *Competition and Entrepreneurship* (Chicago: Chicago University Press, 1973); *Perception, Opportunity and Profit* (Chicago: Chicago University Press, 1979).

20. Minkes, A.L. and Foxall, G.R., 'Entrepreneurship, Strategy and Organisation: Individual and Organisation in the Behaviour of the Firm', *Strategic Management Journal*, vol. 1, no. 4 (1980), pp. 295-301.

21. Littlechild, S.C., *The Fallacy of the Mixed Economy* (London: Institute of Economic Affairs, 1978), Chapter 2.

22. Some of the grounds upon which the social valuation of innovation rests are in need of qualification and further investigation. For example, the simple attribution of growth in productivity to 'technological progress' which is usually operationalised in terms of the physical methods of production raises a number of methodological issues. Productivity increases may result additionally from changes in employee motivation or in working practices. See Bowey, A., 'Productivity Improvements in Engineering — Microprocessors or|Motivation?', *Transactions of the Institution of Engineers and Shipbuilders in Scotland*, vol. 124 (1980-1). Although the authors of empirical studies sometimes acknowledge this, it is often overlooked in the wider debate. The problem is especially apparent in studies in which the growth of output per employee is measured by a 'residual' method. (Here, the effects of quantifiable inputs on aggregate output having been identified, the remaining 'unexplained' growth is attributed to broadly-defined technological change.) Recent investigations by Denison using this method have raised another problem. Although the residual method indicates that technical progress and related factors accounted for over half of the increase in productivity among American employees during the period 1948-73, there is now evidence that this relationship no longer holds. Cf. Denison, E.F., *Accounting for Slower Economic Growth in the United States in the Seventies* (Washington, DC:

Brookings Institution, 1979); Schott, *Industrial Innovation* pp. 26-9. The application of new knowledge appears not to have enhanced the rate of productivity growth in the US during the 1973-6 period. Schott notes that although there is no statistical evidence for similar conclusions in the UK and Canada, the failure of these countries to sustain high levels of productivity growth suggests that similar forces may be at work.

23. Central Advisory Council for Science and Technology, *Technological Innovation in Britain* (London: HMSO, 1968).

24. Schott, *Industrial Innovation*, p. 3.

25. Rockwell and Particelli, 'New Product Strategy', p. 49.

26. Robertson, T.S., 'The Process of Innovation and the Diffusion of Innovation', *Journal of Marketing*, vol. 31, no. 1 (1967), pp. 14-19.

27. Baker has employed the same terminology in reference to the effects on producers of creating and marketing new products. (Baker, M.J., *Marketing New Industrial Products*, London: Macmillan, 1975, pp. 51-3.) Continuous innovations in *this* context are those which can be made available with relative certainty on the part of the manufacturer since they involve only 'a marginal increment in technology which, while offering some improvement over the technology it seeks to replace, is so closely related to it that informed observers can immediately and clearly perceive its relationship with the preceding "state of the art" '. From the producer's point of view, dynamically-continuous innovations involve rather greater uncertainty since they derive from technological 'steps' which may appear logical, orderly and sequential to the manufacturer but which may well prove too expensive, sophisticated or lacking in relevance as far as the market is concerned. Elaborate computer-aided manufacturing techniques are still inappropriate for some engineering companies because their managers are not yet ready to absorb their implications for working arrangements or their costs. In the consumer sphere, 'mixer' drinks such as Schweppes' *Russchian*, designed to be drunk with Vodka, presented no problem to manufacturers and even offered the benefits of manufacturing synergy since they could be produced with existing productive capacity which would otherwise have been idle. In one case, the manufacturer believed that a persuasive televisual advertising campaign which informed customers of the existence of the new mixer would be sufficient to stimulate adoption throughout large sections of the potential market. In fact, customers perceived the product as relatively discontinuous and diffusion in this case was dependent upon prior product legitimation by avant garde innovative customers. A great deal of uncertainty surrounds the manufacture and marketing of products considered discontinuous by companies; such products are usually the result of technological breakthroughs rather than quantifiable and knowable customer demand and, where they succeed, they are usually responsible for the establishment of entirely new industries such as those based upon microelectronics and biotechnology. That products which are judged *discontinuous from the consumer's point of view* need not be based upon new technology requires emphasis, however. Davidson tells of the Carnation Company whose main strengths lay in its 'excellent technology in milk-based and granular food products, together with a strong consumer franchise, through the Carnation name, for any product related to milk'. Through precise market research, it developed products which exploited this existing technology further: an instant breakfast drink, a liquid aid to slimmers, and *Coffee Mate*. See Davidson, J.H., *Offensive Marketing* (London: Penguin, 1975), pp. 129-30.

28. Abernathy, W.J. and Utterback, J.M., 'Patterns of Industrial Innovation', *Technology Review*, vol. 80 (1978), pp. 41-7. See also Utterback, J.M., 'Innovation in Industry and the Diffusion of Technology', *Science*, vol. 183 (15 February 1974), pp. 658-62.

29. The description of changes in the innovative process over time corresponds

closely to that of the concept of the *product class life cycle* which sales for an entire product class from the launch of its first constituent brand to the demise of the last.

30. Howard, J.A. and Moore, W.L., 'Changes in Consumer Behaviour Over the Product Life Cycle' in Tushman, M.L. and Moore, W.L. (ed.), *Readings in the Management of Innovation* (London: Pitman, 1982), pp. 122-30.

31. Howard, J.A., *Consumer Behaviour: Application of Theory* (New York: McGraw-Hill, 1977).

32. Ehrenberg, A.S.C., *Repeat Buying* (Amsterdam: North Holland, 1972).

33. Twiss, B.C., *Managing Technological Innovation* (London: Longmans, 1974, 1980); White, R., *Consumer Product Development* (London: Penguin, 1976).

34. Davies, B., 'High Risks, Few Winners', *Marketing*, vol. 8, no. 11 (1982), p. 54.

35. Urban, G.L. and Hauser, J.R., *Design and Marketing of New Products* (Englewood Cliffs, NJ: Prentice Hall, 1980), pp. 26-7.

36. *Guardian*, 4 May 1976.

37. Ramsay, W., 'Product Launches: The Facts', *Financial Times*, 12 April 1967.

38. Ramsay, W., 'The New Product Dilemma', *Marketing Trends*, no. 1 (1982), pp. 4-6.

39. 'New Products in 1981', *Nielsen Researcher*, no. 1 (1982), pp. 8-11.

40. Mansfield, E., Schnee, J., Wagner, S. and Hamberger, M., *Research and Innovation in the Modern Corporation* (New York: Norton, 1971). See also Cooper, R.G., 'The Components of Risk in New Product Development: Project New Prod', *R&D Management*, vol. 11, no. 2 (1981), p. 47.

41. 'A Drastic New Loss of Competitive Strength', *Business Week*, 30 June 1980.

42. Pavitt, K. (ed.), *Technical Innovation and British Economic Performance* (London: Macmillan, 1980), p. 1.

43. Kraushar, P.M., 'Grocers Take Tougher Line', *Marketing*, vol. 8, no. 11 (1982), pp. 47-51.

44. Ibid.

45. Simon, H.A., *Administrative Behaviour* (New York: Macmillan, 1961), pp. xxiv-xxv.

46. Rothwell and Zegveld, *Industrial Innovation and Public Policy*, pp. 3-11.

47. Shah, K. and LaPlaca, P., 'Assessing Risks in Strategic Planning', *Industrial Marketing Management*, vol. 10, no. 2 (1981), pp. 77-91. This section draws on the framework of Shah and LaPlaca.

48. Shah and LaPlaca, 'Assessing Risks in Strategic Planning', p. 79.

49. Ansoff, *Corporate Strategy*, pp. 97-101.

50. *Marketing*, 6 January 1982, p. 31.

# 3 STRATEGIES OF INNOVATION

## Strategic Management

The management of firms in transition from effective but small entre-preneurial enterprises to established, functionally-structured organisa-tions, and the maintenance in the latter of the capacity to innovate radically have been identified as the two most critical challenges currently facing corporate managements. The management of a single product or product class through its life cycle represents only one dimension of the strategic problem facing companies, however. Most companies are engaged in the management of several (or many) products through their respective cycles and thus with the administra-tion and integration of a number of separate strategic business units (SBUs) which, in organisational terms might be departments, plants, divisions or separate companies owned by a single parent company. The integrated management of a group of SBUs has, during the last decade or so, emerged as the prevailing strategic concept in the study and planning of multi-faceted business organisations. As Claycamp[1] writes:

> The primary task of top management is to manage the composition of the corporate portfolio of *businesses* in order to achieve the corporation's goals. Businesses are made up of product/market combinations that have different resource requirements and profit opportunities. Achievement of corporate success in the marketplace, i.e. leading market share, should lead to advantages of scale, lower costs and higher profits.

Business strategy is usually defined in terms of the relationship of the organisation with its environment. Mintzberg[2] speaks of it as 'a media-ting force' linking organisation and environment and states that 'Strategy formulation therefore involves the interpretation of the environment and the development of consistent patterns in streams of organisational decisions (strategies) to deal with it.' Central to strategic management, however, are the various resource requirements and profit opportunities of the business units managed within the overall corporate portfolio of businesses. The capacities and costs which are attributable to each of the SBUs which compose the portfolio are basic inputs in strategic planning which attempts to achieve the general objectives of the organisation in the context of its business policies. Thus, as Mintzberg[3] observes, 'managing the boundary conditions of the organisation, the managers of the strategic apex develop an understanding of its environment; and in carrying out the duties of direct supervision, they seek to tailor a strategy to its strengths and its needs, trying to maintain a pace of change that is responsive to the environment without being disruptive to the organisation'.

Corporate planners and top management therefore require information and concepts which assist them in defining and segmenting the product-markets which determine the nature and scope of SBUs, creating and delivering effective marketing mixes for each target product-market, and anticipating the actions and reactions of competitors. Thus it is with the way in which corporate resources are allocated or distributed and with the decision to invest in certain SBUs while divesting the portfolio of others that strategic management is intimately concerned. These functions involve the appraisal of internal strengths and weaknesses, the estimation of external opportunities and threats (or, at least their identification) and the adjustments necessary to ensure a satisfactory alignment of corporate resources with the market requirements suggested by analyses of demand and competition. These are the factors made explicit by Ansoff[4] in his listing of the components of corporate strategy: the definition of product-market scope appropriate to the firm's concept of its business, growth vector analysis, competitive advantage and synergy. The considerations which derive from each of these and the decisions they necessitate are directly concerned with the implications of the resource requirements and profit potential of each of the components of the corporation's product mix or business portfolio. And the allocation of resources among product-markets/SBUs involves careful prior appraisal of (i) the extent to which volume production and marketing of each *product* can be expected to make a continuing claim on corporate investment funds and (ii) the attractiveness of the *market* served by the product in terms of its likelihood of contributing to the achievement of the company's financial objectives.[5]

## Strategic Portfolio Analysis

These appraisals and the managerial decisions they prefigure are, in practice, inseparable; the assessment of internal strengths and weaknesses and of external opportunities and threats are interdependent. Threats may diminish, for instance, as strengths are identified, perhaps quantified, and better appreciated; weaknesses may be reduced through the reconceptualisation of threats and problems as opportunities. Nevertheless, it is desirable to find appropriate analytical measures to portray the dimensions of product-market structure in terms of which the various components of the business portfolio may be compared and evaluated (both by reference to one another and with regard to those of competitors). Finding suitable proxy measures of corporate capacity and industry attractiveness is no simple task, however, but an interesting attempt to operationalise these variables has been presented by the Boston Consulting Group[6] (BCG). The portfolio analysis developed by the BCG concentrates upon the positive and negative cash flows associated with businesses (or products) which are classified in terms of their relative market share and the growth rate of the industry in which they are located. High relative market share is indicative of a business which is capable of generating high levels of cash and thus indicates strong industry attractiveness. The association of high levels of cash flow with high market share derives from the expectation that the unit costs incurred in manufacturing and marketing a product vary with the level of output attained. Unit costs decrease as output expands for a number of reasons: physical economies of scale, managerial and financial economies, the generation of synergystic effects, the absorption of fixed costs by a higher level of throughput and so on. The particular source of cost reductions to which the BCG approach draws attention is independent of these, however; it is the familiar *learning effect* which refers to the tendency for experience gained in the previous exercise of a skill (as manifest in the construction of a material product, for example) to render additional practice less demanding and further production less costly per unit of output. The time required to complete a physical task in industry tends to be inversely related to the number of times the task has been performed; the learning effect which is often presented as a generalisation of this observation properly applies only to the decrease in direct-labour time in manufacturing industries, usually by a constant proportion for each doubling of output.[7] *Experience effects*, which underlie not only the BCG analysis but a number of additional managerial techniques, subsume such physical learning effects and other factors which have been mentioned as sources of reductions in the unit costs as output increases.

The observation that a company's competitive advantage, in terms of lower costs of production and/or marketing, varies proportionally with its market share was made in a series of studies known as the PIMS (Profit Implications of Marketing Strategies) investigations.[8] Since every firm in an industry may be assumed to enjoy the same potential experience effects, by virtue of its greater output and the experience effects derived from it, the firm which has the dominant market share incurs lower unit costs than those of its competitors: its executives may choose to earn higher profits than its competitors by maintaining the existing market price structure or to undermine that price structure by undercutting less fortunate rivals. In the case of the first strategy, the dominant firm's rivals are left to operate as before, though their efforts will be less profitable than those of the former; in the second strategy, the competing firms are likely to suffer immediate cash flow or productive difficulties as a result of matching the dominant firm's price reduction. BCG portfolio analysis, as noted, employs *relative* market share — i.e. the ratio of the proportion of sales the business has in a given product market compared with that of its nearest rival. A relative market share (RMS) in excess of unity implies that the firm in question is the market leader: its market share is greater than that of its closest competitor. An RMS of two indicates a market share twice as large as the next firm's, while an RMS which is less than unity implies a smaller share of the market than that attributable to the market leader. The significance of this measure for portfolio analysis and management will be further discussed below.

The second variable employed by the BCG analysis, market growth rate, derives from product life cycle analysis. Critics of the product life cycle concept point out that it is possible to construct life cycle curves only retrospectively after the product has been withdrawn or has entered the decline phase in the absence of any managerial attempt to rescue it. The attempt to locate an extant product within its life cycle inevitably involves considerable quesswork. There is, moreover, a distinct likelihood that managerial decisions based upon such forecasts will reflect exaggerated or defeatist beliefs about the prospects for future sales and cash flow: a product which appears to have reached late maturity might well be abandoned or creatively repositioned rather than modified to conform better with customers' requirements. However, while rigid adherence to product life cycle analysis can be regressive,[9] it is inevitable that marketing-oriented managers will be keenly interested in the growth prospects for the markets in which their products are sold. The growth rate for the future of the product class as a whole is more easily estimated than that for a specific brand, especially during the growth and maturity stages. A measure of annual market growth is incorporated in the BCG matrix from which Figure 3.1 is derived and is intended as a reflection of the cash requirements of the businesses located in that market since products in fast-growing markets require substantial inputs in terms of advertising expenditures, R&D investments and so on if they are to become dominant.

Figure 3.1: The Business Portfolio Vector (Based on the Boston Matrix)

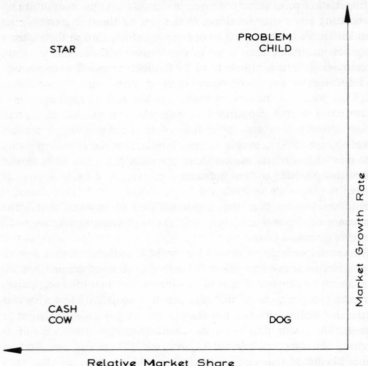

Source: Derived from Henderson, B.D., 'The Experience Curve Reviewed IV: The Growth Share Matrix or the Product Portfolio', *Perspectives*, no. 135 (Boston: The Boston Consulting Group, Inc., 1973).

## Types of Business

Before describing the four types of business (or product) which are identified in the analytical framework depicted in Figure 3.1, it may be useful to summarise the foundations of this approach to business portfolio analysis. Relative market share provides a direct indication of the contribution to net cash flow made by a given business unit: the expectation that a business will achieve market dominance increases the expectation of its being associated with lower costs and high earnings.

Market growth rate provides a measure of the probable investment requirements of the business: a fast-growing market is likely to require larger financial commitments to production, technological research and development and marketing if the products for which that business is responsible are to gain or retain a dominant market share and thus reap the benefits that derive from experience. By dividing these two dimensions it is possible to identify four types of business. The RMS dimension, which is expressed on a log scale in view of the nature of the experience curve effect, is divided at the RMS=1 point to distinguish products which have a dominant share of their markets from those which are followers. The division of the growth rate dimensions is more arbitrary; an annual growth rate of ten per cent or more denotes high growth. The four business types thus delineated are known as *problem children*, *stars*, *cash cows* and *dogs* respectively; consideration of the cash flow implications of each demonstrates the value of portfolio analysis for planning and management.

*A Problem Child* is a product, product line or business unit which enjoys a position in a growth market but suffers because this is not a dominant position. The responsible SBU is thus forced to support it heavily with investment funds while bearing relatively high unit costs of production and distribution. New products in particular begin life as problem children and imitative continuous innovations are likely to remain in this position making very substantial financial demands on the corporation. As long as such new products are responsible for large negative cash flows, the danger remains that they will fail to develop into stars and, ultimately, into cash cows. The key strategic decision with respect to these questionable products (the term 'question mark' is sometimes substituted for 'problem child') is when to abort their slow development, cease the heavy flow of funds and eliminate them from the product portfolio. To do so too early is to forego entirely returns on the investments made and to lose a possible star.

*A Star* has a dominant share of a relatively fast-growing market. In spite of its strategically-advantageous position, however, its net contribution to cash flow is low since the investment requirements of such a product-market combination are so high as to offset the comparative advantage afforded by the favourable experience effects attributable to high levels of manufacturing and marketing. Although there is a temptation to reduce these investments in order to gain immediate cash flow benefits from a star, this often proves to be a myopic strategy since the long term possibility that the product will develop into a lucrative cash cow is jeopardised. As Jain comments:[10]

> The ultimate value of any product or service is reflected in the stream of cash it generates net of its own reinvestment. For a star, this stream of cash is in the future, sometimes the distant future, and to obtain real value, the stream of cash must be discounted back to the present at a rate equal to the return on alternative opportunities. It is the future payoff of the star that counts, not the presented reported profit.

If the star shows strong intentions of becoming a cash cow, that is.

*Cash Cows* also enjoy dominant positions within their markets but those markets exhibit relatively low growth. As a result, the investment commitment they require is low and they can be 'milked' of the high cash contributions they earn as a consequence of the high experience effects attributable to their manufacture and marketing. Cash cows not only pay for themselves but provide the funds for investment in new projects upon which the future survival and growth of the organisation depends. Diversification programmes and the development of radical innovations rely heavily upon the funds provided by cash cows.

Cash cows are among the products or businesses which strategic management has decided should be 'harvested' (to mix agricultural metaphors) but this does not mean that their management (especially their marketing) does not demand the highest level of executive commitment. The stagnant markets in which cash cows are located often feature strong competition and both promotional (competitive) action designed to maintain market share and innovative (strategic) action may be required in order to ensure that the required levels of cash flow are maintained from cash cows. If cash cows are to play their required role in the portfolio, i.e. the generation of sufficient cash to support other projects, they require careful attention within the overall marketing strategy and customer policy of the corporation. As Cotton[11] writes:

> Harvest brands should concentrate on existing users and existing uses. The conventional wisdom is that penetration determines brand size and that the main marketing thrust should therefore be to increase awareness and penetration. This is appropriate for new or growth products but, for harvest products, the emphasis should be

on maintaining penetration and increasing frequency of use. Successful harvesting usually reinforces existing uses or finds a niche by focussing on very particular uses, as Fairy Household Soap did when moving from being an all-purpose product to being the answer to grimy collars and cuffs.

The task of maintaining cash cows is essentially that of ensuring the effectiveness of any product, making sure that its attributes continue to deliver the benefits demanded by buyers, and this hinges upon the development and exploitation of an appropriate market mix. Given that integrated marketing management in these circumstances involves both competitive reactions and product innovation, the problem of co-ordinating the marketing mix is immense. Since each marketing mix presented by the firm has implications for other mixes it presents (see below), the problem of integration is multi-dimensional. Cotton continues by pointing out that

> This kind of analysis points towards multiple packaging and pricing and promotion strategies aimed at intended uses and current users. It does not necessarily involve withdrawal from advertising. 'Reminder' advertising may be fundamentally important, as can the kind of advertising which revives powerful properties, frequently associated with a brand's origin; the return by Cadbury to its campaign featuring thick chocolate and 'a glass and a half of milk' is a good example.

The same fundamental thinking applies equally to industrial products and services, even though, as Carman and Langeard[12] note, there are subtle differences in the strategic analysis and management which are applicable to services as opposed to physical products.

*Dogs* are products or businesses which occupy weak competitive positions in markets which evince only slow growth. The net contribution of such products to cash flow is zero or even negative and, except in unusual circumstances, the strategic need is to eliminate such products or businesses. Such circumstances are not necessarily infrequent; it may, for example, be necessary to retain a dog in the product portfolio as a loss leader or as a complementary product to a star or cash cow. The effectiveness of the overall portfolio, whose elements may be bound together by all manner of synergystic effects which impinge upon customer choice and usage, is the supreme factor.

*Strategic Portfolio Management*

The number of companies reported to use planning techniques based upon the BCG approach and alternatives which are akin to it now runs into several hundreds.[13] Their popularity derives in part from the provision of categories by which the present positions of SBUs can be identified, measured and analysed and suggestions of patterns of life cycle management which allow objectives to be formulated, their feasibility assessed and strategic programmes for their attainment devised. The essential features of corporate strategic planning and the basis for strategic management are made available; above all managers are attracted by the operational measures of corporate capacity and industry attractiveness, factors which are absent from so many business policy prescriptions. Strengths, weaknesses, opportunities and threats can be located, quantified and amalgamated into generic measures of the key internal and external ingredients of strategic decision-making. Scenarios for future growth can be formulated and compared in standard terms and competitors' positions can also be mapped on the same basis.

The most desirable sequence for the progress of businesses or products follows that of the classic product life cycle: from *problem child* to *star* to *cash cow* (introduction, growth and maturity) and, if unavoidable, to *dog*. If this is the intended route, the status of business units and the products for which they are responsible can be determined and strategic decisions with respect to investment and divestment made accordingly. Those which appear to be following an undesired sequence — from *cash cow* to *dog*, from *star* to *problem child*, from *problem child* to *dog* — require very serious attention. The likelihood of achieving the desired sequence and that of avoiding the undesirable routes are increased if portfolio planning is directed towards the attainment of balance in the strategic configuration of businesses or products. A balanced portfolio would typically contain two or three cash cows, generating the relatively high positive cash flows upon which business development depends, one or two stars which are moving towards cow status, several problem children *en route* for stardom, and perhaps a small number of dogs. As long as clearcut decisions with respect to the dogs have been or are capable of being made, they should not unbalance the portfolio. A genuinely unbalanced portfolio is typified by the following: a single cash cow, no star to take its place, numerous dogs and a small number of problem children located towards the right hand pole of the RMS dimension. The creation and maintenance of a balanced portfolio requires determination and courage;

courage is required most resolutely in the elimination of products, the deliberate withdrawal or planned obsolescence of products which are not contributing adequately to the overall profitability or cash generation of the portfolio.[14] An example of deliberate elimination is provided by the Cadbury chocolate and confectionary group which has continued to introduce new chocolate bars while consistently withdrawing products such as *Tiffin* and *Old Jamaica* during the 1980-2 period. The benefits of reduced unit costs made possible by volume production of the remaining brands were partly responsible for the increase in the group's profit in 1981 which exceeded the 1980 total by some £20m, an increase of about one third.[15]

Portfolio planning and analysis are not without their faults, however. While they were enthusiastically welcomed some years ago, it is now more fashionable in the management literature to criticise them and emphasise their shortcomings. The most realistic interpretation is no doubt that they have settled into the repertoire of managerial techniques and that the tendency to criticise them is a natural development as their limitations are realised, just as the tendency to seize upon new approaches to management as though they represented the strategic panacea appears to be a natural part of management education, consultancy and practice. It is necessary to point out, however, that the variables incorporated in the BCG approach are not universally applicable proxy measures of corporate capacity or industry attractiveness; nor are they unambiguous and independent in every instance. Day[16] notes that the BCG analysis ignores elements of the firm's competitive environment such as barriers to industrial entry, legal and political constraints, demand elasticity and cyclicality. Furthermore, cash flows do not always adhere to one of the four postulated patterns; nor are experience effects necessarily constant or predictable in the face of technological innovations available either to one's own company or to one's competitors. Learning phenomena cannot be indefinitely exploited; indeed, considerable managerial ingenuity and flexibility are required in order to continue to derive experience effects throughout their feasible range. There are, moreover, notorious difficulties involved in the definition and measurement of market share and market growth rate.[17] The assumptions that products located in high growth markets require greater investment than those in slower markets and that cash flow varies with market share are not ubiquitously valid. The problems of defining markets, arriving at accurate (or even useable) estimates of target market growth rates and the possibility, mentioned already, of a synergystic relationship between stars and dogs which impedes or at least complicates the elimination of the latter remain.[18] Furthermore, despite the conceptual and practical promise of portfolio planning, its effective use, even where it is directly relevant and applicable, rests heavily upon managerial judgement with respect to the appropriate levels of investment required in each target market, the assessment of *future* as well as past rates of growth, balancing the mix of SBUs and integrating marketing mix management. It is a diagnostic tool which indicates, at best, the direction of necessary change but which cannot take the place of managerial judgement and decision-making any more than can any analytical method.

*Alternative Approaches*

Two other approaches to portfolio analysis and planning, developed in industry partly in response to the difficulties mentioned above, also serve to illustrate the strategic problems involved in product management and innovation and thus deserve brief mention. Both rely upon measures of return on investment as indicators of industry attractiveness rather than cash flows as indicated by market growth rate and market share indices (the BCG criteria). The Business Assessment Array (BAA) approach employed by the General Electric Company (USA), is illustrated in essence in Figure 3.2. (Business postures are usually shown as discrete areas: since the purpose of this discussion is to illustrate the corporate strategic problem rather than to advocate specific solutions, continua have been used in Figures 3.1, 3.2 and 3.3 to avoid the suggestion made by the arbitrary cut-off points that SBUs and products can be neatly categorised and decision-making with respect to strategic options simplified.) The summary variables employed in this mode of analysis are labelled Business Strengths and Industry Attractiveness but these are not unidimensional measures: each represents the weighted sum of a range of relevant factors which have hitherto included: (for *industry attractiveness* – market size, market growth, market diversity, competition, vulnerability to inflation, cyclicality of demand, customer finances, energy impact and international scope); and (for *business strengths* – size, growth, relative market share, profitability, profit margins, technological advantage, product quality, image, personnel, vertical integration and productivity).

Businesses or products are shown in Figure 3.2 as circles whose radii are proportional to their sales. The nine categories of business posture indicate the desired strategy *ceteris paribus*. Broadly, the three postures in the top left area of the figure (1, 2 and 4) suggest that high levels of investment be made available either to maintain the present position of the SBU or product (say, in the face of growing competition) or to grow by achieving a better match between company capabilities and market opportunities. The three diagonal postures (3, 5 and 7) indicate selective investment allocation in order that returns from all of the products involved may reach overall balance. In the lower right area of the figure, businesses which require elimination are shown. As in any

Figure 3.2: The Business Assessment Vector

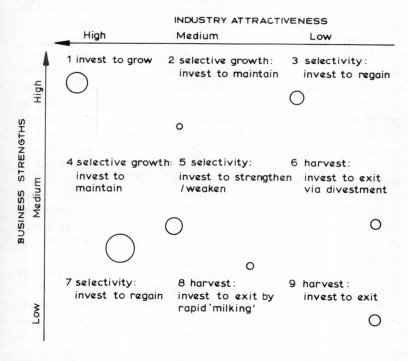

Source: Derived from *Maintaining Strategies for the Future Through Current Crisis* (Fairfield, Connecticut: General Electric Company, 1975).

other portfolio approach, the comparison within a single framework of products operating in a variety of markets, whose performance can properly be evaluated only in terms of the characteristics of their unique produce-market circumstances, remains problematic. But the BAA approach with its weighting of the relevant factors attempts to reduce the biases inherent in unidimensional measures of internal and external elements. The third approach to SBU assessment and the

formulation of product strategy has been employed in the UK and elsewhere in Europe by the Shell Chemical Company. Like the BAA
approach its 'directional policy matrix' (illustrated in essence in Figure
3.3) employs multi-factorial measures of industry attractiveness (labelled 'business sector prospects') and business strengths (the 'company's
competitive capabilities') and indicates the requisite strategies.

Figure 3.3: The Directional Policy Vector

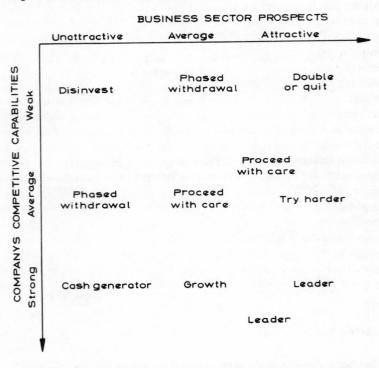

Source: Derived from Robinson, S.J.Q., Hichens, R.E. and Wade, D.P., 'The
Directional Policy Matrix: tool for strategic planning', *Long Range Planning*,
vol. 11, no. 3 (1978), pp. 8-15

Analytical frameworks for the appraisal and planning of business
strategies such as those which have been outlined here are attractive
in view of the corporate need for means by which uncertainty may be
reduced by the specification of probable outcomes and the more
accurate assessment of risks. Like the BCG matrix, the frameworks

constructed by General Electric and Shell are not without drawbacks. Managerial judgement is still essential in the classification of businesses as attractive or unattractive, in the determination of what constitutes a balanced and what an unbalanced portfolio, the extent to which unattractive business units or products should be tolerated because of their assumed symbiotic interactions with more attractive units or products, and so on.[19] Above all, in common with most extrapolative forecasting and planning techniques, strategic business analysis depends upon *ex post* judgements of business status and performances as bases for decision-making with respect to the future. The result is that strategic choice, corporate decision-making under conditions of uncertainty, remains inescapable. Ironically, portfolio methods of analysis exemplify but do not remove the strategic problem. They have been presented here not by virtue of their capacity to solve the strategic problem outright but precisely because their widespread use indicates that many company managers are seeking strategic planning tools which promise to help in the assessment of business capacities and environmental attractiveness (and, therefore, that the tenor of this chapter is justified) and because their drawbacks illustrate graphically the difficulties inherent in that assessment. However, there is one important respect in which business portfolio planning underestimates the complexities of new product development: it fails to incorporate adequately the realities of marketing a multiplicity of products. Multiproduct marketing involves the attempt to influence sales not simply through the agency of the products themselves but by means of an array of interrelated marketing mixes. We propose to term this array the firm's Marketing Portfolio.

## Marketing Portfolio Analysis

A balanced product portfolio represents a unique match of business capabilities and market opportunities. To rearrange that mix by the introduction of a new product requires a deliberate innovation policy and appropriate strategic awareness and capacity for action. The more reactive strategies can be expected to result in relatively continuous innovations, while proactive businesses may have more flexibility and scope for stealing competitive leads by producing discontinuous new products which impinge to a far greater extent upon customers' behaviour. Strategy is, moreover, dynamic: as companies grow, for instance, they often adopt a more assertive approach to new product development which transforms the nature of at least some of their constituent business units from reactive to proactive. Attention has been drawn in this chapter to the recent development of business portfolio analysis which addresses the fundamental strategic problems which companies face: how to allocate internal resources among the components of the current product mix and new ventures that may justify investment. According to this framework of analysis and planning, the selection of new product ideas for development depends upon matching their probable financial contribution and demands for resource inputs which they are likely to make upon the business. Portfolio analysis improves upon more simplistic methods of business planning by stressing the need to manage harmoniously the overall entity composed by businesses or products which are the basic units of analysis rather than striving to administer each component of the portfolio separately.

The portfolio concept nevertheless tends to simplify the reality behind the management of the component businesses or products by portraying them monolithically as tangible discrete and self-contained structures when in fact they comprise multi-dimensional marketing mixes. Customers certainly purchase the benefits which are generated in the uses to which they put the products or services they consume but their purchases and consumption behaviours are affected by wider considerations – for instance, corporate image, marketing communications effects, reputation, distribution and availability, value for money, status symbolism, and so on. The responsibility of business management is thus not confined to the supply of discrete and homogeneous products but encompasses in addition their whole amorphous accompaniment, the non-product elements of the marketing mix and the joint effects they create. The *ultimate* components of the portfolio which top executives manage are not, therefore, businesses or products (and still less 'product/market combinations'). They are the various marketing mixes which the company presents to its customers and prospective customers. The true strategic task is the management of this array of marketing mixes as a unified whole which contributes effectively to the economic objectives of the enterprise. This is a more onerous job than the integrated planning and administration of a series of related but essentially separate products or businesses which are conceived as uni-dimensional, difficult as that alone would be.

The task of managing effectively the collection of marketing mixes which constitute the *Marketing Portfolio* involves the co-ordinated use of a group of interactive mix elements, each of which contains numerous components which impinge upon and have consequences for the others, in such a way as to encourage that pattern of customer behaviour through which corporate needs are fulfilled. This requires the synergystic interaction of each of the interdependent marketing mixes with the rest and of their various sub-components (*price* might, for example, include credit facilities, net or non-net agreements, customer discounts) so that they harmonise with and mutually reinforce one another. Corporate image and reputation and the level of customer service provided by the firm communicate to buyers something over and above the elements of the marketing mix with the result that any marketing offering is greater than the sum of its parts. Thus it is possible that two identical mixes offered by different businesses, each accompanied by a unique customer image, convey quite distinct meanings to potential purchasers. Figure 3.4 hints at the demands made upon the planners and administrators of multi-marketing mix companies.

Not only must the price of product *a* be integrated with the other elements of the marketing mix A: this use of price must be integrated with the use of price throughout the marketing portfolio. The same is true of the elements of the marketing mixes that surround and incorporate products *b* and *c* and of any innovative products which are subsequently added to this portfolio. There is, for instance, little point in a firm which has employed price to reflect high levels of product quality launching a new item at so low a price as to be incongruous with the name, image and reputation previously built up. (It might, however, launch a distinctive portfolio of marketing mixes based upon lower prices and/or less high quality distribution outlets; the links, if any, with the existing portfolio would then have to be carefully considered and decisions with respect to the development of novel brand names and images would follow.)

The task represented by the need to plan and manage a dynamic marketing portfolio in an integrated and profitable manner is part of the complex reality of the multi-product business. It cannot be escaped and the optimisation techniques of 'management science' can do no more than ameliorate slightly the problem it poses for those who are responsible for the asssessment of the internal and external business environments, the investment in marketing mixes which contribute collectively to corporate needs and the elimination of those which make no such contribution even as loss-leaders. While effective marketing portfolio management cannot be ignored, however, the difficulty it poses can be reduced if innovation strategy is considered and planned in relation to the general strategic mode pursued by the company, and designed to reduce the particular uncertainties it poses.

Figure 3.4: The Marketing Portfolio

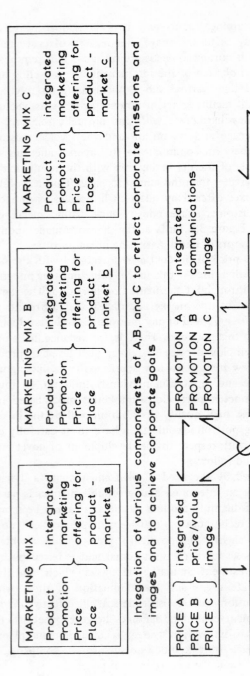

Integation of various componenets of A,B, and C to reflect corporate missions and images and to achieve corporate goals

## The Strategic Need to Innovate

Companies face these uncertainties in differing combinations and managerial perceptions of the salience of the problems which face them vary from company to company. Just as the contexts within which strategic management and innovation occur are far from homogeneous, so the outcomes of these processes show distinct differences as they reflect diversity of concerns and objectives. An overriding determinant of the strategic need to innovate and of the mode of innovation adopted by companies is the extent to which economic conditions, notably market structures, encourage and alert general and functional managements to adopt a marketing- or customer-oriented philosophy which reflects accurately the attractiveness of innovative products *to their customers and potential customers*. It follows from the strategic analysis considered above that the rate and method of innovation pursued by a company derive from its managers' perceptions of the viability of attempting to benefit from the market opportunities they believe to be available and of the comparative advantages and innovative capacities they believe the company offers. Part of these perceptions depends upon the need managers feel to pursue a marketing-oriented style of management. Marketing-orientation is not an isolated virtue which some managers happen to possess and which manifests itself in an altruistic, customer-directed approach to business: it is an approach to business management which is enjoined upon companies which confront a special set of productive and marketing factors. Notably, such marketing-oriented management is essential − if the business is to survive and prosper − when (i) supply of the product in question, by an industry which comprises two or more serious competitors, exceeds or is capable of exceeding demand, and (ii) when customers' discretionary income, time and mobility are relatively great. The degree and kind of marketing-orientation shown by a given company depends, therefore, upon the demands of its customers and the capability of its competitors to supply them efficiently.[20] A continuing task of innovative strategy is thus the *matching* of the firm's competitive, marketing-oriented response to the desires and demands of customers for new products. Where the demand for innovation is strong on the part of customers, the appropriate strategic response naturally demands the creation of novelty; but there is no strategic logic in the pursuit of so high a rate of innovative development that new products are always produced more frequently than the market demands of competitors can supply. Failure to be as innovative as technology and productive ability permits is not necessarily a sign of production-orientation, especially when customers and competitors permit a slower rate of development. Effective corporate strategy reflects this.

## Strategic Options

The judgement of market requirements and the estimation of competing firms' capacity and willingness to supply them are, of course, huge tasks but there are in any case limited strategic options available to most companies to respond to their judgements and estimates. Broadly-speaking, the alert management team has two choices: it may, in response to its strategic analyses of the marketplace and its position in it, select an essentially *reactive* approach, waiting for customer demands to become clear and responding subsequently to their fulfilment, or a *proactive* strategy which requires the active forecasting and anticipation of customer requirements. Within each of these broad strategies there exists a range of positions. Urban and Hauser[21] describe four variants of reactive strategy — defensive, imitative, second-but-better and responsive — and four kinds of proactive strategy — research and development, marketing-based, entrepreneurial and acquisitive. Each of these may be appropriate to a particular business, depending upon its internal abilities and the externally-imposed need to be marketing-orientated. Further, the same organisation may, over time, adopt differing strategic modes as internal and external circumstances alter, as different stages in the product class life cycle are entered or as different segmental product-markets are entered. However, while any business may be vulnerable to the six sources of uncertainty and risk described in Chapter 2 at some time, each of these broad strategies emphasises particular sources of danger. When different SBUs are pursuing alternative policies, the overall strategic management task becomes the more complicated not only in determining the distribution of resources among them but in assessing overall risks.

## Reactive Strategies

Of the reactive strategies, the defensive, imitative and second-but-better all represent direct responses to competitive actions and only indirect reactions to customers' behaviour and needs. The defensive approach involves modifying existing products in such a way as to ward off competitors' incursions: a number of detergent manufacturers, taken somewhat by surprise when 'biological' washing powders were introduced through strong televisual advertising which stressed the innovations' effectiveness in removing stains, responded by a promotional campaign which emphasised their existing products' ability to remove all known stains and so obtained breathing space to develop their own 'biological' powders. Their longer-term strategy was proactive but in the short-term they were forced into a defensive posture. Defensiveness is usually a short-term tactic rather than a long-term strategic mode and, as such, it may be used from time to time by even the most customer-oriented businesses since few can avoid being overtaken by competitive events at some time. Imitative businesses employ reaction as a general response, imitating competitors' products as soon as they become available. 'This . . . "me too" strategy is common practice in the fashion and design industries for clothes, furniture and small appliances.'[22] Imitation provides a sound strategy of concentrated marketing when the business has the resources and capabilities necessary to mass produce quickly products for which there is heavy demand from segments which are not catered for by the original designers and/or producers. The instant copying of dresses worn at celebrity weddings is an example. When customer interest and economic demand cannot be so easily and accurately gauged, however, a 'second-but-better' strategy affords greater security because the imitative firm enjoys whatever benefits are to be derived from the prescience of the originator who bears in full the initial costs of research, market development and commercialisation together with the basic risks. As a result, much of the uncertainty of new product development is removed for the second-to-market firm. It is essential, nonetheless, that the second-but-better product offers distinct advantages over the original which may enjoy considerable customer awareness, familiarity and acceptance by the time the derived products appears. Timing is, therefore, crucial to success. Many second-but-better firms have only one opportunity, because of their limited resources, to enter the market; to do so too early runs the risk that a dominant design will emerge subsequently and that most manufacturers will be in a position to supply the mass market while the premature product is quickly perceived by customers as outmoded; to wait too long, however, runs the risk that customers will have come to trust the original product and company. This is especially salient in the case of many industrial markets where buyers are likely to require substantial inducements in terms of product superiority and performance to switch to a second-comer. In consumer markets, a number of retail chains take advantage of manufacturers' product and market development efforts by bringing out their own brands of products which range from convenience foods to anti-freeze. By employing an area of the marketing mix in which they have preeminence, i.e. widespread distribution, and possibly by adding price or quality premia, the retailers avoid the high costs involved in the design and creation of the other elements of an integrated mix (notably the product itself and initial advertising and promotion).[23]

But second-but-better does entail an alertness to market factors which is missing in those companies which attempt to survive and prosper by means of extended defensiveness. Both imitation and second-but-better may require detailed market intelligence and the entrepreneurial insight to detect unfulfilled customer wants. Indeed, far from suggesting moribund production-orientation, reactive strategies generally may be adopted and successfully exploited by companies which are being *as marketing-oriented as they need to be*, given their environments and strengths. The skilful accommodation of their resource bases to their market requirements via the efforts of their competitors may represent sound customer-oriented management. The chief ingredient of any strategy which depends upon the revealed actions of competitors is, nevertheless, the capacity to make realistic judgements of rivals' abilities. In a world where most new products fail to live up to expectations, reactive strategies of this kind pose several strategic problems. Competitors may themselves fail to produce a product which is worth imitating; they may gain scale advantages due to experience effects which preempt profitable pursuit by reactors; their marketing process may outstrip that of their imitators because of its being based upon more comprehensive and relevant marketing research than that of second-to-enter firms; and their size, highly-differentiated marketing base and generally proactive stance may enable them to take advantage of technological leaps which their reactive followers cannot match. They may also ward off reactive threats by the use of aggressive marketing tactics like price-cutting. Most significantly, however, in view of the earlier discussion, reactive firms are allowing their business portfolios to be determined entirely by their competitors who may, for instance, be capable of tolerating a new product which quickly becomes a dog or which remains a problem child for longer than expected because they have the cash cows to do so; reactive firms are seldom in so favoured a position.

Responsive strategies actually stand at the centre of the reactive-proactive continuum. They represent a direct reaction to customers' requirements and are especially apparent among those industrial companies which develop products suggested by their customers. In some cases, user-companies have gone as far as conceptualising a product of process for their own use, building a prototype and conducting in-house tests before approaching a manufacturer who commercialises the item.[24] This tendency will be further considered in Chapter 9.

The responsive strategy is subject to some of the uncertainties and risks associated with purely reactive approaches to new product development. It is especially the case that the responsive business's portfolio is externally-determined and the organisations or other customers which originate the innovative process may have a peculiar need for the product they invent which is not generalisable and thus not a secure basis for widespread commercialisation. Unless the originator of the product or idea is sufficiently large a user to justify adequate sales on its own account, the responsive firm must carry out its own investigations of the generic demand pattern before it incurs further development expense. The wisdom of the responsive strategy is that, when customer-originators are reliable and willing to co-operate in developmental work, costs and uncertainties of both development and market acceptance are relatively low. The risks which do feature in this strategy — primarily financial and technological in kind — support the argument that innovative responsiveness is a strategy which is most suitable for small, flexible jobbing firms or for business units which constitute part of a larger company whose main strengths lie in proactive strategies. While some companies or SBUs make a habit of innovative responsiveness, this is not a strategy by which all can live. Responsiveness is a necessary strategic mode for companies which have the internal capacity to benefit from customers' ideas; even if it is employed only from time to time as opportunities arise, it requires constant managerial alertness, but it is unlikely of itself to offer long term growth prospects for the majority of businesses.

## Proactive Strategies

Distinct types of proactive strategy are less easily distinguished. Large business organisations in particular tend to rely upon heavy R&D expenditures, well-executed marketing-oriented management, risk-seeking entrepreneurship and may undertake innovation by means of acquisitions when speed of entry and market conditions dictate that overall supply should not be increased (since this would depress prices). Proactive strategies require a balanced approach which incorporates all of these strengths in the aggressive initiation of product development programmes and the launch and nurturing of effective innovations. All proactive strategies attract high levels of financial uncertainty and risk; strongly customer-oriented entrepreneurial and acquisitive approaches are also likely to attract governmental regulation since they may impinge upon consumer protection, environmental pollution and antitrust issues.

The outgoing nature of proactive strategy means that the resulting innovations are frequently (though not universally) discontinuous or at least provide the customer with demanded benefits that are not made available by existing models or brands. This is true in both industrial and financial markets. The UK market for agricultural tractors was severely hit by recession during the late 1970s and early 1980s (as was that of much of the world);[25] this recession and the competitive reaction which accompanied it resulted in Ford's market share falling from over 31 per cent to just over 25 per cent in the four years to 1981. Ford used extensive marketing research before tailoring its Series 10 range of tractors, which took five years and $100m to develop, to British farmers' expressed requirements in an effort to outperform its competitors. 'What the research showed above all was a demand for more power, and as a result the new tractors develop a near 10 per cent increase in output compared with their predecessors, while at the same time offering a 6 per cent improvement in fuel economy. All the models now have synchromesh gears, with transmission systems that provide up to 16 forward and eight reverse gears and with four-wheel drive available as an option on all the bigger machines. There are lots of improvements too which make the tractors easier to use and more comfortable and convenient for the farmer.'[26] Many of the inventions and innovations incorporated in the new range are incremental; indeed, Ford specifically ruled out radical change on this occasion (during the 1960s its market share had been severely reduced after the introduction of automatic gearboxes). The evolutionary changes involved suggest that the dominant design for the product was available and that the innovative process was now dominated by technological changes firmly governed by customers' actual requirements.

Similar proactive but (from the producer's point of view) relatively continuous innovation is apparent in the development of many consumer products. Product modifications which are, at most, dynamically-continuous from the manufacturing stance succeed in consumer markets only if the buyer perceives them to offer distinct benefits. The marketing vice-presidence of the Mennen Company,[27] describes the process in which a company created and marketed a new indigestion remedy which contained the comparative advantage of fast relief for heartburn sufferers; such

> product improvement must be on a critical dimension that is perceived as important by the consumer. Major product improvements

must be created. It is not possible to take away the business that P&G [Proctor and Gamble] has with Crest simply by offering the consumer another anti-cavity toothpaste. In these highly competitive markets, it is not possible to enter the market with any hope of being successful with a me-too product. When Miles Laboratories launched Alka-2 into the antacid market, it was the 38th chewable antacid launched into the market. The world was not waiting for another chewable antacid. In that setting you really have to have something new, different and important to say to the consumer if you expect the product to sell. In product development you are changing consumer purchase habits and to do that the product must have a major consumer advantage over existing brands.

## Conclusions

Innovation is not a homogeneous concept. Product innovations differ over the innovative process from highly discontinuous to increasingly continuous; purchasers of new products over the generic life cycle differ from one another in terms of social, psychological and economic characteristics. And companies differ from each other and of themselves over time as various strategic responses to their environments become necessary. Whatever strategy is adopted by a business, certain specific areas of risk and uncertainty are inevitably incurred but by *matching* their chosen strategies to their strengths and weaknesses, opportunities and threats firms are able to minimise the risks they take and increase the certainty of effective innovation. Reactive and proactive strategies suit specific circumstances and the same corporation may pursue variants of these strategies concurrently (perhaps through separate SBUs) in order to reduce the vulnerability of the total organisation to one or two sources of environmental change. Companies whose policies tend towards corporate growth, are willing to explore directions of growth other than market penetration, are able to protect their new products by patent cover or by using superior market positions, are seeking success in target markets which require high volume throughout or high margins, and can commit the necessary human and financial resources, are likely to be attracted to proactive strategies. Businesses whose comparative advantage derives from the management of their current product mixes, whose markets are not sufficiently large to ensure the recovery of development expenses, which enjoy little protection from imitative competitors, and lack the resource commitment required for more aggressive approaches, can reduce their uncertainties and risks by pursuing reactive strategies.[28] Reactive strategies do not, however, invariably entail relatively continuous innovation; reactive businesses may be involved in the marketing of comparatively complex or discontinuous brands, especially when those businesses are components of large companies which can provide the resources which the SBU in question may initially lack. Similarly, proactive organisations may proceed by innovating by means of novel combinations of continuous innovations. The overriding consideration is the requirement of the customer which should evoke the appropriate style of marketing-orientation.

## Notes

1. Claycamp, H.J., 'Portfolio Planning', *Journal of Marketing*, vol. 44, no. 3 (1980), p. 116. The contemporary literature of strategic management speaks of 'product-market elements', 'strategy centres', 'businesses' and 'strategic units'. These terms are essentially synonymous and refer to 'the smallest unit of a company for which strategic decisions can be made'. Baker suggests that this means a *product*. See Baker, M.J., 'Innovation – Key to Success', *Quarterly Review of Marketing*, vol. 7, no. 2 (1982), pp. 1-11. Strategic business unit (SBU) is perhaps the most widely-understood for the business component which 'serves a set of outside markets with a family of products which makes it essentially independent of other SBU's'. This description of the function of the SBU is suggestive of an administrative unit responsible for a line or range of products. See Lorange, P., *Corporate Planning* (Englewood Cliffs, NJ: Prentice-Hall, 1980) p. 70. Lorange points out that the American General Electric Company identifies some fifty of its constituent groups, divisions and departments as SBUs. The important things to grasp are that the strategic unit must be consistently defined over time and companies and that it must be capable of isolation in terms of its contribution to cash flow, profit or return on investment so that its performance can be appraised and controlled.

2. Mintzberg, H., *The Structuring of Organisations* (Englewood Cliffs, NJ: Prentice-Hall, 1979), pp. 25-6. See also: Mintzberg, H., 'Strategy-making in Three Modes', *California Management Review* (Winter, 1973), pp. 44-53; 'Patterns of Strategy Formation', *Management Science*, vol. 24 (1978), pp. 934-48.

3. Mintzberg, *The Structuring of Organisations*, p. 30.

4. Ansoff, H.I., *Corporate Strategy* (London: Penguin, 1968), Chapter 6.

5. Lorange, P., *Corporate Planning* (Englewood Cliffs, NJ: Prentice-Hall, 1980), p. 70.

6. Henderson, B.D., 'The Product Portfolio', *Perspectives* (Boston: The Boston Consulting Group, 1970).

7. Conley, P., 'Experience Curves as a Planning Tool', IEEE Spectrum, vol. 7, no. 6 (1970), pp. 63-8. Cf. Abernathy, W.J. and Wayne, K., 'Limits of the Learning Curve', *Harvard Business Review*, vol. 52, no. 5 (1974).

8. Schoffler, S., Buzzell, R.D. and Heany, D.F., 'Impact of Strategic Planning on Profit Performance', *Harvard Business Review*, vol. 52, no. 2 (1974), pp. 137-45; Buzzell, R.D., Bradley, G.T. and Sultan, R.G.M., 'Market Share – a Key to Profitability', *Harvard Business Review*, vol. 53, no. 1 (1975), pp. 97-106.

9. Dhalla, N.K. and Yuseph, S., 'Forget the Product Life Cycle Concept!', *Harvard Business Review*, vol. 54, no. 1 (1976), pp. 102-12; Foxall, G.R., *Strategic Marketing Management* (London: Croom Helm and New York: John Wiley, 1981), pp. 73-8.

10. Jain, S.C., *Marketing Planning and Strategy* (Cincinnati, Ohio: South-Western 1981), pp. 417-18; see also: Day, G.S., 'Diagnosing the Product Portfolio', *Journal of Marketing*, vol. 42, no. 2 (1977), pp. 29-38.

11. Cotton, P., 'Milking the Cash Cows', *Marketing*, vol. 8, no. 10 (11 March, 1982), pp. 29-32.

12. Carman, J.M. and Langeard, E., 'Growth Strategies for Service Firms', *Strategic Management Journal*, vol. 1, no. 1 (1980), pp. 7-22.

13. Brownlie, D., 'Analytical Frameworks for Taking Product-Market Strategy Decisions' in Flood, P., Grant, C.L. and O'Driscoll (eds.), *Marketing: Future Imperfect* (Proceedings of the Annual Conference of the Marketing Education Group, Dublin, 1981). See also: Thomas, M.J., Linneman, R. and Kennell, J.D., 'A 10-step, Common Sense Approach to Portfolio Planning' in Flood, Grant and O'Driscoll (eds.), *Marketing*, pp. 240-1.

14. Avlonitis, G., 'Product Elimination: A Neglected Phase of Innovation' in Flood, Grant and O'Driscoll (eds.), *Marketing*, pp. 2-50.

15. Wheatcroft, P., 'Cadbury Bars that have Melted Away', *Sunday Times*, 14 March 1982.

16. Day, G.S., 'A Strategic Perspective on Product Planning', *Journal of Contemporary Business* (Spring, 1975), pp. 1-34.

17. Thomas, Linneman and Kennel, 'A 10-step, Common Sense Approach', pp. 240-1. Abernathy, W.J. and Wayne, K., 'Limits of the Learning Curve', *Harvard Business Review*, vol. no. 5 (1974). For an up-to-date review of marketing strategy within its corporate context which critically appraises the BCG, PIMS and other work, see Day, G.S., 'Analytical Approaches to Strategic Market Planning' in Enis, B.M. and Roering, K.J. (eds.), *Review of Marketing 1981* (Chicago: American Marketing Association, 1981), pp. 89-105. Day concludes, p. 103, that 'Perhaps the greatest contribution of these models is that they provide a data base – in the case of PIMS – and a conceptual framework to guide further research.'

18. E.g. Sissors, J., 'What is a Market?', *Journal of Marketing*, vol. 30, no. 3 (1966), pp. 17-21; for an economics viewpoint, see Nightingale, J., 'On the Definition of "Industry" and "Market" ', *Journal of Industrial Economics*, vol. 27, no. 1 (1978), pp. 31-40.

19. Jain, Marketing Planning and Strategy, pp. 426-33.

20. Foxall, G.R., 'Marketing's Domain', *European Journal of Marketing*, vol. 17 (forthcoming).

21. Urban, G.L. and Hauser, J.R., *Design and Marketing of New Products* (Englewood Cliffs, NJ: Prentice-Hall, 1980), p. 20.

22. Ibid.

23. Morris, D., 'The Strategy of Own Brands', *European Journal of Marketing*, vol. 13, no. 2 (1979), pp. 59-78.

24. Hippel, E. von, 'A Customer-Active Paradigm for Industrial Product Idea Generation' in Baker (ed.), *Industrial Innovation*, pp. 82-110.

25. Foxall, G.R., 'Industrial Buying during Recession: Farmers' Tractor Purchases, 1977-78', *Management Decision*, vol. 17, no. 4 (1979).

26. Rines, M. 'Ford Fields a $100m Hope', *Marketing* (22 September 1981), pp. 19-24.

27. Hatch, T., 'New Product Development – A Manager's Viewpoint' in Urban and Hauser, *Design and Marketing of New Products*, p. 65.

28. Urban and Hauser, *Design and Marketing of New Products*, pp. 572-4

# 4 MARKETING-ORIENTED INNOVATION

## Entrepreneurship and Marketing-orientation

Strategic management, which as we have seen, addresses the company's relationship with its environment, has two modes. *Competitive* action is that mode of strategic response which is concerned with stable environments while *entrepreneurial* actions involve the achievement of the economic objectives of the enterprise 'by reinventing the firm's structure and its transactions with the world about it, in an unstable or dynamic environment'.[1] Murray[2] notes that competitive action refers not to the competition assumed by orthodox economic theory but to 'strategic behaviour focused on system maintenance, on doing a known job more effectively, and above all behaving within an accepted set of strategic parameters'. Entrepreneurial behaviour demands the 'reconceptualisation of these parameters, leading to entirely new combinations of productive resources and market potentials'. In the light of Abernathy and Utterback's analysis of processual innovative patterns, competitive strategy is appropriate for the incremental progression of continuous innovation which follows the establishment of a dominant design for recently-created products. Entrepreneurial strategy is, of necessity, concerned with discontinuities: it is the mainspring of the technological and economic advance which inaugurates the innovative process. Yet as the following analysis indicates, competitive and entrepreneurial strategies are closely related by virtue of their common reliance upon a style of administrative behaviour known as marketing-orientation. Marketing-oriented management is a concept well-understood by practitioners and students of marketing. It refers not to a specific set of operations but to a component of business policy which in the case of organisations which have fully adopted and implemented the marketing concept pervades the attitudes and behaviour of all members of the company and is thus expressed in the performance of *all* operations. It has not been more accurately yet succinctly described as in the works of King[3] for whom it is that 'managerial philosophy concerned with the mobilisation, utilisation, and control of total corporate effort for the purpose of helping consumers solve selected problems in a way compatible with the planned enhancement of the profit position of the firm'.

## The Nature and Locus of Entrepreneurship

The identification of entrepreneurship is a notoriously difficult task. The old idea of risk-bearing individuals whose personal achievement stems from the courageous and perceptive grasping of opportunities which elude their peers, who design and build responsive organisations and mobilise resources to yield spectacular economic and social rewards remains attractive, and therefore, pervasive.[4] A rather more sophisticated view emerges from the writings of Kirzner[5] who draws attention to the role of those individuals within the economic system who are *alert* to opportunities for profit, of which others are oblivious, and who possess the qualities required to exploit those perceived opportunities. By stressing the functions performed by these entrepreneurs, members of the 'Austrian School' of economics — who include Hayek[6] and Mises[7] as well as Kirzner — present an economic paradigm which takes a view of the nature and operation of markets that is distinct from the familiar tenets of mainstream neoclassical economics. Instead of depicting markets as essentially static devices subject to inhibiting monopolistic pressures such as entry barriers and other assumed impediments to the pattern of resource allocation inherent in the perfect competition model, the Austrians view markets as dynamic *processes*, subject at all times to new developments, novel sources of competitive behaviour which result from the entrepreneurial pursuit of profit. Entrepreneurial alertness is vital to this view of market operations and Kirzner[8] writes that

> Human beings tend to notice that which it is in their interest to notice. Human beings notice opportunities rather than 'situations'. They notice, that is, concatenations of events, realised or prospective, which offer *pure gain*. It is not the abstract *concatenation* of these events which evokes notice; it is the circumstance that these events offer the promise of pure *gain* — broadly understood to include fame, power, prestige, even the opportunity to serve a cause or to help individuals.

The capacity to distinguish previously unnoticed opportunities resides in individuals who are able to *benefit* from the chances they identify. This is not an entirely truistic statement since, while the entrepreneurial capacity is common to all men and women, alertness to a specific opportunity in particular circumstances is governed by the incentive of personal gain which arises in that situation. Not all individuals are likely to identify the same opportunity for *personal* gain in any given objectively-common situation. It is the actions of individual entrepreneurs, behaving privately and personally (but thereby creating opportunities for others who may or may not be alert to them) which are the mainspring of innovation and new product development. Ignorance and intuition, the sort of alertness which enables connections (say between buying and selling prices) to be made and gestalts to be formed from partially-known situations, are the stuff of entrepreneurial behaviour according to this view. In contrast to the mainstrain micro-economic view in which everyone's objectives, means of achieving them and level of attainment are fully known and predictable in the equilibrium state, the processual view of markets stresses that individuals' plans are more often than not unfulfilled. It is through continual trial and error and the perpetual revision of plans and objectives on the parts of both producers and consumers, acting under conditions of comparative ignorance, that any measure of co-ordination occurs. Entrepreneurship consists in the ability to spot opportunities to co-ordinate (albeit usually temporarily) the plans of others, spurred by one's own seeking for gain.

But industrial societies are increasingly characterised (indeed some would say already dominated) by large, bureaucratised business organisations in which entrepreneurship is rarely traceable to specific individual enterprise. Even among writers of the Austrian School of economics such as Kirzner, 'the entrepreneur is an elusive being and what these authors actually depict is a creative impulse rather than a living individual. In one-man or very small firms, at the moment of discovery of product-market opportunity, this impulse may be clearly identifiable with a specific person. Beyond this stage, when once the firm has grown into an organisation, the entrepreneurial role is generalised and becomes, in the words of Alford,[9] "diffused entrepreneurship".[10] The depiction of entrepreneurship as a process diffused among departments, divisions, layers of management, groups and teams implies that it can never be conceptualised as confined to a single functional area of the company such as R&D, production, engineering or marketing. It is true that an argument can be made for Murray's proposition that the marketing functions of the firm constitute that subset of corporate activities most posed and prepared to appreciate the potential rewards of reconstructed technological production and marketing environments and capable of providing the intelligence and insights required to construct innovative marketing mixes through which the consequent opportunities for effective business development may be advantageously exploited. But it is not in fact the definable marketing department or function within the firm that is exclusively identified with the locus of entrepreneurship: rather it is the amorphous, 'invisible department' which comprises marketing-oriented management wherever its members are found within the enterprise.[11] Perhaps marketing-orientation is a misnomer since it is *customer*-orientation which is to be emphasised but there is no intention in retaining this entrenched label to contribute to the internecine conflicts which, in spite of a generation of managerial thought which has stressed the need for integrated management, still persist. Rather it is to argue against the view presented by some marketing texts to the effect that the marketing department's *functional* role is inherently superior to that of other operational specialisms. There is a world of difference between the concept of *marketing functions* which include the assembly and administration of the marketing mix and *marketing-oriented management* which, on the basis of King's definition, is evidently closely linked with the entrepreneurial role of overall corporate strategy and which, therefore, carries implications for the entire organisation, guiding the operations of production, R&D, finance, personnel and design as well as the marketing function itself.[12]

## The Role of Marketing-oriented Management

The attitudes and behaviours which constitute marketing-oriented management are an indispensable part of entrepreneurship but the two are not coterminous. Marketing-oriented management has relevance also to the execution of effective competitive strategy for this, as well as entrepreneurship, relies vitally upon the fulfilment of consumers' needs as a prerequisite of achieving the economic goals of the business. Relating entrepreneurship to marketing-orientation corroborates the argument that the former is diffused throughout the organisation; but when the contribution of marketing-oriented management to the entrepreneurial process is appreciated it becomes clear that even the constitutional frontiers of the firm do coincide with the bounds of entrepreneurship because customers and other groups are, on occasion, responsible for initiating the process of entrepreneurial innovation and, indeed, for sustaining it.[13] There is, moreover, another consideration arising from the role of marketing-oriented management which clarifies further the nature and locus of entrepreneurship. Entrepreneurship can be judged and attributed only *ex post*: a company is not entrepreneurial because if managers *propose* to produce innovative products for gain or *intend* to fulfil customers' expectations and thus their own or make *ex ante* forecasts of their willingness to succeed. Minkes and Foxall[14] write that entrepreneurship is displayed in the *successful* extension of product-market scope. While it is doubtless legitimate to speak of entrepreneurial characteristics — flair, risk-taking, alertness — failed entrepreneurship is, strictly, a contradiction in terms. Entrepreneurship does not consist of the development and market launch of products which are perceived as novel by their originator; the individual who is engaged in *this* productive process is an inventor-cum-developer. Invention becomes innovation, enterprise merits the title *entrepreneurship*, only when the market favourably judges the new product placed before it by purchasing it in sufficient volume to allow the firm to achieve its business objectives: its profit or sales' goals at its threshold level of return on investment, and its other aims. Thus, since successful commercial exploitation is a prerequisite of entrepreneurship, innovation and entrepreneurship are ultimately determined by the market rather than by management's appropriation of these functions to itself.

The importance of this reasoning is that the process of entrepreneurial behaviour links sellers and buyers as does the market process itself; its actors severally perform the roles of both producers *and* consumers. Entrepreneurial alertness and behaviour can be ascribed only after the establishment of the product and this is not usually until the product has entered the mature stage of its life cycle when further new product development consists largely in incremental or continuous change. This is also the stage at which *competitive* strategy comes into its own but it is now clear that entrepreneurial strategy depends vitally upon this competitive phase and that marketing-oriented management must be the managerial philosophy which relates and sustains the two strategic modes.

The problem with the marketing concept of marketing- or consumer-oriented management is an operational one: if this orientation is a prerequisite to commercial success, it follows that successful companies exhibit it, while failures deserve criticism for ignoring it. To attribute a marketing-oriented managerial philosophy to effective firms says little in itself to clarify the content of such a philosophy and to locate its operational effects. The search for the ingredients of effective innovation demands more than this — the identification of the *operational* factors which discriminate between successful and unsuccessful developers of new products. It will be time enough to deduce differences in managerial philosophy when such factors have been found. Nevertheless, the volume of empirical research into the factors associated with success and failure in new product development is now sufficiently large to enable some preliminary conclusions to be drawn. Most of the basic sources of product success and failure identified in this research apply to final consumer products and to industrial products equally. The separation of consumer and industrial innovation in the following sections reflects no more than that empirical work is usually undertaken in one or other sector and that this provides a convenient approach to summarising the findings and drawing conclusions.

## Effective Consumer Product Innovation

The high rate of new product failure in consumer markets has already received comment. The tendency for the product itself or its packaging to be at fault has been shown to be a prominent and increasing source of failure[15] and, although the contributions of individual elements of the marketing mix cannot be clinically separated to the extent that this might suggest, the general conclusion must be that most consumer innovations are judged by potential adopters to be incapable of delivering the required benefits. Several American surveys suggest that the reasons for this state of affairs lie in poor marketing research, product defects, substandard marketing, high costs, greater-than-expected competition, mistiming and difficulties in production including the use of technology.[16] In the UK a survey by Kraushar and Eassie Ltd published in 1982, presents the factors involved in successful development of fast-moving consumer goods: 'They tend to be distinctive in some way or other, are in line with general consumer trends, are suitable for the companies marketing them, and are marketed with a great deal of commitment, singlemindedness and attention to detail.' As Kraushar[17] points out, these are mundane conclusions but there is still far too little evidence that the majority of firms practice sound new product development. 'This is apparent from the low calibre of many executives entrusted with new products, the lack of resources given to them, the absence of coherent and long-term policies and the lack of commitment within the company. In the circumstances, it is not surprising that so many new products fail; indeed, it is surprising that so many succeed.' The overwhelming impression is that far too few innovative consumer products offer distinctive advantages over existing brands.

Most research into product failure and success has identified factors which are consistently associated with one or other of these outcomes. The difficulty which arises in the interpretation of such work is that even actions which are *always* encountered in the case of, say, success-ful new products in the sample may not be linked to the *causes* of success in general: they may be equally prevalent among products which fail. Davidson[18] reports an attempt to overcome this problem by comparing fifty successful new brands of grocery product with fifty innovative grocery failures and employing a relatively unambiguous criterion of failure — failed products are identified as those eliminated during test marketing or withdrawn after national launch because of poor profitability. Successful new brands differ significantly from failures in three respects: value, distinctiveness and timing.

*Value.* Successful fast-moving consumer goods offer distinct and con-siderable value benefits which are not already available. Value may derive from lower prices and similar or better performance *or* a similar or higher price coupled with superior performance. Eighty-two per cent of the successful innovations offered one or other of these advantages. Only 20 per cent of failures fall into this category and all ten such items were offered at a higher-than-usual price which may have over-come their performance advantages; alternatively they failed because their merits were not sufficiently well communicated to prospective buyers or because their target segment proved too small to support profitable production and distribution. Sometimes failing products offered the wrong consumer benefits: if flavour is the discriminatory variable employed by smokers, crush-proof packs will not overcome its absence. While 18 per cent of successful brands offered buyers no discernible advantage, the proportion of failed brands offering none was *eighty* per cent.

*Distinctiveness.* Sixty-eight per cent of the successful new brands in Davidson's sample were 'drastically different' or 'very different' from those they rivalled; seventy per cent of the failures were 'marginally different from' or 'similar to' competitors. As he notes, these are ultimately subjective assessments but the work appears to employ the same ideas of conspicuous discontinuity or appearance or performance with a high degree of consistency. The lesson is clear in any case: the effective introduction of products which are discontinuous innovations — new products which radically modify consumer and consumption behaviour — demand not only a physical product which offers con-sumers notable improvements over what is available but also the con-struction and delivery of an integrated marketing mix to inform, distribute and offer distinct value for money. A significant difference alone is not sufficient to guarantee successful innovation, however. Davidson categorises the thirty per cent of new product failures which were dramatically or very different as (a) those which suffered from poor functional performance (e.g. *Kellog's Freeze Dried Fruit with Cereal*), (b) products whose high price was not compensated by their distinctive attributes (e.g. *Downy* fabric softener) or (c) unsuccessful, relatively discontinuous innovations (e.g. *Campbell's* condensed soups).

*Timing.* For reasons which will become clearer from the analysis of innovative buying (in Part II) there are advantages in launching the first brand of a new product class. Briefly, they accrue from the fact that the initial brand stands to benefit from the 'innovativeness' or 'venturesomeness' of the earliest adopters (innovative buyers) upon whose experience and conspicuous product use subsequent diffusion of the new item through the social system and market depends. Davidson's analysis of the status of pioneer brands in 18 post-war grocery and related product-markets[19] from washing-up liquids and detergents to cakes and frozen desserts confirms this: although pioneer brands were displaced during the survey period by competing brands in seven of the markets investigated, the remainder maintained dominance and there were good reasons for the deviation from this pattern in the seven former areas, predominently the dissipation of these brands' novel features through inadequate and unimaginative use of the full marketing mix.

## Effective Industrial Innovation

As is the case with empirical investigations of consumer innovations, many earlier studies of innovation in industrial products and services concentrated upon a single dimension of the new product experience of firms, namely success *or* failure rather than attempting to isolate factors which discriminate between the two. Nevertheless, useful investigation has been reported by Cooper[20] who examined 114 industrial product failures in Canada. The criteria of failure were devised by managerial respondents to a postal questionnaire which was designed to elicit relationships among the *general* reasons for product failure (e.g. low profitability due to lower sales than expected), *specific* cause of failure (e.g. a poor pricing strategy) and *latent* causes of failure (e.g. the failure of marketing research to determine customers' perceptions of value). The dominant pattern identified was poor sales results (general) which were a consequence of inadequate market awareness or marketing competence (specific and latent) rather than technical impediments. Cooper[21] comments that 'This result is quite provocative, particularly when one considers the relatively minor amounts spent on marketing research compared to the large sums spent on R&D. Under-estimated competitive strength, overestimating the number of potential users, and overestimating the price customers would pay for the new product were the three major causes of low sales. The majority of the dimensions or factors which appeared to explain many of the causes of low sales were also market-related — a lack of understanding of the marketplace, the customer and the competition.' The internal-orientation of the companies responsible for failure was manifested in the lack of the strategic skills which enable successful firms to impinge effectively upon their environments: particularly marketing intelligence and the provision of the resources demanded for effective product launches. The lack of a sufficient study of the market and, conse-quently, of a clear impression of target market segments appeared to stem from the belief that 'a good product sells itself'.

Cooper's analysis is valuable for its insights into the relationship between effective innovation and marketing-orientation but there are many other studies which throw light upon the nature of the orienta-tion and competence possessed by the members of those companies which are successful in this particular form of strategic response. On the basis of an analysis of nine empirical studies of over a thousand indus-trial innovations, Rothwell[22] identified six characteristics of firms which were effective innovators and/or technologically progressive: such firms showed greater commitments to innovation, perceived inno-vation as a company-wide task, gave particular attention to marketing strategy, user needs and after-sales service, conducted design and development work more efficiently, had good communications and possessed high levels of managerial skills and performance. Table 4.1 summarises the results of this survey.[23]

Table 4.1: Characteristics of Successful Innovators and Technically Progressive Firms

---

1   COMMITMENT TO INNOVATION — Innovative capacity is associated with an active policy of finding and developing new products. Successful innovators undertook a deliberate search for innovation. Successful projects are initiated by the firm's top management. Success is promoted by enthusiastic and committed top management. The executive in charge of success has more involvement with, and enthusiasm for the project; he has more status, power

Table 4.1 continued

and authority. The clear will of management to innovate is essential to achieve successful innovation.

2 INNOVATION AS A CORPORATE-WIDE TASK — Innovation is a corporate task not R&D in isolation; it cannot be left to one functional department. The balance of functions of production, marketing and R&D is important to success: it is a question of qualitative as well as quantitative balance. Successful firms, on average, out-perform failures in *all* the areas of competence encompassed by the innovation process. Harmonious co-operation among research, development, production and financial departments contributed to the project's success and was an important characteristic of the technically progressive firm. Successful firms took steps to co-ordinate the efforts of the various functional departments.

3 ATTENTION TO MARKETING, USER NEEDS AND AFTER-SALES SERVICING — Successful innovators understand user needs better and pay more attention to marketing and sales; successful innovations arise in response to a market need. Technically progressive firms also adopt an effective selling policy. Knowledge of demand is an important factor in success. Successful firms have a formal marketing policy. Technically progressive firms offered good technical service to customers. Successful firms provide an efficient and reliable after-sales maintenance and spares supply service. Successful firms paid more attention to user education and to adequate preparation of customers.

4 EFFECTIVE DESIGN AND DEVELOPMENT WORK — Successful innovators perform their development work more efficiently than failures. Successful innovators eliminate technical defects before commercial launch. A characteristic of technically progressive firms is conscientiousness in R&D. Success was considerably facilitated if the enterprise succeeded in overcoming operational problems before commercial launch, and by adequate preparation of facilities for solving emergencies during the course of pilot production. Successful innovations suffer from fewer after-sales problems.

5 GOOD INTERNAL AND EXTERNAL COMMUNICATION — Good internal communication is associated with success, as is good intra-firm co-operation. Successful innovators had better contacts with the scientific and technical community in the specific area associated with the innovation. Technically progressive firms enjoyed better contacts with outside technical establishments and a higher quality of incoming information. Successful innovators collaborated with potential suppliers and customers during development, and maintained frequent contact with customers thereafter. Technically progressive firms showed a willingness to share knowledge and to co-operate with outside agencies.

6 MANAGEMENT SKILLS AND PROFESSIONALISM — A characteristic of technically progressive firms is the good use of management techniques. In the case of successful innovations, planning was more highly structured and sophisticated. Most successful innovators formulate explicit innovation policies. Characteristics of technically progressive firms are: good recruitment and training policies and good-quality — and enough — intermediate managers. Technically progressive firms possess an open-minded, high-quality chief executive. Senior staff are often engineers, but other graduates are included. Successful firms have an ability to attract talented and qualified people and provide ample scope for management training.

Source: Rothwell, R., 'Policies in Industry' in Pavitt, K. (ed.), *Technical Innovation and British Economic Performance* (London: Macmillan, 1980), pp. 300-1, Copyright 1980, Science Policy Research Unit. Used by permission.

The general conclusions of Cooper's research and of the studies summarised by Rothwell are corroborated by two comparative studies of industrial innovation, one British, the other North American, both of which have added to the clarification of the factors which assist in distinguishing effective and ineffective innovation. The British work, conducted by the Science Policy Research Unit at the University of Sussex is known as Project SAPPHO and focused upon the differences between successful and unsuccessful innovations launched into the same product-market.[24] Its two-phase investigation included examination of 43 innovations, 22 of them chemical processes, the remainder scientific instruments. The other investigation, Project NewProd, also sought to compare success and failure and involved 102 studies of successful innovations and 93 of unsuccessful new products. A mailed questionnaire required managers to select a successful and an unsuccessful innovation defined in terms of the company's financial criteria and to describe each venture in terms of 77 separate dimensions, covering technical and production synergy and proficiency, marketing knowledge and proficiency, market need, growth and size, and marketing communications and launch effort.[25]

*Project SAPPHO*

Project SAPPHO identified five major respects in which successful projects differed from unsuccessful ones. First, those firms which innovated successfully possessed a superior understanding of *user needs*. Because of this practical orientation, their product or process was much more likely to meet buyers' expectations with a minimum of further adaptation. Secondly, the successful businesses gave more attention and effort to *marketing*, understanding the need to find adopters of the product if it was to contribute to general corporate strategy. Thirdly, such companies carried out *more thorough product development* work, employing (fourthly) *external technological expertise* and advice particularly in the specific area to which their product innovation concerns related. Finally, in successful cases the individuals responsible for new product development had more authority, status and personal commitment to the project than did those individuals engaged on similar projects which failed. Table 4.2 presents ten composite variables in terms of which successful innovation may be explained; the rank orders of importance for the two industries separately and in aggregate are shown. (The rankings are based upon the percentage of cases in which successful projects used more of or used better the factor included in the summary variables.) The high rankings of marketing and user needs in every column confirm the general explanation of innovative effectiveness in terms of marketing orientation. Rothwell[26] explains the second order ranking of marketing in the case of chemical processes by the tendency of the companies involved to be their own customers for the new processes − thus having less need for external marketing-orientation − and by the good relationships and understandings which exist between the manufacturers of chemical processes and their relatively few external customers. This should not detract from the fact that the necessary research, development and technical skills were present in the successful companies; indeed, the reports of Project SAPPHO emphasise that the successful innovators outperformed those who failed on *all* of the five general discriminating factors listed above.

Project SAPPHO was based upon a consciously commercially-oriented definition of innovation which conforms to the general needs of definitional statements developed in the last chapter: 'The technical, industrial and commercial steps which lead to the marketing of new manufactured products and to the commercial use of new technical processes and equipment.'[27] The selection of projects for case analysis also reflected a market-orientation: each of the 43 pairs of innovations contained products or processes which were similar in that they competed for the same market rather than that their technological bases coincided.[28] The exercise of the marketing *function* emerged certainly and unambiguously as a factor which discriminated between effective and ineffective innovators[29] but so did a number of other factors such as R&D strength, the quality of management, efficiency of manufacturing processes and so on. Marketing and marketing-related functions differentiated between success and failure more frequently than other variables but the results of the project point to marketing-oriented management as a prime ingredient of successful innovation; where this was lacking numerous functional areas of the responsible companies required attention, including, of course, marketing. But the conclusion which must be drawn from this research is surely that managerial perspective is the key to effective innovation: the implementation of the marketing concept in its fullness ought to lead to the remedying of functional deficiencies but without a marketing-oriented approach to integrate and co-ordinate them no amount of tinkering with departmental responsibilities and actions is likely to be conducive to the achievement of success through innovation. As Rothwell[30] summarises: '. . . a highly developed market awareness, coupled with understanding of, and a desire to meet, the needs of potential customers, are prime requisites for successful industrial innovation. Failure, on the other

hand, is associated with ignorance of, and indifference to, the requirements of the market place.'

Table 4.2: Rankings of Composite Explanatory Variables

| Rank Order | Chemicals | Scientific instruments | Aggregate |
|---|---|---|---|
| 1 | R&D strength | Marketing | Marketing |
| 2 | Marketing = User needs = | User needs = Communication = | R&D strength |
| 3 | | | User needs |
| 4 | Management strength | R&D strength | Communication |
| 5 | Communication = Risk = | Management strength = Familiarity = | Management strength |
| 6 | | | Familiarity |
| 7 | Pressure | Techniques = Organic organisation = | Techniques |
| 8 | Familiarity = Techniques = | | Pressure |
| 9 | | Pressure | Organic organisation |
| 10 | Organic organisation | Risk | Risk |

Source: Derived from Rothwell, R., 'Marketing and Successful Industrial Innovation' in *Innovation in Marketing* (Department of Marketing, University of
Strathclyde, 1973), p. 2.10.

## Project NewProd

Project NewProd produced results which are broadly corroborative of
those of SAPPHO and isolated three dominant dimensions which
discriminate between successful and unsuccessful industrial innovations:
*product uniqueness and superiority* (including such factors as highly
innovative product, new to market; and cost reduction possibilities for
buyers), *market knowledge and marketing proficiency* (good preliminary market assessment; good test marketing; good launch; understanding
of buyers' needs, behaviour and price sensitivity), *and technical and
production synergy* (compatibility of engineering skills and production
resources for project; good preliminary technical assessment; good
knowledge of product technology; good prototype and development
testing; and appropriate production processes and readiness). The
effects of a company's showing high levels of prowess on each of these

dimensions (the top 20 per cent of firms scored on each dimension) are compared in Table 4.3 with the performance of firms showing low or medium levels of competence (the bottom 20 per cent and middle 60 per cent respectively).

Table 4.3: Dominant Dimensions of Effective Industrial Innovation

| Dimension | Percentage of successes among: | | |
|---|---|---|---|
| | Top 20% | Middle 50% | Top 20% |
| Product uniqueness and superiority | 82 | 50 | 28 |
| Marketing knowledge and marketing proficiency | 79.5 | 51 | 28 |
| Technical and production synergy and proficiency | 64 | 56 | 31 |
| Number of innovations = 195, of which 102 successes, 93 failures | | | |

Source: Cooper, R.G., 'Project NewProd: Factors in New Product Success', *European Journal of Marketing*, vol. 14, no. 5/6 (1980), pp. 277-92.

The three dimensions naturally interact and, of those launches which enjoyed high rating on all three, 90 per cent were successful, while only seven per cent of those with a low rating on all three succeeded. The product factor — 'having a product with a differential advantage in the eyes of the customer' — is crucial, however; in those cases where marketing and technical/productive capacity and proficiency were judged low but whose product uniqueness and superiority were highly rated, 62 per cent of the new products were nevertheless successful. Furthermore, only 38 per cent of products rated high on marketing but low on the other dimensions succeeded and only 26 per cent of products showing high technical and productive support but low ratings otherwise were successful. Cooper[31] concludes nonetheless that the overriding impression of his analysis is 'the essential presence of all three factors — product, market(ing) and technical/production as the key to success . . . and that deficiency in any one area [reduces] the success rate dramatically'. Cooper's work in the NewProd programme is particularly useful in that the precise components of marketing-oriented effort which discriminate successes from failures are specified; fifteen specific factors which discriminate in this way are listed and include (in order of importance): efficient execution of the launch including the appropriate and integrated use of selling, promotion and distribution; creating a unique new product which has competitive advantages in the way it meets customer requirements; undertaking a satisfactory prototype test *with the customer*; effective targeting of the sales force and distribution function; good test marketing; undertaking full scale production smoothly and efficiently; knowing customers' sensitivity to price; developing an innovation which allows the customer to reduce his costs; having good fit between the company and the product in terms of the work of sales forces and distributors; a similar accommodation in terms of marketing research skills; and an efficient idea screening device. (Cooper's papers contain a wealth of additional information for the innovator.)

## The Crucial Role of Marketing-oriented Management

Further use will be made of these studies of consumer and industrial innovation in later chapters but the pre-eminent conclusion which emerges from this brief review is the vital role played by marketing-oriented management in effective new product development. Although both Project SAPPHO and Project NewProd individually attract some criticisms — e.g. the narrow product range of the former, the reliance upon managerial diagnoses in the latter — their combined scope and concurrence of conclusions make some generalisation possible. The fundamental discriminators of successful and unsuccessful innovations coincide: the results of both surveys are supported by independent research and by research into consumer innovation. To ignore the implications of these projects' results for the management of innovation would be perilous. The surprising conclusion which must be drawn from observation of the innovative process and its outcomes is that so few companies appear to adopt and implement the marketing philosophy. Krausher[32] expresses amazement that 'large and sophisticated companies, well-staffed with marketing executives, can have failures for reasons which would often be apparent to the most junior marketing assistant. How can a company risk a large expenditure . . . without knowing what the customer thinks of the product? How can a company not bother to obtain a feel of the market? How can a company aim for long-term investment in a market known for its fickleness and absence of continuous brand loyalty? How can a company launch a new product these days which is found to be unacceptable by the consumer?' His answer is that such companies lack the objectivity to assess ideas for new products accurately and courageously in terms of corporate capacities and external opportunities, to abort projects which the company cannot harmoniously accommodate, and to resist the 'compulsive urge to go ahead unless there are strong negatives'.

White[33] underscores these enemies of customer-orientation by identifying, on the basis of wide practical involvement in new product development, reluctance to cancel projects which have begun, partly because of excessive executive commitment, and 'corporate arrogance' about the quality of the product or the ability of the company to influence sales of an inferior item. Davidson[34] also identifies factors which dissipate objectivity in new product development. First, there are sources of imbalance which involve *timing*: self-imposed pressures which derive from a desire for action that results in the speedy introduction of new products, especially in response to competitors' innovations, even if the new products are of the 'me-too' variety and offer no comparative advantage; self-imposed targets for the launch of an arbitrary number of brands each year, regardless of market needs and buyer behaviour. Secondly, there are the *vested interests* which favour the acceptance of new product ideas generated by high-status managers and which benefit from the lack of courage to drop the consequent projects even when they show little sign of eventual market success. Thirdly, the previously-mentioned *arrogance* that whatever products a successful and well-placed company offers the market will inevitably be accepted by it also contributes to innovative failure. Finally, *absorption* in the process of new product-development distracts managerial competence from the essential task of matching corporate resources with buyers' purchase and consumption behaviour via the medium of effective marketing mixes. In industrial companies it is often absorption in technical processes and research, which are justified on the grounds that they underlie product development, that stymie innovative development that satisfies market needs. This is fully consistent with the repeated finding that approximately three-quarters of product ideas for effective innovations originate in the recognition of opportunities to fulfil market demands or improve processes, while in only about one quarter of cases is the possibility of utilising technological advance the mainspring of successful innovative development.[35]

These findings are in stark contrast with the tendency for technical rather than marketing personnel to predominate in the generation of ideas for R&D in new product development practice in spite of the evidence that ideas inaugurated by R&D specialists have been shown to have a much higher probability of leading to products which fail in the marketplace.[36] The import of this is (at risk of repetition) not that one or other sectional interest ought always to determine the direction of innovative effort; rather it is that those who are in closest touch with the requirements of the marketplace must be associated with effective innovation to the end that it contributes usefully to the achievement of the strategic objectives of the business. Of course, marketing managers of competence should play a part in the innovative process – the responsibility for doing so lies in part with them – but unqualified customer-orientation requires the integration of all functional areas of management and operation. If marketing-oriented management, which is the ultimate responsibility of top management, is absent then the improvement of marketing functions contributes little to effectiveness. Of the failures studied by Cooper[37] 'At every stage of the product development process, market-oriented activities fared much worse than corresponding technical/production activities. By far the most deficient activity undertaken was the detailed market study. The message for industrial product firms is clear. A greater market orientation is required as part of the new product development effort. This means industrial goods firms must be prepared to balance their heavy R&D expenditures with research of another kind – marketing research.'

The design and proper use of marketing research investigations and the data they yield are, nevertheless, only the beginning of a procedure which involves creating and maintaining a balanced interaction between marketing and R&D personnel. General Electric Laboratories are reported to apply R&D resources to the goal of meeting market requirements which have previously been identified by marketing research and to employ good communications between R&D scientists who make clear the possibilities of forthcoming technological advances at such a time and in such a manner that marketing research may be undertaken to appraise the probability and strength of demand and, in turn, assist product development.[38] This suggests not the persistent predominance of a single function upon which sectional interests depend but the prevalence of the integrating philosophy of customer-oriented management upon which the future of the entire enterprise depends. Flexibility and the appreciation by R&D scientists and marketing specialists of one another's perspectives and capabilities make possible the adaptation of product ideas and technical/productive potentials to the features of the market.

## Conclusion

Finally, one other important conclusion may be drawn from the research which has been assessed here. The ability of managers to increase the effectiveness of their strategies of innovation is apparent from the fact that the variables which discriminate success from failure are those which are under executive rather than environmental control. A central contribution of Project NewProd to increasing the effectiveness of the innovative process is the understanding that 'certain activities, information areas and elements of the commercial entity [i.e. the product offering and launch strategy] were so strongly linked to new product success that they were, on their own, able to account for a considerable proportion of variability in outcomes. The eventual outcome of the new product venture thus lies in the hands of the company people involved . . . The message clearly is that "it matters not what situation you face; it matters more what you do about it!" '[39] Insofar as international differences in the effectiveness of innovation and export performance derive from differences in the management of innovation, the efficiency of firms new product development programmes may be capable of remedy through changes in managerial action rather than through state intervention. In the mechanical engineering industries, for instance, British companies appear to produce less sophisticated products than their overseas competitors.[40] Parkinson[41] notes that 'One of the features of an advanced, industrialised economy is the gradual substitution of improvement in product quality for price as a major competitive tool' but that 'many British companies have continued to base their marketing strategy on price competitiveness, rather than product quality, and accordingly have become increasingly less competitive'. From his empirical investigation of the marketing of machine tools by British and West German companies, he observes several important differences between the two countries: West German firms tend to collaborate more often with universities and research bodies *and* with other machine tool manufacturers; their design engineers tend to be in closer touch with customers at all stages of the new product development process from idea generation to the building of a prototype and to test the product in a customer's factory rather than in their own laboratories; and German companies concentrate more than their British counterparts on continuous rather than discontinuous innovation.

All of these factors imply a greater understanding of the importance of user needs in the technical design and development processes than appears to exist among many companies in the UK. Rothwell[42] draws similar conclusions from his comparison of British and West German manufacturers of agricultural tractors from which he generalises that

'Britain's inability to keep pace with the steady development of technology, coupled with the lack of attention to marketing needs, is the reason for our national decline.' The solution is less in the realm of the manipulation of macro-economic policy than in the hands of those who are — or should be — responsible for the intrafirm new product development process.

## Notes

1. Murray, J.A., 'Marketing is Home for the Entrepreneurial Process', *Industrial Marketing Management*, vol. 10, no. 2 (1981), pp. 93-9.

2. Ibid.

3. King, R.L., 'The Marketing Concept' in Schwartz, G. (ed.), *Science in Marketing* (New York: John Wiley, 1965), pp. 70-97.

4. An interesting discussion of the history and significance of entrepreneurship is provided by Thwaites, A.T., *The Industrial Entrepreneur: A Definitional Problem* (Newcastle upon Tyne: Centre for Urban and Regional Development Studies, University of Newcastle upon Tyne, 1977).

5. Kirzner, I.M., *Competition and Entrepreneurship* (Chicago: University Press, 1973); *Perception, Opportunity and Profit* (Chicago: University Press, 1979); Kirzner *et al.*, *The Prime Mover of Progress* (London: Institute of Economic Affairs, 1980).

6. E.g. Hayek, F.A., *Individualism and Economic Order* (London: Routledge, 1949).

7. E.g. Mises, L. von, *Human Action: A Treatise on Economics* (New Haven, Conn.: Yale University Press, 1949).

8. Kirzner, 'The Primacy of Entrepreneurial Discovery' in Kirzner *et al.*, *The Prime Mover of Progress*, p. 16. See also: Minkes, A.L. and Foxall, G.R., 'Entrepreneurship, Strategy and Organisation: Individual and Organisation in the Behaviour of the Firm', *Strategic Management Journal*, vol. 1, no. 4 (1980), pp. 295-301.

9. Alford, B.W.E., 'The Chandler Thesis — Some General Observations' in Hannah, L. (ed.), *Management Strategy and Business Development* (London: Macmillan, 1976).

10. Minkes, A.L. and Foxall, G.R., 'The Bounds of Entrepreneurship: Interorganisational Relationships in the Process of Industrial Innovation', *Managerial and Decision Economics*, vol. 3, no. 1 (1982), pp. 41-7.

11. Foxall, G.R. and Minkes, A.L., 'On the Locus of Entrepreneurship in the Modern Corporation', Presented at the Journal of Management Studies Conference, Qualitative Approaches to Organisations, University of Bath, 1982.

12. Foxall, 'Marketing's Domain', *European Journal of Marketing*, vol. 18 (forthcoming).

13. Hippel, E. von, 'Industrial Innovation by Users', Working Paper 953-77 (Alfred P. Sloan School of Management, Cambridge, Mass.: Massachusetts Institute of Technology, 1977).

14. Minkes and Foxall, 'The Bounds of Entrepreneurship', p. 42.

15. Cf. 'How to Strengthen Your Product Plan', *Nielsen Researcher*, 1966; 'Test Marketing Reduces Risks', *Nielsen Researcher*, 1973.

16. Angelus, T.L., 'Why Do Most New Products Fail?', *Advertising Age* (24 March 1969), pp. 85-6; Hopkins, D.S. and Bailey, E.L., 'New Product Pressures', *Conference Board Record* (June 1971), pp. 16-24.

17. Kraushar, P.M., *New Products and Diversification* (London: Business Books, second edition, 1977), pp. 27-8.

18. Davidson, J.H., 'Why Most New Consumer Brands Fail', *Harvard Business Review*, vol. 54, no. 2 (1976), pp. 11-21; reprinted in *Marketing* (April 1977), pp. 55-7.

19. Davidson, J.H., *Offensive Marketing* (London: Penguin, 1975), p. 251.

20. Cooper, R.G., 'Why New Industrial Products Fail', *Industrial Marketing Management*, vol. 4 (1975), pp. 315-26.

21. Ibid., p. 325-6.

22. Rothwell, R., 'Policies in Industry' in Pavitt (ed.), *Technological Innovation and British Economic Performance*, pp. 299-309; 'The Characteristics of Successful Innovators and Technically Progressive Firms', *R&D Management*, vol. 7, no. 3 (1977), pp. 191-206.

23. This table summarises the results of nine important empirical studies: Carter, C.F. and Williams, B.R., *Industry and Technical Progress* (Oxford: Oxford University Press, 1957); Hayvaert, C.H., *Innovation Research and Product Policy: Clinical Research in 12 Belgian Industrial Enterprises* (Catholic University of Louvain, unpublished, 1973); Langrish, J. *et al., Wealth from Knowledge* (London: Macmillan, 1972); Myers, S. and Marquis, D.G., 'Successful Industrial Innovation', (Washington, D.C.: National Science Foundation, 1969); Rothwell, R. *et al.*, 'SAPPHO Updated: Project SAPPHO Phase II', *Research Policy*, vol. 3 (1974); Rothwell, R., *Innovation in Textile Machinery: Some Significant Factors in Success and Failure* (University of Sussex: Science Policy Research Unit, 1976); Schock, G., *Innovation Processes in Dutch Industry* (Apeldoorn, The Netherlands, 1974); Szakasits, G.D., 'The Adoption of the SAPPHO method in the Hungarian Electronics Industry', *Research Policy*, vol. 3 (1974); Utterback, J.M., *The Progress of Innovation in Five Industries in Europe and Japan* (Cambridge, Mass.: Massachusetts Institute of Technology, 1975).

24. Reports of Project SAPPHO include: SPRU, *Project SAPPHO — A Study of Success and Failure in Industrial Innovation* (London: Centre for the Study of Industrial Innovation, 1972); Rothwell, R., 'Marketing and Successful Industrial Innovation' in *Innovation in Marketing* (Glasgow: Department of Marketing, University of Strathclyde, 1973); Robertson, A., 'Innovation Management', *Management Decision*, vol. 12, no. 6 (1974), pp. 329-72; Rothwell, *et al.*, 'SAPPHO Updated — Project SAPPHO Phase II'.

25. Reports of Project NewProd include: Cooper, R.G. and Little, B., 'The Dimensions of Industrial New Product Success and Failure', *Journal of Marketing*, vol. 43, no. 3 (1979), pp. 93-103; 'Identifying Industrial New Product Success: Project NewProd', *Industrial Marketing Management*, vol. 8 (1979) pp. 136-44; Cooper, R.G., 'Project NewProd: Factors in New Product Success', *European Journal of Marketing*, vol. 14, no. 5/6 (1980), pp. 272-92; 'New Product Scenarios: Prospects for Success', *Journal of Marketing*, vol. 45, no. 2 (1981), pp. 48-60.

26. Rothwell, R., 'Marketing — A Success Factor in Industrial Innovation', *Management Decision*, vol. 14, no. 1 (1976), pp. 43-53.

27. Rothwell, R., 'Factors for Success in Industrial Innovation', *Journal of General Management*, vol. 2, no. 2 (1976), pp. 57-65. This is the definition provided by the Central Advisory Council on Science and Technology.

28. Ibid.

29. Rothwell, 'Marketing — A Success Factor in Industrial Innovation'.

30. Ibid., p. 52.

31. Cooper, 'Project NewProd: Factors in New Product Success'.

32. Kraushar, *New Products and Diversification*, pp. 27-8.

33. White, *Consumer Product Development*, p. 69.

34. Davidson, 'Why Most New Consumer Brands Fail', pp. 57-8.

35. E.g. Carter and Williams, *Industry and Technical Progress*; Myers and Marquis, *Successful Industrial Innovations*; Langrish *et al.*, *Wealth from Knowledge*; Utterback, J.M., 'The Process of Innovation', *IEEE Transactions on Engineering Management*, vol. EM-18, no. 4 (1971); Baker, N.R., Siegman, J. and Rubenstein, A.H., 'The Effects of Perceived Means and Needs on the Generation of Ideas for R&D', *IEEE Transactions on Engineering Management*, vol. EM-14, no. 4 (1967).

36. Seiler, R.E., *Improving the Efficiency of R&D* (New York: McGraw-Hill, 1965); Peplow, M.E., 'Design Acceptance' in Gregory, S.A. (ed.), *The Design Method* (London: Butterworth, 1960); Baker, *et al.*, 'The Effects of Perceived Means and Needs on the Generation of Ideas for R&D'.

37. Cooper, 'Why New Industrial Products Fail', pp. 325-6.

38. Roberts, R.W. and Burke, J.E., 'Six New Products – What Makes them Successful?', *Research Management* (May 1974), pp. 21-4.

39. Cooper, 'Project NewProd', p. 287.

40. Rothwell, R., 'The Relationship between Technical Change and Economic Performance in Mechanical Engineering: Some Evidence' in Baker (ed.), *Industrial Innovation*, pp. 39-51.

41. Parkinson, S.T., 'Successful New Product Development – An International Comparative Study', *R&D Management*, vol. 11, no. 2 (1981), pp. 79-85.

42. Reported in Massey, A., 'Why a New Product Fails', *Marketing*, vol. 6, no. 5 (1981), pp. 23-4.

PART TWO

INNOVATIVE BUYING

# 5 INTRODUCTION TO PART TWO

## Innovative Buying

Innovative buying is a subset of buying generally and in the context of marketing management, merits special attention only if it can be shown to be behaviourally distinct in such a way as to signal opportunities for differential marketing strategy. The innovative process is incomplete until the new product has been fully accepted and adopted by the members of relevant social and economic systems — i.e. until it has been purchased (and usually repurchased) sufficiently to achieve corporate objectives set for it — and the primary interest of marketing executives in innovative buying thus stems from the need to use business resources in ways which are appropriate to the acceleration of product diffusion. As the earlier discussion of the innovative process indicates, successful corporate innovation is dependent upon the requisite market responses over time — a positive reaction by innovative buyers and users leading to subsequent adoption by less- or non-innovative purchasers.

### Purchase Strategy

The depiction of strategy in terms of the purposive interaction with the environment renders buyer behaviour as well as the actions of the corporate subsystem capable of conceptualisation as a strategic response: indeed, the view of the innovative process as parallel changes in the behaviour of both producers and customers (which was also developed in Chapter 2) reinforces this understanding. Corporate strategies of innovation must, therefore, dovetail and harmonise not just with 'buyer behaviour' as it is statically monitored and forecast but with the strategic behaviour of customers and consumers as they too interact purposefully with their environments, pursuing their apparent objectives through entrepreneurial alertness to opportunities for personal gain. The purchasing behaviour of organisational buyers may appear more readily to resemble the strategic responses of producers than that of final consumers whose prepurchase plans and consumption behaviours are far less amenable to empirical investigation simply because they seem more erratic, changeable and unpredictable to the observer. It is certainly true that organisational buying behaviour appears superficially more orderly and strategic and one of the most fascinating strands of research interest is the attempt to ascertain relationships between such buying and overall corporate strategy.[1] It is also evident that one of the questions to which subsequent discussion must be addressed is, In what sense can marketing behaviour (i.e. that of both producers and customers) be said to be strategic? The present point, however, is that buyer behaviour may be conceptualised in the same strategic terms as producer behaviour, that they are broadly similar processes: in that all buying and consumption, like all marketing management, occur within a framework of uncertainty and ignorance, the possibility that final as well as organisational consumers may use whatever information is available to them to form patterns or gestalts whose exploitation leads to personal gain suggests that buyer behaviour may justly be considered entrepreneurial or strategic. (Final consumers are rarely in competition as are marketers or industrial buyers but are nevertheless likely to behave in ways consistent with the pursuit of gain.) The role of marketing-oriented business thus involves the provision of information which enables and encourages potential buyers to act entrepreneurially through making specific purchases, an approach to corporate responsibilities which recalls King's definition of marketing-orientation itself as 'helping consumers solve selected problems in a way compatible with planned enhancement of the profit position of the firm'.

## Innovative Buyers

The interest of marketing researchers and managers in customer innovation derives from this orientation but focuses upon the fact that the products involved are new in the sense of having been recently launched on to the market. Since customer innovators are, in many markets, crucial to the diffusion of the product, it is important that managers understand their behaviour in order to judge the probable pace of diffusion and, where necessary, to catalyse that process. This is not the focus adopted by several important writers on the subject, however, who restrict the term *innovation* to the purchase of a product (or the adoption of an idea) which is perceived as new by its purchaser or user regardless of how long it has been generally available. For instance, Rogers and Stanfield[2] state that within their frame of reference, 'It really matters little so far as human behaviour is concerned, whether or not an idea as "objectively" new as measured by the amount of time elapsed since its first use or discovery,' a sentiment which finds repeated expression in the work of Rogers[3] who explains its logic by pointing out that 'It is the newness of the idea to the individual that determines his reaction to it.'

Without denying the value of the work of social scientists whose primary interest is in subjective innovation, it is clear that the strategic interest of marketing researchers and managers in customer innovators confines their frame of reference for the most part to just a proportion of the individuals who are of concern to the former group. Many purchasers of 'objectively' new products *are*, of course, encountering them for the first time and thus perceive them as new. These earliest buyers and users of new products evince a distinct attraction to the purchase of innovations (at least within a certain range), requiring little if any social legitimation of their behaviour in this respect (by definition little or none is available at an interpersonal level since few if any other customers have as yet tried the new product). Midgley[4] goes so far as to define innovativeness as the 'degree to which an individual makes innovation decisions independently of the communicated experience of others'. The majority of customers for any given product do not show high levels of innovativeness: although they may become aware of new products at or shortly after their launch, they delay purchase until an innovation has become socially acceptable, legitimated by the endorsement of earlier adopters, so that it may be perceived as 'less new' or 'more established', 'tried and tested' or 'a necessity rather than a luxury'. *Some* later adopters undoubtedly become aware of products only after they have become firmly established in their life cycles and are thus innovators in Rogers's sense but, except in relatively unusual circumstances, such customers are of marginal strategic significance because their numbers are too small to justify a differential marketing programme.

Marketers' attention is thus concentrated upon the earliest adopters of innovations upon whose behaviour the inauguration of the diffusion process relies and who require and justify differentiated marketing appeals. In this chapter and those which follow, buyer innovators are understood in this marketing sense as the first adopters of a new product: *first* may be operationalised in terms of a given span of time elapsed since launch, though in those cases where it is possible to draw upon previous experience in the introduction of similar products or upon research which identifies innovators, it is likely to be operationally defined by reference to some empirically demonstrated correlate of innovativeness such as heavy buying, socio-economic status or inner-directed behaviour. The behaviour of customer innovators has received a great deal of research attention during the last decades and, concurrently, there have been numerous attempts at modelling innovative buying in order to make possible more general statements about the nature of innovativeness. Before turning to consider these attempts, it is useful to distinguish two concepts upon which models and research depend. These are product *trial*, which refers to the initial purchase and use (usually though not necessarily on one occasion) of a new product, and *adoption*, which is the continued use of the item, exclusively or as an alternative, subsequent to its proving itself in trial. These terms refer to the behaviours of both innovative and non-innovative customers.

## Notes

1. Kennedy, A., 'Industrial Innovation and Marketing Strategy: A Longitudinal Analysis', Proceedings of the Annual Conference of the Marketing Education Group, Dublin, 1981.

2. Rogers, E.M. and Stanfield, J.D., 'Adoption and Diffusion of New Products: Emerging Generalisations and Hypotheses' in Bass, F.M., King, C.W. and Pessemier, E.A. (eds.), *Applications of the Sciences in Marketing Management* (New York: Wiley, 1968), p. 228.

3. Rogers, E.M., *Diffusion of Innovation* (New York: Free Press, 1962) p. 13.

4. Midgley, D.F., *Innovation and New Product Marketing* (London: Croom Helm, 1977), p. 49.

# 6 PATTERNS OF ADOPTION AND DIFFUSION

## Modelling Innovative Adoption

Accounts of strategic decision-making in the context of either marketing or buying behaviour inevitably abstract from observed reality. Abstraction is simply an outcome of the attempt to generalise, to make statements which are not restricted by constant reference to the particular and which are not therefore descriptively accurate of all individual cases. The test of theory in the social sciences is not descriptive correspondence between the tenets of the theory and observable phenomena; it is the capacity of theory to predict. Confidence in the explicative power of a theory derives largely from its ability to facilitate valid forecasting.[1] The import of this is not to deny the usefulness of description but to limit theorisation particularly in the sphere of policy formulation and strategic planning, for the very pressures which encourage abstraction and generalisation in theoretical work militate against the value of theory in policy-making at both macro and micro levels of analysis. By dint of the necessity of abandoning complete descriptive correspondence between observation and the assumptions by which theory simplifies in order to generalise, the *specific* consequences of government, corporate or buyer behaviour in *specific* circumstances which the theory of necessity cannot embrace but which can, nevertheless, not be separated from the devising of policy and strategy, remain largely beyond the predictive power of the theory and thereby the usefulness of theorisation in much applied work is reduced. In matters of policy and strategy description must therefore play a part, albeit aided by theoretical predictions when they are available and when their underlying model's comprehension of the specific case to which the policy applies renders them credible for this purpose.

A scientific model comprises three components: (i) a statement of key explanatory variables, (ii) statements or hypotheses which posit specific relationships among these variables and (iii) rules of correspondence which indicate how the model's variables (which, as has been argued, need not correspond descriptively to observable reality) may be validly operationalised in order to permit empirical testing.[2] Further requirements of models or theories are that they should be parsimonious and refutable; a model which explains or predicts a wide range of phenomena parsimoniously is, moreover, judged superior to one which is of more restricted scope.[3]

Models of buyer behaviour have tended to avoid the rigour and the practicality required by these criteria (and, as a result, the term *model* is used rather more loosely than is desirable). The economic theory of consumer behaviour proceeds at such levels of abstraction that its operationalisation is often beyond human capacity while marketing models of buyer behaviour have tended to stress descriptiveness or have failed to include either relational hypotheses to link their variables or rules of correspondence which make possible empirical test.[4] Further obfuscation has arisen in marketing as a result of an artificial distinction between models of 'general buyer behaviour' and those which purport to make peculiar reference to innovative buying. The result is that models which are essentially similar in scope and range are assigned somewhat arbitrarily to one or other of these categories as though they applied to different orders of reality or levels of analysis. On occasion, this classification of models is said to be justified on the grounds of differential emphasis: models of innovative buying are portrayed as concerned with new product purchase alone and, furthermore, with the full adoption process, while general models are presented as concerned with a single instance of purchase of an 'objectively' old project.[5] This dichotomisation is misleading on several counts. A number of widely-accepted 'composite' models of general buyer behaviour actually concentrate upon new product acceptance thus blurring any distinction between unrestricted models and so-called models of innovative buying.[6] A major advance claimed by many authors of general models, moreover, is the ability of their constructions to cope with repeat buying (or adoption as well as trial) by their incorporation of feedback loops and the assumption of need and purchase continuity. Some general models actually emphasise trial and adoption to a greater extent than do models which are said to be restricted to innovative buying and use. And at least one approach to the modelling of new product purchase behaviour has been generalised without major modification to cover buyer decision-making at large.[7] Although the initial purchase of a product may differ descriptively from routine purchasing (perhaps in ways akin to those suggested by Howard's concepts of extended problem-solving, limited problem solving and routinised response) and, while the individuals involved in each may differ, both innovative and general buyer behaviour are embraced by the paradigm within which models of buying have usually been constructed in marketing.

*Buyer Behaviour: Paradigm and Model*

The essential coincidence of what are variously termed general and specific models of buying is demonstrated in van Raaij's paradigm[8] which is illustrated in Figure 6.1. This relatively simple diagram whose author describes it as a metatheory rather than a specific model[9] is based upon a series of functional relationships among the *economic environment* (E): which includes personal finances, market conditions, employment factors and sources of income; *general environment* (GE): economic growth, government policy, social factors; consumers' and businessmen's *perceptions of the economic environment* (E/P): notions of business climate, market conditions, predictions of the price level, alertness to opportunities, costs; *personal characteristics* (P): expectations, aspirations and lifestyle; the *economic behaviour* (B) of the individual customer or marketer: purchase, consumption, investment and saving; anticipated and unanticipated *situations* (S); *subjective wellbeing* (SW): satisfaction with consumption, employment, living standards, life chances, social relationships; and *social discontent* (SD): dissatisfaction with social, economic and political arrangements and their outcomes. The functional relationships derived from these summary variables are as follows (where → denotes 'is a function of' and ↔ suggests two-way influence: $E \leftrightarrow GE$; $E \rightarrow SW$; $E \rightarrow B$; $E/P \rightarrow E$; $E/P \rightarrow SW$; $P \leftrightarrow E/P$; $B \rightarrow E/P$; $B \leftrightarrow S$; $SW \leftrightarrow B$ and $SW \leftrightarrow SD$.

What characterises van Raaij's approach as a paradigm rather than a model is its inclusion of *generic* influences and outcomes by way of its broad summary variables rather than specifications of variables, relationships and rules of correspondence; as he notes, it is only 'after filling in the boxes with more detailed concepts that a buyer behaviour model may arise'.[10] So comprehensive a framework is of little predictive value in itself but may subsume numerous other models and suggest theoretical developments. In pointing to the possibility of relationships between economic behaviour and buyers' economic perceptions, for instance, van Raaij incorporates the idea of a hierarchy of psychological effects between these initial perceptions and final behaviour, a decision process akin to that used in the more specific model of innovative buying advanced by Rogers and Shoemaker.[11]

This model (which is actually a powerful summary model of buying behaviour in general) is shown in essence in Figure 6.2. The purchase decision process is portrayed as a sequence comprising *knowledge* (awareness/alertness), *persuasion*, *decision* and *confirmation*, and the salient influences upon that sequence are depicted as *receiver characteristics* (personal features and attributes of the individual to whom the innovation is communicated such as personality, attitude towards change, social interactions and perspectives such as cosmopolitenness, and the perceived need for the innovation); *social system variables* (such as norms, toleration of deviance and the integration or cohesiveness of the community); formal and informal *communication*; and *perceived characteristics of the product* (relative advantage, compatibility, complexity, trialability and observability). The specific foci of each of these influences as predicted by the model are also shown:

Figure 6.1: Economic Psychology: van Raaij's Paradigm

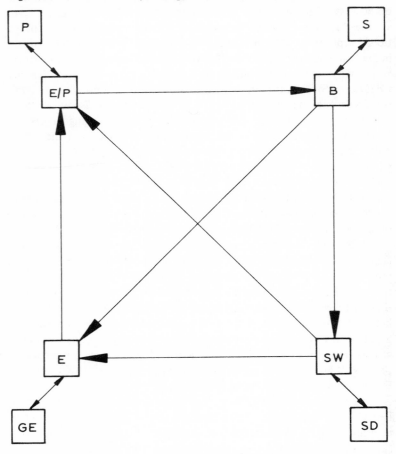

Source: van Raaij, W.F., 'Economic Psychology', *Journal of Economic Psychology*, vol. 1, no. 1 (1981), p. 9. Used by permission.

Figure 6.2: The Innovation-Decision Process

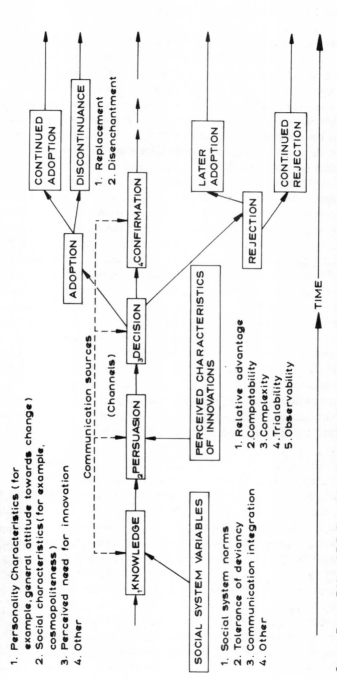

RECEIVER CHARACTERISTICS

1. Personality Characteristics (for example, general attitude towards change)
2. Social characteristics (for example, cosmopoliteness)
3. Perceived need for innovation
4. Other

SOCIAL SYSTEM VARIABLES

1. Social system norms
2. Tolerance of deviancy
3. Communication integration
4. Other

Communication sources
(Channels)

1. KNOWLEDGE
2. PERSUASION
3. DECISION
4. CONFIRMATION

ADOPTION

CONTINUED ADOPTION

DISCONTINUANCE

1. Replacement
2. Disenchantment

REJECTION

LATER ADOPTION

CONTINUED REJECTION

PERCEIVED CHARACTERISTICS OF INNOVATIONS

1. Relative advantage
2. Compatability
3. Complexity
4. Trialability
5. Observability

TIME

Source: Rogers, E.M. and F.F. Shoemaker, *Communication of Innovations* (New York: The Free Press, 1971). Reprinted by permission of the Macmillan Publishing Co. Inc. Copyright © 1971, The Free Press, a division of the Macmillan Company.

the personal characteristics of the individual and his social environment are shown as exerting predominant effect at the initial *knowledge* stage, the perceived characteristics of the innovation primarily the *persuasion* process, while communications constitute a pervasive influence. All individuals presented with a new idea or product are assumed to move through this decision sequence (though presumably with varying levels of involvement) and to accept or reject the innovation: the possibility of revising their first decision is always available, however, and even the 'decision to make full use of a new idea as the best course of action' (i.e. adoption) may be rescinded. The model presented in Figure 6.2 harmonises well with the general framework of conceptualisation and analysis shown in Figure 6.1: the environment (E and EG) subsumes social norms and values with respect to change, innovation and modernisation as well as patterns of interpersonal and mass communication; E/P includes both the potential earlier and later adopters' perceptions of E and the perceived characteristics of the innovation; trial, adoption or rejection are the outcome of E/P and P; the latter includes the personal characteristics which serve to distinguish innovators from non-innovators and non-adopters (see Chapter 7); adoption and non-adoption are the outcomes which determine economic behaviour, B, which is a function of circumstances as well as the perceptions and characteristics of the buyer; continued adoption is dependent upon the subjectively evaluated results of trial and adoption (SW) which are shaped by the innovation's relative advantage in use, social approval of the item's purchase and use, and consequent legitimation, and evaluations of the future availability and performance of the product.[12]

## Rationality vs. Successive Approximation

As has been noted, even simple description of observed events involves abstraction and the least sophisticated of models attribute to human decision-makers a rationality of purpose and behaviour which may not be justified. The very assumption of purposefulness which suggests the description of innovative buying as strategy is questionable; while it may be necessary for theory to make this assumption, purposeful intention often appears to be absent from observed instances of the behaviour of customer innovators (and from that of customers generally, and, for that matter, from the actions of producers). Decision-making in the context of policy and strategy is, nonetheless, frequently shown as a series of rational actions which follow logically and consistently the unambiguous specification of ends. Lindblom[13] notices the similarities of this type of formalisation of the decision process and the procedures of modern 'management science'; 'the hallmarks of these procedures', he writes, 'are clarity of objective, explicitness of evaluation, a high degree of comprehensiveness of overview, and, whenever possible, quantification of values for mathematical analysis'. But, while this may be an appropriate description of the solution of problems of severely limited scope in which comparatively few variables are involved, it provides no adequate basis for the resolution of complex issues which are characterised by multiplicity of variables and by uncertainty as to the nature of opportunity costs and outcomes. The resolution of such difficulties is, in practice, usually accomplished by a much more rough and ready procedure than the notion of a logical and all-embracing process of information-seeking and appraisal conveys. Lindblom refers to the latter, which underlies so many models of human decision-making, as the 'rational-comprehensive' depiction of problem-solving and contrasts it with the method of 'successive, limited comparisons' by which he denotes decision processes in practice.

In practice, ends are often unspecified until the available means have been identified; analysis (including search and evaluation) is seriously constrained because certain valuable outcomes are overlooked; and, rather than decision-making relying upon the application of administrative theory, it comprises a 'succession of comparisons' of limited, relevant, known outcomes from which policy and strategy emerge. The making and implementation of decisions thus tend to reflect past decisions (whose procedures and results are generalised to include the present instance), are incremental, founded upon experience rather than radically based upon the leaps of faith suggested by theoretical predication. They are subject to trial and error, the result of mistakes and their correction as well as of intentional processes and manoeuvres. The theoretically-valid ascription of greater rationality than observation warrants is a result of imposing patterns upon the phenomenal world for purposes other than the direct improvement of practice.

The view that human decision-making proceeds in fact by means of successive approximations to particular, acceptable outcomes is reinforced by theoretical and empirical researches elsewhere in the social sciences. In the first case, it has much in common with the description of entrepreneurial behaviour in 'Austrian' economics which consists in alertness to opportunities to co-ordinate profitably the otherwise incomplete plans of the entrepreneur and others. In the absence of such co-ordination, individuals' plans are likely to remain unfulfilled, being revised continually in a trial and error sequence. It is also consistent with the findings of social psychological investigations of the predictability of behaviour from verbal statements of attitude and behavioural intention. Fishbein and Ajzen[14] have shown that such a statement of behavioural intention is predictive of overt behaviour only when both statement and behaviour are carefully specified in terms of the particular action to take place, the target of that action, the timing and circumstances of the overt behaviour *and* when the statement of behavioural intention is the immediate antecedent of the overt behaviour. Thus, what is often called decision-making is actually no more than the statement of a behavioural intention which can be predictive of behaviour only if referent and circumstances remain unchanged, i.e. if there are no situational interventions between statement and behaviour which render possible some other course of explicit action. Consequently, the behavioural intentions which relate to specific behaviours cannot always be known by either the actor or observers before opportunities to act become available. Hence, despite the development of elaborate decision-making techniques and procedures, behavioural intentions are frequently inchoate prior to the commitment which behaviour itself enforces. It is possible, therefore, to surpass Lindblom in accounting for the selection of ends and means in the decision/behaviour process: if, as he points out, decision-makers adopt simultaneously a means of attaining an objective and the objective itself, it is feasible that ends are ascribed to behavioural outcomes *after the means have been employed*, in order to present rational, logical and consistent patterns of choice and outcome. *Ex post* outcomes are rationalised and described as though they were the result of *ex ante* objectives.

This is highly relevant to the modelling of adoption since most models of buyer behaviour ('general' or 'specific') are based upon the ascription of rational, pre-purchase sequences of decision-making to the buyer. The customer is portrayed as moving through a series of psychological states prior to becoming *convinced* that the product or brand in question is right for him: his continuity of purchase is then assured. This type of formal representation of consumer decision processes and behaviour is clear, for instance, in the 'hierarchy of effects' model presented by Lavidge and Steiner[15] (though it underpins virtually every commonly-accepted model of marketing communication and buyer behaviour).[16] In the Lavidge and Steiner formulation, the customer passes through the mental states of Awareness → Knowledge → Preference → Conviction → Purchase, a sequence which is unlikely for two related but distinct reasons. First, measures of the key intervening variables of affect and behavioural intention (Liking, Preference and Conviction) correlate with measures of behaviour only, as discussed earlier, when the level of situational correspondence is so high as to suggest that situational rather than psychological factors mediate behaviour. Secondly, since the model does not take situational intervention into consideration, it can take no account of the effects of consumption on subsequent purchase decisions and choices. Experience with the product in terms of the benefits gained form its use are ignored: once the state of psychological conviction has been reached as a result of market-dominated circumstances, evaluation and choice are eliminated.

This is in stark contrast to the representation of customer behaviour advanced by Ehrenberg and Goodhardt[17] (which resembles a paradigm rather than a model in terms of the earlier reasoning). Although this was originally constructed to account for patterns of consumption of fast-moving consumer goods it has been generalised to include consumer durables and industrial products and is equally applicable to the purchase of new products and established brands. The $A \rightarrow T \rightarrow R$ paradigm consists of three major summary variables: Awareness, Trial and Reinforcement and lays much greater stress than other models upon trial and adoption, i.e. the *behavioural* aspects of customer choice. Prepurchase persuasion is viewed as having minimal effect upon subsequent behaviour: at most it results in *trial* and it is the evaluation of the product or brand's performance during such trial which determines whether adoption occurs and the pattern of further choice, i.e. the degree of 'loyalty' to a given manufacturer or brand which is apparent from the buyer's post-trial pattern of consumption.

The $A \rightarrow T \rightarrow R$ approach which attributes only relatively weak effects to advertising and promotion on the argument that experience with the product is reinforced primarily by the consequences of that experience appears to accord descriptively with observable market events to a greater extent than does the hierarchy of effects model in which marketing communications assume a much more powerful role. The Rogers and Shoemaker model is also capable of de-emphasising the extent to which pre-purchase (pre-trial) persuasion determines adoption; its *persuasion* stage may be interpreted to conform to a hierarchy of effects approach but it may also harmonise with the idea that minimal pre-trial mental progression occurs and that it is trial and its consequences which decide the pattern of adoption, if any. Persuasion refers to the totality of pre-decisional processes and their outcomes and not merely to the modification of attitudes by advertising. Pre-adoptive trial of the innovation, where this is possible, is essential to the decision process and its results depend firmly upon the 'persuasive' effects of certain subjectively evaluated characteristics of the innovation itself, full appraisal of which *needs* active trial or demonstration. The ascription to the product of high *relative advantage* (relative, that is, to other known and available means of fulfilling the need in question), *compatibility* (with present methods and patterns of usage), *trialability* (which facilitates direct comparison and performance appraisal), *observability* or conspicuousness (which allows the experience of earlier adopters to be monitored, interpreted and judged) and of relatively low *complexity*, is likely to induce a more positive response to full adoption of the product. Where direct trial is impossible, vicarious trial often takes its place but the sequence is rarely if ever from persuasion to adoption, as is the case in the hierarchy of effects models.

Sequential models of buyer behaviour tend, in spite of their apparent descriptive virtues and thus increased suitability for policy analysis and strategic planning, to suggest that customer behaviour is an essentially rational process based upon known objectives and extensive deliberation and assessment of known outcomes rather than a succession of approximations to assumed intentions which themselves vary according to circumstance and the opportunities they ostensibly offer. The belief that prospective buyers can make some sort of objective economic cost/benefit analysis and performance appraisal before making an essentially rational decision looms large in the entire literature of buyer behaviour. Few model-builders (Rogers and Shoemaker, Ehrenberg and Goodhardt being among the exceptions) present approaches which may be seen as behaviourally-based. It is vital to appreciate the extent to which statements of behavioural intention (decisions) may fail to correlate with subsequent actions because of situational interventions. Van Raaij[18] points out that 'Behavioural intentions lead to behaviour if no anticipated or unanticipated situations $S$ arise and prevent realisation . . . These situations may be emergencies, accidents, illnesses, a bank refusing credit, sudden unemployment, marriage, birth of a child. The longer the time lag between behavioural intention and actual behaviour, the higher the probability of situational intervention. Economic behaviour is also influenced by anticipated situations: a party, a weekend trip, being with your partner. Consumers tend to differentiate their product selection according to anticipated usage situations.' Similarly, industrial purchase behaviour including innovation is subject to unexpected, non-logical influence. Sheth[19] presents a model of industrial purchasing in the familiar form of a computer-type flow diagram which implies that 'the choice of a supplier or brand is the outcome of a systematic decision-making process in the organisational setter' but he also points out quite emphatically that 'there is ample empirical evidence in the literature to suggest that at least some of the industrial buying decisions are determined by *ad hoc* situational factors and not by a systematic decision-making process'. The implication is that, at least a subset of purchase situations are such that behaviour rather than its assumed antecedent states should be the focus of research attention and managerial action. The more advanced the innovative process and the more continuous the nature of the products produced and marketed within it, the more probable is low involvement decision-making or routinised responses in which pre-purchase deliberation and evaluation are minimal and in which the scope for influencing customers other than directly through the attributes of the product itself is small.

Thus the possibility of predicting accurately the course of individual buyers' pre-purchase behaviour is small: the stages assumed to constitute the decision process vary from model to model (some positing a cognitive → affective → conative hierarchy, while others employ a conative → affective → cognitive or a cognitive → conative → affective sequence)[20]; the number of stages varies from model to model as does the sequence in which they are presented.[21] Furthermore, the description of buyer behaviour as strategic in the senses of orderly, systematic and purposeful interaction with the environment requires qualification: it may be possible to build up *ex post* a pattern of apparent ends-means relationships from data which describe consumers' decision and behavioural processes; it is quite another task to attempt to predict from decisional statements of intention what strategies will be employed and it is often difficult to predict from such decisions what ends will actually be pursued. Unpredictable situational factors may always intervene and the most powerful theoretical predictions cannot cope with such factors. Nevertheless, while individual purchase and consumption behaviours remain largely unpredictable, the actions of customers in the aggregate (e.g. those of given market segments) are more amenable to forecasting. Of especial interest in the context of this chapter is the segment of initial purchasers or customer innovators which, in many markets can be identified and whose behaviour is usefully accounted for during the early stages of the product or brand life cycle. The creation of a market which is sufficiently large to justify new product development relies to a considerable extent upon the diffusion process for whose inauguration this strategic segment is responsible.

**The Diffusion of Innovations**

Diffusion, cumulative adoption, raises a number of issues which are not only of research interest but impinge directly upon the use of marketing resources over the innovative process. These issues are principally concerned with the manner in which innovation is communicated among individuals and groups and, given that most companies wish the diffusion process to be as temporally short as possible, suggest that markets might be segmented over time.

*The Nature of Diffusion*

Robertson[22] conceptualises the process of diffusion in the context of modern marketing as '(1) the adoption, (2) of new ideas and services, (3) over time, (4) by consumers, (5) within social systems, (6) as encouraged by marketing activities', a definition which makes a useful starting point because of its succinctness but which nevertheless requires qualification. First, it seems unnecessary to point out that buyers are members of some social system or other but the implication that the adopters of a given product constitute *a* social system is misleading. *System* suggests orderly interaction and there is no reason to infer that the consumers or firms that eventually come to make up the market for a new product should constitute a group whose members interact systematically. Rather, it is more probable that such buyers are scattered and belong to different social and economic systems. Perhaps the idea that buyers of new products form a social system is a hangover from the work of rural sociologists who laid the foundations for so much innovation theory and research. The notion of diffusion is clearly of immense practical value in studying the spread of new ideas and practices in local communities as evidenced in the work of anthropologists and medical as well as rural sociologists,[23] whose investigations often employed models of relatively small-scale, primary *communities* nominated *Gemeinschaften* by Tönnies[24] and within which communication flows and influence processes could be identified with comparative ease. *Gemeinschaft* relationships tend to be primary (or face-to-face), intimate and lasting. Some industrial buying relationships contain elements of gemeinschaft interactions but the majority of consumer buying situations and many industrial purchase processes resemble more closely *associations* of disparate individuals linked by limited, contractual agreements; Tönnies referred to such associations as *Gesellschaften*, which are exemplified by large-scale, impersonal organisations 'in which rationality, efficiency and calculation appear to play a more important part than kinship and close face-to-face relationships'.[25] Gemein-schaften individuals 'remain essentially united in spite of all separating factors, whereas in Gesellschaften, they are essentially separated in spite of all uniting factors.'[26]

The second qualification of Robertson's definition of diffusion con-cerns the role of marketer-dominated communication and influence. Marketing activities naturally exert some influence upon the whole pro-cess of innovation and they perform an especially vital part in informing the earliest adopters, the innovators, of a new product of its attributes and availability. However, great emphasis must be given also to the part played by buyer-dominated sources of information during the spread of innovations where the information-provision attributable to informal change agents is often decisive in encouraging direct trial, rendering possible vicarious trial and stimulating adoption.

## Patterns of Diffusion

Although it is commonplace to speak of the diffusion of innovations, by the time 'new' products have been adopted by the majority of the members of their effective markets, they may be far from innovative in that they are no longer products 'recently launched'. Not only may the time elapsed since their introduction to the market have rendered them too well-known to be thought of as innovative: they may well have been partially or wholly superseded by even more recent market-ing offerings. Diffusion is a process in which innovative buyers play a role of central strategic importance − that of making new products socially as well as physically available − but it is usually the later adopters whose purchases enable the financial objectives of the firm to be fulfilled. The process of diffusion is often depicted as in Figure 6.3 (after Rogers) whose categories of adopters are still widely em-ployed. In practice, buyers cannot of course be separated into discrete groups with such precision before diffusion is complete and the actual pattern of diffusion can be mapped only when the life cycle of the innovation is itself at an end.

The identification of the earliest adopters, whether they are defined as the first two and one-half per cent of buyers as is frequent practice in rural sociology, the first ten to fifteen per cent as is often the case in marketing, or whatever, can be finally accomplished only *ex post*, and marketers rely upon the description of the innovators who initiate the diffusion process in the economic and/or behaviour terms discussed above and in Chapter 7 if they are to tailor their marketing programmes to the needs of the primary segments implied by this 'normal curve of diffusion'. The general pattern of diffusion was discovered and used in the earliest work of sociologists and social psychologists whose interests lay often in the communication of new ideas and products among farmers and physicians. Although not all of the assumptions and conclusions which apply to and derive from these innovative contexts are equally valid in marketing, both rural and medical innovation and diffusion involve professional buying in economic settings and provide relatively straightforward opportunities to identify buying centres and decision-making units. Decisions in these contexts are, moreover, closely related to personal factors and the informal influence of the social and professional community. They provide valuable, albeit frequently overlooked, examples of small scale industrial buying and innovation and allow the non-task factors which influence buyers generally to be observed more easily than is often the case in organisational buying.[27]

Figure 6.3: Adopter Categories

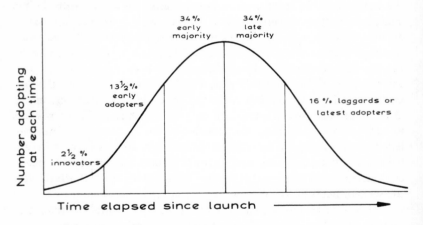

*The Communication of Consumer Innovation*

The communication of novelty in consumer markets depends significantly upon the social legitimation of new products especially where these are conspicuous and have an element of discontinuity. At its simplest, the conspicuousness of the earliest adopters' consumption behaviour leads to their imitation by later adopters. While consumer innovators are thus overwhelmingly dependent upon market-dominated sources of information which operate via the formal media of mass communication and distribution, later purchasers rely less on marketing communications and are influenced to a far-reaching extent by other buyers. The name *opinion leaders* has generally been applied to individuals who exert a disproportionate amount of behavioural influence both by example and by word-of-mouth. The concept of opinion leadership originated in the empirical studies of voting behaviour published from the 1940s onwards by Lazarsfeld, Katz and others[28] whose interpretations of behavioural choices in the political sphere led to the formulation of the hypothesis of a two-step flow of communication. This hypothesis is posited upon the assumption that the majority of the population are essentially passive, not seeking information (about political policies, new products or whatever) from the formal mass media yet internalising and acting upon informal communications from other members of their communities. The informational and persuasive roles of the mass media are thus confined by and large to their effects upon those disproportionally-influential community members upon whom the rest rely, the opinion leaders.

The great merit of the two-step hypothesis lies in its rebuttal of the notion that the mass media communicate directly and with similar and equal effect with each and every member of their audience rather as a physician's hyperdermic needle acts upon each of his patients receiving vaccination (hence the somewhat disparaging references to the 'hyperdermic needle theory of communications' which the two-step theorists saw themselves as replacing). The idea of a one-step flow of communications summarises well the tendency to attribute strong effect to the mass media which still underlies much research and writing in spite of social scientists' demonstrations to the contrary. Nevertheless, the observation that the majority of citizens are informed and their behaviour changed principally by their fellows rather than by mass communicated opinion is only the starting point for the investigation of the social process in which innovations are communicated.

Opinion leadership is a central concept in communications research, even in those theories which postulate that most individuals are rather more active seekers of information and opportunity than does the two-step hypothesis.[29] But recent empirical work has established that opinion leaders themselves are not 'hyperdermically-injected' with information by the mass media: they communicate avidly among themselves too, receive information *from* non-leaders as well as dispensing it to them, and they are not the sole channels of informal communication for consumers, most of whom inform and persuade each other in particular product-specific situations. Communication is multi-phasic rather than a two-step process. Opinion leaders do have certain social, economic and psychological characteristics in common but their verbal and overt behaviours are largely product and situation specific and the sphere of influence of an opinion leader is usually limited to a small number of related products or categories. Like consumer innovativeness itself, opinion leadership tends to be a universal characteristic which is brought to the fore by situational cues and opportunities. Virtually all consumers are capable of providing this form of leadership in some context or other especially since opinion leadership may be passive as well as active.[30]

The strategic importance of word-of-mouth communication is obvious from the work of numerous researchers including Holmes and Lett[31] whose report of the tendency for consumers whose brand opinions are positive to act as opinion leaders and inform more potential buyers than do individuals whose brand-use reactions are negative is of considerable interest to marketing managers. Furthermore, their investigation of the information-seeking behaviour of potential buyers indicates that individuals with strong intentions to buy actively look for information from previous purchasers before making their own choices in the marketplace, a result which adds weight to the contention that the statement of an attitude or purchase intention towards a new brand (even if the attitude or intention is strongly held) is alone unlikely to provide accurate prediction of purchase choice in the absence of information about pre-purchase situational interventions including word-of-mouth reports and their attendant personal influence.

The relationship between interpersonal communication and interpersonal influence is the subject of a paper by Sheth[32] which argues that word-of-mouth information is likely to be of immense importance in the purchase of innovative, fast-moving consumer goods which involve little risk. Marketer-dominated communications for such products are avoided by consumers who believe them to be highly-exaggerated but interpersonal communication may be freely offered in precisely these circumstances because of the low risk of friendships being harmed if the new brand fails to meet the expectations of the influenced party. From his study of the introduction of stainless steel razor blades, Sheth concludes that there is a 'strong relationship between awareness from word-of-mouth and influence of word-of-mouth' which confirms the hypothesis that 'the total market may have a single segment which relies on word-of-mouth for both information and influence'. Those consumers whose own adoption of an innovative brand has been influenced by interpersonal communications are, moreover, likelier than others to stimulate trial of the product by other prospective adopters (which again adds complexity to the fundamental notion behind the two-step formulation). This also confirms the awareness → trial → adoption sequence. More importantly than Sheth concludes, however, this evidence and the line of thought it provokes suggests that only a segment of the market may be especially vulnerable to marketer-dominated influence and that as the innovative process proceeds and more continuous innovations are offered such influence declines significantly. The complexity of information and influence processes which have developed by this stage in the innovative process permit a much wider range of opinion leadership influences than Katz and Lazarsfeld suggested: almost any consumer might exhibit this behavioural trait when personal experience and situational opportunities permit its expression.

As noted above, opinion leadership appears to be product or product group specific;[33] the social, demographic and communications characteristics of leaders seem also to vary with the type of product in question — all of which enhances the view that opinion leadership is a universal institution whose expression is situationally-determined and depends primarily upon perceived risk, the availability of 'objective' information, product cost and the social or cultural meanings of the adoption and usage of the innovation. The identification of opinion leaders *per se* and attempts to influence them separately and directly are thus unlikely to be effective unless the situations in which opinion leadership is an active and acceptable influence can be pinpointed; this has sometimes proved the case among farmers and physicians and industrial buyers but is seldom possible in the case of consumer buying. Rather, the planning, creation and application of innovative marketing mixes requires appreciation of the phenomena of interpersonal influence and their role in the adoption process. Marketing communications in particular require to be designed in such a way as to stimulate information seeking and to provide information which may be assimilated by opinion leaders and transmitted to other potential consumers.

Not only do different segments of consumer markets play distinct roles during the various stages of the innovative process: so do different producer organisations. As the product becomes increasingly continuous, so its development and marketing become the responsibility of more bureaucratised departments or firms which are geared to incremental change and less willing to assume risks. An interesting example of this phenomenon is inherent in the observation of the interaction of parallel processes of communication and diffusion; Midgley and Wills[34] hypothesise that fashion goods diffuse simultaneously among retailers, whose marketing is usually segmented, and final consumers; thus 'every season, or few seasons, the more innovative organisations launch one or more style innovations. Some of these are acceptable to a significant proportion of the public, and spread or diffuse to the general population, probably over a period of years. However, the majority of style innovations are not acceptable to the consumer and are not adopted by more than a small minority of the market. Those fashions that do succeed within this innovative market segment are noticed by the merchandising executives of the larger and less innovative retail organisations who in turn put the new style into their outlets and thus accelerate its diffusion through society.'

## Diffusion in Industrial Markets

Upon the rate of diffusion of new products depends the timing of the stream of strategic benefits which producer innovators can expect; indeed, the availability of any benefit is generally felt to be contingent upon the fulfilment of the sequence of cumulative adoption shown in the familiar S-shaped logistic curve of diffusion which has been frequently observed. Additionally, upon the speed with which effective industrial innovations spread depends the release of higher levels of productivity which are expected to result in enhanced economic growth and material wellbeing. There is some evidence that the life cycles of consumer products are becoming significantly shorter but the innovative process for major industrial products has generally been characterised by slow diffusions.[35] Mansfield[36] concluded from his studies of innovation in the bituminous coal, iron and steel, brewing and railway industries that 'Measuring from the date of the first successful commercial application, it took twenty years or more for all the major firms to install centralised traffic control, car retarders [on the railroads], by-product coke ovens and continuous annealing [in iron and steel]. Only in the case of the pallet-loading machine, tin container [in brewing] and continuous mining machine [in bituminous coal] did it take ten years or less for all the major firms to install them.' Closely related is the rate at which innovations can be imitated: 'Sometimes it took decades for firms to install a new technique, but in other cases they imitated the innovator very quickly. For example, fifteen years elapsed before half the major pig-iron producers had used the continuous-mining machine. The number of years elapsing before half the firms had introduced an innovation varied from 0.9 to 15.' The same point is made by Davies[37] in his more recent study of the diffusion of 22 industrial process innovations:

> . . . diffusion is often a long drawn out process. Whilst four of the sample innovations had been adopted by about half, or more, of all potential adopters only six years after their first introduction, for another sixteen, 50 per cent diffusion (measured in this way) had not been attained eight years after their first introduction. Indeed for seven of those, over half of all potential adopters had still not adopted even fourteen years after the first appearance of the innovation.

General patterns of industrial diffusion vary, moreover, quite substantially with economic and social circumstances as international comparisons indicate well. Nabseth and Ray[38] investigated the diffusion of eight industrial processes (numerically-controlled machine tools, float glass, an acid used in malting, shuttle-less looms, oxygen steel, continuous steel casting, tunnel kilns for brick-making and special presses for paper-making) in the USA, UK, Austria, France, West Germany, Sweden and Italy during the late 1940s to 1960s period. The speed of diffusion was shown to be a function of the time of initial national adoption, potential profitability of adoption, positive managerial attitudes, access to investment capital and the national rate of growth of investment. The countries involved differed from each other in terms of diffusion rates for the various processes and a wide range of social, structural, economic and behavioural factors was used to explain these international differences. The assessment of these factors — e.g. wage levels, the quality of information systems, managerial competence and trades union attitudes — insofar as they impinge upon corporate planning and the implementation of strategy have a profound effect upon the overall geography of diffusion and product life cycles.[39]

The linking of diffusion rates with the strategic context of the potential universe of adopters is of especial interest in view of the discussion of innovation and strategy in Chapter 3 in which levels of cost and the speed of their reduction with volume loom large. As Sciberras[40] notes from his study of innovation in UK semiconductors, 'The *pattern* of diffusion of innovations has in the past reflected the price-elasticities of demand of various applications, from the price-insensitive military market to the highly price-conscious consumer market. The pace of diffusion is linked to the process of steep cost reduction through cumulative production volume and experience which pervades the industry. This process is described by the learning curve and is made up of a technological and a manufacturing element.' For the semi-conductor industry it was found that the doubling of output volume reduced manufacturing costs by 27-30 per cent. The subjective meaning of cost reductions depends upon the strategic mode of the adopting organisation, the relatively proactive or reactive outlook of its senior executives and the slope of its experience curves in the manufacture and marketing of the various components of its product/business portfolio. Only if cost reductions elsewhere harmonise with the strategic mode made possible and desirable by this combination of factors is the innovation in question likely to be adopted. Where even a small number of major firms adopt an innovation, however, the effects on the process of diffusion can be enormous. Sciberras continues 'The rapidly falling costs of componentry are passed on as lower costs for the sub-systems and systems of end-equipment manufacturers. Such reductions encourage the wider use of end-equipment and applications in areas previously excluded for reasons of cost. This increased end-use demand further stimulates semiconductor production and a further round of cost falls, and so on.'[41]

At the early stages of the life cycle of the innovative product or brand, managerial concerns revolve around the need to initiate as quickly as possible a successful diffusion sequence; the dynamics of this process are in many ways beyond the control or influence of the innovative producer, however, and a complementary concern is the elimination of those new products which early show signs that the desired pattern of cumulative adoption will not occur. The general pattern of diffusion depicted in Figure 6.3 thus takes on considerable strategic significance. Baker[42] claims that 'once initial adoption has occurred, diffusion will follow, given the existence of the necessary enabling conditions, and exhibit an S-shaped growth curve'. He refers to this as a law-like chain reaction in which diffusion, up to the point at which fifty per cent of potential adopters have bought, can be most accurately viewed as an exponential process: 'once an initial sale has been made, sales will double in each succeeding period of time equivalent in length to the first period'. If this pattern can be taken as representative of diffusion processes in general, producer innovators have a benchmark by which to measure the progress of their new products and according to which marketing strategy decisions with respect to the commitment of (further) resources, the modification of the marketing mix and product elimination can be taken. There are two reasons for urging caution upon those who incline to this simplistic view. First, in practice, the pattern and speed of diffusion (as depicted in diffusion curves) can vary considerably from innovation to innovation: no single curve has universal validity as applied to empirically-discerned patterns of diffusion. Reynolds and Wells[43] have, for instance, pointed out that the pattern of diffusion of a real product may follow one of several forms. 'In general,' they write, 'it is believed that discontinuous innovations tend to follow the S-shaped growth curve and that continuous innovations tend to exhibit an exponential growth curve,' though they admit to the sparsity of empirically-derived evidence for this precise belief. Secondly, the key phrase in Baker's statement of the principal of diffusion is 'given the existence of the necessary enabling conditions'. Once again, this raises the issues of the situational context of adoption and diffusion and the need to study adoption decisions at the intra-firm level of analysis. These points deserve amplification.

## Towards Understanding Patterns of Industrial Diffusion

Basic marketing texts often simplify the process of diffusion, casting its pattern as unitary and ubiquitous. There are, in actuality, several apparent patterns of diffusion and managerial decision-making with respect to both the marketing and adoption of innovations does well to recognise relevant variations. Much depends, for instance, upon the relative continuity of the product or process in question. If the diffusion of consumer goods is most usefully and accurately depicted as a communications process, it may well be because of the continuous nature of most of the products involved in it. Schon[44] is critical of those who confine the study of diffusion to such items by considering 'the diffusion only of new products or techniques which presuppose a relatively stable technological system of which they are components'. This limitation of viewpoint can be particularly dangerous in the case of industrial products such as a new agricultural weedkiller:

If the weed-killer could be shown to be relatively effective and innocuous in its side-effects, and if it promised an increase in land productivity or a further reduction in farm labour, then managers of middle- to large-sized farms might accept it fairly readily. Its diffusion might then very well consist of disseminating information, conducting trials, influencing opinion-leaders, and the like. But this would be because the weed-killer meshes with a pre-existing technological system whose objectives it seems likely to enhance with relatively little disruption. For that system, it is not . . . a very significant innovation.

The process by which discontinuous innovations diffuse is, however, 'more nearly a battle than a communication' because of the 'dynamically conservative plenum into which information moves . . .'. Indeed,

> The situation is quite different where the introduction of the innovation requires significant disruption of the entire technological-social system and the system of ideas related to it. In such a case, diffusion of an innovation looks less like the dissemination of information than like a sequence of related disruptions of complex systems, resulting in each case in a new configuration. Here the unit of diffusion is not a product or technique but a whole technological system.[45]

Davies,[46] whose work on the diffusion of industrial process innovations received brief mention above is also critical of mechanistic models of the diffusion process founded upon grossly unrealistic assumptions.[47] His own model of industrial diffusion is based upon the recognition that potentially adoptive firms respond differently to a given innovation: their perceptions of its likely profitability, their attitudes towards risk-taking and, in particular, towards innovation are among the factors which account for this. Furthermore, there are likely to be considerable variations in the effects and effectiveness of innovations over time. Different industrial innovations permit the exploitation of quite distinct learning curve phenomena for both producers and adopters with the effect that 'the post-invention improvements in the specification of major, technologically complex processes are likely to occur over a long period, with little tendency for them to "tail off" after the first few years of the innovation's life as is likely for cheaper and more simple innovations'. This distinction between process innovations which are relatively, technically-simple, inexpensive and produced off-site and those which are more elaborate and costly, custom-made and frequently requiring long periods of on-site installation is crucial to Davies's model. The former are known as 'Group A' innovations, the latter as 'Group B' innovations and Table 6.1 lists the actual new processes studied. Figure 6.4 shows the essential difference in learning effects shown by the two types of new process.

The model's author comments that:

> Learning effects (as reflected by declining labour inputs, both in the *production* of the innovation and *when using it*) for group A might be initially quite large, but soon falling away drastically. For group

B, they are likely to be much longer lived and, in the long run, more substantial. Nevertheless, over the early years, whilst the manufacturer is overcoming teething troubles and building up a portfolio of knowledge about his customers' different operating conditions, learning might be quite limited for group B.[48]

Figure 6.4: Learning Effects for Group A and Group B Innovations

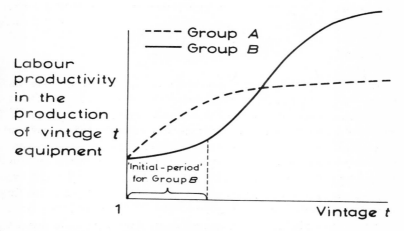

Source: Davies, S., *The Diffusion of Process Innovations* (Cambridge: Cambridge University Press, 1979), p. 51. Used by permission.

The elements of this distinction between essentially continuous and discontinuous innovations are operative in determining the pattern and pace of diffusion shown by a particular new process and thus for the shape of the diffusion curve. Davies's model predicts that group A innovations will exhibit a positively skewed cumulative lognormal diffusion curve while those of group B will follow a symmetrical cumulative normal S shaped pattern (see Figure 6.5). Both the predictions of the model and the empirical patterns of diffusion which generally support it depart from the expectations of many writers on innovation in economics and marketing. The widely-assumed logistics curve depicts diffusion as a sequence in which cumulative adoption accelerates until half the eventual population has adopted; thereafter the adoption level continues to increase but at a decelerating rate.[49] This pattern is disconfirmed by the majority of Davies's empirical observations: 'the curves predicted by the model performed better [in all but one case, though sometimes marginally] than the logistic, the latter often proving to be an apparent misspecification'. Group B innovations typically show a pattern of diffusion which can be represented by a symmetrical S-shaped curve similar to the logistics curve, while for group A processes, the typical curve is positively-skewed which suggests that the adoption rate peaks at an early stage and then slows appreciably.[50]

Table 6.1: Types of Industrial Process Innovation

| Innovation | Industry | Nature | Initial adoption |
|---|---|---|---|
| **GROUP A** | | | |
| Special presses | Paper and board | Supplementary | 1962 |
| Foils | ditto | ditto | 1962 |
| Synthetic fabrics | ditto | ditto | 1962 |
| Wet suction boxes | ditto | ditto | 1957 |
| Gibberellic acid | Malting | ditto | 1959 |
| Accelerated drying hoods | Weaving | ditto | 1948 |
| Electric hygrometer | ditto | Involving automation | 1935 |
| Automatic Size box | ditto | ditto | 1951 |
| **GROUP B** | | | |
| Paper machine control by computer | Paper and board | Involving automation | 1965 |
| Automatic track lines | Car manufacture | ditto | 1947 |
| Tunnel kilns | Clay brick making | Replacing capital-embodied old technology | 1953 |
| Basic oxygen process | Iron and steel | ditto | 1958 |
| Continuous casting | ditto | ditto | 1959 |
| Vacuum melting | ditto | Involving new function | 1958 |
| Vacuum degassing | ditto | ditto | 1955 |
| **UNCLASSIFIED*** | | | |
| Computer typesetting | Provincial newspapers | Involving automation | 1964 |
| Photo-electrically controlled cutting machines | Shipbuilding | ditto | 1957 |
| Shuttleless looms | Weaving | Replacing capital-embodied old technology | 1958 |
| Tufted carpet machines | Carpet manufacture | ditto | 1962 |
| Numerically-controlled machine tools | Turning machine manufacture | ditto | 1956 |
| Ditto | Turbine manufacture | ditto | 1957 |
| Ditto | Printing press manufacture | ditto | 1962 |

Note: *The innovations have characteristics of both group A and group B.
Source: Derived from Davies, S., *The Diffusion of Process Innovations*, (Cambridge, Cambridge University Press, 1979) pp. 38-9; for full details see these pages.

Figure 6.5: Diffusion Curves Predicted by Davies' Model

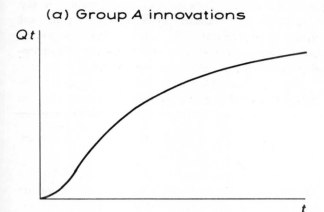

(a) Group A innovations

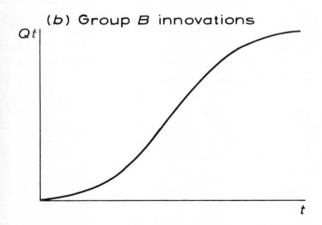

(b) Group B innovations

Note: $Qt$ is the probability that a randomly-selected firm will have adopted by time $t$.
Source: Davies, S., *The Diffusion of Process Innovations* (Cambridge: Cambridge University Press, 1979), p. 79. Used by permission.

The different learning effects associated with innovations of types A and B imply differences in the flows of information and the competitive pressures felt by non-adopters during their respective diffusion processes. The more profitable an innovation, the more quickly it spreads and the entry of highly profitable innovations to an industry puts those firms which have not yet introduced them at a disadvantage *vis-à-vis* their competition. Furthermore, there is no evidence to suggest that more expensive innovations diffuse more slowly, probably because they are the more profitable processes and word of their efficacy spreads comparatively quickly through the industry and helps reduce the uncertainties and risks associated with adoption. In addition, the speed of diffusion varies directly with the profitability of the new process, the labour intensity of the purchasing industry, and less significantly, the growth rate of that industry; it varies inversely with the number of firms in the adopting industry and the size inequalities among its firms.

## Situation-specific Adoption

Diffusion of industrial innovations depends upon managerial attitudes and organisation, the communicability of the comparative advantages of the new product or process and a host of additional specific factors. The search for a single generalised determinant of the rate of industrial diffusion seems pointless in the light of the situation-specific variety of empirical patterns available. This should not imply that the relevant situational variables and their environmental causes cannot be identified and used to predict adoption and diffusion in particular cases: but it is entirely consistent with the difficulties inherent in attempts at drawing generically-applicable conclusions from the welter of empirical studies of interpersonal communication and influence in the industrial adoption process. Indeed, evidence of the incidence and effect of industrial opinion leadership leads only to the confusing conclusion of apparent contradiction if the results of individual studies are taken at face value. The following examples illustrate the paradox.

The well-known investigations of Webster[51] and Martilla[52] indicate quite distinct approaches to interpersonal communication in industrial marketing and purchasing. The former, a study of American manufacturing companies serving a variety of markets, revealed insignificant patterns of *interfirm* opinion leadership:

> Only two of 50 respondents indicated there were certain companies they consistently looked to because those companies' acceptance of new purchased products was important to them. The majority agreed that specific companies were not important because each company's problems are different and it is unlikely for two companies to have the same needs and experience at the same points in time. Opinion leaders, if they exist at all, seem to be rare in industrial markets.

Matilla's investigation of companies in the US paper industries not only led him to emphasise *intrafirm* opinion leadership, an area which Webster ignored, but to argue that, 'Contrary to Webster's findings, buying influentials in the converting markets also reported seeking information about paper from persons in competing firms, in much the same way as within the firms.'[53]

Two British studies confirm the apparent contradiction. From investigations of rates of diffusion in flour milling industries, Hayward[54] noted that 'Purchasers and potential purchasers repeatedly stated that they gained information from colleagues after having obtained initial details of new products from sales engineers, advertising leaflets and trade journals. Further study demonstrated that the same people were visited time and time again . . . These opinion leaders play a major role in the successful introduction of new products and highlight the importance of good communications.' Extra-firm reference groups included other millers and the milling engineers who produced the innovations in milling equipment.[55] However, the examination of the adoption and diffusion of chemicals and dyestuffs in the UK textile industry reported by Lancaster and White[56] revealed that 'the communications approach could not account for the observed pattern because of the infrequent incidence of interfirm opinion leadership'. It is hardly surprising that reviewers of the organisational buying literature have reached only very tentative conclusions about the role of inter-personal information and influence in industrial purchasing.[57]

Yet, the confusion which surrounds the study of the processes in which industrial innovations are communicated and diffused is reduced when the situational factors associated with these procedures are taken sufficiently into consideration. These factors have been accorded only passing reference in a lot of cross-sectional studies of industrial buying but Czepiel[58] gives them greater than usual prominence in his socio-metrically-based studies of interpersonal interactions in the American steel and electrical utilities industries. Czepiel draws attention to the social nature of innovation and the social environment of the firm in ways which are reminiscent of the stress placed upon the contextual variables in terms of which organisational structure, behaviour and performance is explained by members of the contingency theory school of organisation studies. He shows that decision-makers within competitive industries are linked by patterns of communications that reflect their joint interests and problems. Although communications networks vary from industrial setting to industrial setting, each context displays a degree of homogeneity. The major points of industrial structure and process upon which variations in communications networks depend are the similarity of production processes, organisational and managerial behaviours (especially the allocation of responsibility), industrial competition, and the age and maturity of the industry. Thus, the existence of common productive processes and methods implies that firms share the same problems and information needs and that other members of the industry are capable of providing the necessary information. Similar managerial and technical organisation implies the presence of institutions (formal ones such as trade associations and informal such as social events) which allow frequent exchanges of information to take place. The degree of competition in the industry has obvious repercussions on the flow of information. And, finally, the age of the industry has implications for the continuity of personal relationships, feelings of competitiveness, production methods and the recognition of common problems and interests. Moreover, the particular nature of any given buying situation, its causes and consequences, determines managers' information needs and their willingness to seek the views and experiences of opinion leaders.

Consideration of some of the individual empirical studies of industrial diffusion in the light of these comments concerning situational influences, begins to reduce the apparent paradoxes thrown up by those studies' results. Webster[59] notes, for instance, that the two firms whose personnel did engage in opinion leadership relationships possessed a number of the features of technically-progressive firms: large size, commitment to the development of new products, intent upon growth, financial success and progressive general management. Further, Martilla[60] points out that patterns of information exchange within the paper industries do indeed vary with levels of perceived competition: thus paper converters serving regional markets with standardised products were quite prepared to divulge to one another information on price, quality and delivery; but greetings card manufacturers who compete severely on a national basis in terms of design novelty refused to share information. Again, as Hayward points out the flour milling industry in which opinion leadership was rife is characterised by age, maturity and positive managerial attitudes to innovation; but Lancaster and White detail at some length the fierce competition in the textile industry which impedes the flow of innovation-related discussion.

These examples have not been selected because they appear to justify Czepiel's conclusions; rather they have puzzled the author for some time in the absence of any unifying framework which 'explains' their diversity of results.[61] A great deal of empirical exploration and theoretical interpretation is evidently required before a completely convincing statement of the contextual factors which contribute to the explanation of variations in patterns of industrial communications in the context of innovation can be made. Nevertheless enough has been said to indicate the importance of situational influences upon the diffusion of industrial innovations and to suggest the relevance of Czepiel's framework of analysis.

## Conclusion

The validity and usefulness of the concepts of buyer awareness, product trial and post-trial reinforcement/confirmation which are the principal components of the simplest models of the adoption process are supported by the analysis presented in this chapter as well as by current empirical evidence.[62] These variables have also proved to be of decisive, strategic importance in the prediction of new product sales and later chapters will return to this theme. One of the crucial needs of effective innovative strategy by producers continues to be the requirement to perceive and understand the innovative strategies of buyers. Awareness, trial, reinforcement and the search and evaluation behaviours which accompany them constitute buyers' strategic action as they attempt to satisfy their own needs, to attain their peculiar objectives. These actions are, in part, capable of modelling in terms of economic rationality: to a large degree, however, they are not. There is clear evidence that many companies fail to take buyers' strategic needs into consideration in their own marketing plans and management.[63] But there is also proof that companies may take definite steps to increase the effectiveness and efficiency of the new product development process in ways which improve the rate of fulfilment of the strategic needs of buyers and, thereby, those of innovative producers.

The match of strategic strengths and opportunities should also influence the point at which a producer of new products enters the innovative process as depicted by Abernathy and Utterback. Those strengths, opportunities and the probability that they will match are largely determined by the probable pattern and pace of diffusion. The timing of innovative entry depends therefore upon the strategic assessment of internal capacities *in relation to* the external market processes which have been considered in this chapter. In the context of international innovation in steel industries, Aylen[64] states that being the leading innovator is not always desirable or necessary: 'A world leader like Japan bears the cost of innovation, yet the resulting benefits are only partially internalised in the form of licence fees or additional sales and profits for plantmakers. Latecomers are able to learn cheaply from these and similar mistakes.' To enter the innovative process early may be to wait longer years for one's basic new product model to diffuse; to enter later may be to take advantage of dominant designs especially if one has the capacity to adapt quickly to demand for product modifications. Similarly, many adopters may prefer to try to accommodate the innovation only after it has benefited from development based upon the experience of earlier users and the applications to which it has been moulded by earlier users.

## Notes

1. Friedman, M., *Essays in Positive Economics* (Chicago: Chicago University Press, 1953), pp. 14-15.

2. Cushman, D.P. and McPhee, R.D. (eds), *Message – Attitude Behaviour Relationship* (New York: Academic Press, 1980); see the editors' opening chapter, especially pp. 8-14. Although the authors are psychologists, their remarks are pertinent to marketing.

3. Popper, Sir Karl, *The Logic of Scientific Discovery* (New York: Basic Books, 1959).

4. Foxall, G.R., 'Marketing Models of Buyer Behaviour: A Critical Review', *European Research*, vol. 8, no. 5 (1981), pp. 195-206.

5. Robertson, T.S., 'A Critical Examination of "Adoption Process" Models of Consumer Behaviour' in Sheth, J.N. (ed.), *Models of Buyer Behaviour* (New York: Harper and Row, 1974), pp. 271-95.

6. E.g. Nicosia, F.M., *Consumer Decision Processes* (New Jersey: Prentice-Hall, 1966); Howard, J.A. and Sheth, J.N., *The Theory of Buyer Behaviour* (New York' Wiley, 1969).

7. Baker, M.J., *Marketing New Industrial Products* (London: Macmillan, 1975). Cf. Baker, M.J., *Marketing: An Introductory Analysis* (London: Macmillan, 1979), Chapter 4.

8. van Raaij, 'Economic Psychology', *Journal of Economic Psychology*, vol. 1, no. 1 (1981), pp. 1-25.

9. Personal communication, 24 February 1982.

10. Ibid.

11. Rogers, E.M. and Shoemaker, F.F., *Communication of Innovations* (New York: Free Press, 1971), Chapter 3.

12. van Raaij, 'Economic Psychology', pp. 17-18.

13. Lindblom, C.E., 'The Science of Muddling Through', *Public Administration Review*, vol. 19, no. 2 (1959), pp. 79-88.

14. Ajzen, I. and Fishbein, M., 'Attitude-Behaviour Relations: A Theoretical Analysis and Review of Empirical Research', *Psychological Bulletin*, vol. 84 (1977), pp. 888-918.

15. Lavidge, R.J. and Steiner, G.A., 'A Model for Predictive Measurements of Advertising Effectiveness', *Journal of Marketing*, vol. 25, no. 6 (1961), pp. 59-62.

16. Foxall, G.R., *Consumer Choice* (London: Macmillan, 1983).

17. Ehrenberg, A.S.C. and Goodhardt, G.J., 'How Advertising Works' in *Essays on Understanding Buyer Behaviour* (New York: J. Walter Thompson/ MRCA, 1980). See also Ehrenberg, A.S.C., 'Repetitive Advertising and the Consumer', *Journal of Advertising Research*, vol. 14, no. 2 (1974), pp. 25-34.

18. van Raaij, 'Economic Psychology', p. 11.

19. Sheth, J.N., 'A Model of Industrial Buyer Behaviour', *Journal of Marketing*, vol. 37, no. 4 (1973), pp. 50-6.

20. Ray, M.L., 'Marketing Communication and the Hierarchy of Effects' in Clarke, P. (ed.), *New Models for Mass Communication Research* (Beverly Hills: Sage, 1973), pp. 147-76.

21. Robertson, 'A Critical Examination of "Adoption Process" Models of Consumer Behaviour', pp. 281-4.

22. Robertson, T.S., 'New Product Diffusion' in Kassarjian, H.H. and Robertson, T.S. (eds), *Perspectives on Consumer Behaviour* (Glenview, Illinois: Scott Foresman, 1981), pp. 350-6.

23. The earliest study is generally thought to be that of an anthropologist: Tarde, G., *Laws of Imitations* (New York: Henry Holt, 1903). Some of the most interesting studies of innovation and diffusion have been carried out by social scientists whose primary interest was in fields other than marketing. A review of diffusion research that focuses upon rural communities is found in Jones, G.E., 'The Adoption and Diffusion of Agricultural Practices', *World Agricultural Economics and Rural Sociology Abstracts*, vol. 9, no. 3 (1967), pp. 1-34. Other selected references are: Beal, G.M. and Bohlen, J.M., *The Diffusion Process* (Iowa Agricultural Extension Service, 1957); Bohlen, J.M., Conghenour, C.M., Lionberger, H.F., Moe, E.O. and Rogers, E.M., *Adopters of New Farm Ideas: Characteristics and Communications Behaviour* (Michigan Cooperative Extension Service, 1961); Grilliches, Z., 'Hybrid Corn: An Exploration in the Economics of Technological Change', *Econometrica*, vol. 25, no. 4 (1957), pp. 501-22. Kennedy, L., 'Evaluation of a Model Building Approach to the Adoption of Agricultural Innovation', *Journal of Agricultural Economics*, vol. 28, no. 1 (1977), pp. 55-61; Jones, G.E., 'Agricultural Innovation and farmer Decision Making' in *Agriculture* (Milton Keynes: Open University, 1972). In the context of medical sociology, see Coleman, J., Katz, E. and Menzel, H., 'The Diffusion of an Innovation among Physicians', *Sociometry*, vol. 20, no. 4 (1957), pp. 253-70; Menzel, H. and Katz, E., 'Social Relations and Innovation in the Medical Profession: The Epidemiology of a New Drug', *Public Opinion Quarterly*, vol. 19, no. 4 (1955/6), pp. 337-52. *Medical Innovation: A Diffusion Study* (New York: Bobbs-Merrill, 1966). Cf. Ryan, J.F. and Murray, J.A., 'The Diffusion of a Pharmaceutical Innovation in Ireland', *European Journal of Marketing*, vol. 11, no. 1 (1977), pp. 31-42.

24. Tönnies, F., *Gemeinschaft und Gesellschaft*, first published in 1887, translated and edited by Loomis, C.P. and published as *Community and Society* (Michigan: Michigan State University Press, 1957).

25. Woolacott, J., 'Community', in *Social Relations* (Milton Keynes: Open University, 1975), p. 97.

26. Ibid.

27. Foxall, G.R., 'Farmers' Tractor Purchase Decisions: A Study of Interpersonal Communication in Industrial Buying Behaviour', *European Journal of Marketing*, vol. 13, no. 8 (1979) pp. 299-308; 'Adoption of a Discontinuous Innovation in Agriculture: Rough Terrain Forklift Trucks', *European Journal of Marketing*, vol. 14, no. 1 (1980), pp. 75-82; 'Industrial Buying During Recession: Farmers' Tractor Purchases', *Management Decision*, vol. 17, no. 4 (1979), pp. 317-25.

28. Lazarsfeld, P.F., Berelson, B. and Gaudet, H., *The People's Choice* (New York: Duell, Sloan and Pearce, 1942); Katz, E. and Lazarsfeld, P.F., *Personal Influence* (New York: The Free Press, 1955); Katz, E., 'The Two-Step Flow of Communication', *Public Opinion Quarterly*, vol. 21, no. 1 (1957), pp. 61-8.

29. Cox, D., 'The Audience as Communicators', *Proceedings of the American Marketing Association* (Chicago: American Marketing Association, 1963).

30. See Foxall, G.R., *Marketing Behaviour* (Aldershot: Gower, 1981), Chapter 4.

31. Holmes, J.H. and Lett, J.D., 'Product Sampling and Word of Mouth', *Journal of Advertising Research*, vol. 17, no. 5 (1977), pp. 35-40.

32. Sheth, J.N., 'Word-of-Mouth in Low-Risk Innovations', *Journal of Marketing Research*, vol. 11, no. 3 (1971), pp. 15-18.

33. On the question of the specificity of opinion leadership, see Katz and Lazarsfeld, *Personal Influence*: Silk, A.J., 'Overlap amongst Self-designated Opinion Leaders', *Journal of Marketing Research*, vol. 8, no. 3 (1966), pp. 255-9; Robertson, T.S. and Myers, J.H., 'Personality correlates of Opinion Leadership and Innovative Buying Behaviour', *Journal of Marketing Research*, vol. 6, no. 2 (1969), pp. 164-8; King, C.W. and Summers, J.O., 'Overlap of Opinion Leadership across Consumer Product Categories', *Journal of Marketing Research*, vol. 7 no. 1 (1970), pp. 43-50; Gross, E.J., 'Support for a Generalised Marketing Leadership Theory', *Journal of Advertising Research*, vol. 9, no. 6 (1969), pp. 49-52; Montgomery, O.B. and Silk, A.J., 'Patterns of Overlap in Opinion Leadership' in McDonald, P. (ed.), *Marketing Involvement in Society and the Economy* (Chicago: American Marketing Association, 1969), pp. 377-81. 'Clusters of Consumer Interest and Opinion Leaders' Spheres of Influence', *Journal of Marketing Research*, vol. 8, no. 3 (1971), pp. 317-21. See also Turnbull, P.W. and Meenaghan, A., 'Diffusion of Innovation and Opinion Leadership', *European Journal of Marketing*, vol. 14, no. 1 (1980), pp. 3-33.

34. Midgley, D.F. and Wills, G.S.C., 'The Management of Fashion', *Cranfield Research Papers in Marketing and Logistics*, no. 9, 1974/5, p. 134.

35. Olshavsky, R.W., 'Time and the Rate of Adoption of Innovations', *Journal of Consumer Research*, vol. 6, no. 4 (1980), pp. 425-8; Mahajan, V. and Schoeman, M.E.F., 'Generalised Model for the Time Pattern of the Diffusion Process', *IEEE Transactions on Engineering Management*, vol. EM-24, no. 1 (1977), pp. 12-18.

36. Mansfield, E., *The Economics of Technological Change*, (New York: Norton, 1968).

37. Davies, S. *The Diffusion of Process Innovations* (Cambridge: Cambridge University Press, 1979), p. 160.

38. Nabseth, L. and Ray, G.F. (eds), *The Diffusion of New Industrial Processes* (Cambridge: Cambridge University Press, 1974).

39. Ibid.

40. Sciberras, E., 'The UK Semiconductor Industry' in Pavitt, K. (ed.), *Technical Innovation and British Economic Performance* (London: Macmillan, 1980), p. 290.

41. Ibid.

42. Baker, *Marketing New Industrial Products*, pp. 40-2.

43. Reynolds, F.D. and Wells, W.D., *Consumer Behaviour* (New York: McGraw-Hill, 1977), p. 310.

44. Schon, D., *Beyond the Stable State* (London: Penguin, 1971). See Chapter 4, 'Diffusion of Innovation'.

45. Ibid.

46. Davies, *The Diffusion of Process Innovations*, pp. 158-62.

47. Mansfield, E., *Industrial Research and Technological Innovation* (New York: Norton, 1968); Grilliches, 'Hybrid Corn'.

48. Davies, *The Diffusion of Process Innovations*, p. 50.

49. Ibid., pp. 10, 78.

50. Ibid., p. 78.

51. Webster, F.E., 'Informal Communication in Industrial Markets', *Journal of Marketing Research*, vol. 7, no. 2 (1970), pp. 186-9.

52. Martilla, J.A., 'Word-of-Mouth Communication in the Industrial Adoption Process', *Journal of Marketing Research*, vol. 8, no. 2 (1971), pp. 173-8.

53. Cf. Schon, D., *Technology and Change: The New Heraclitus* (Oxford: Pergamon, 1967), Chapters 3 and 4.

54. Hayward, G., 'Market Adoption of New Industrial Products', *Industrial Marketing Management*, vol. 7, no. 3 (1978), pp. 193-8.

55. Hayward, G., 'Diffusion of Innovation in the Flour Milling Industry', *European Journal of Marketing*, vol. 6, no. 3 (1972), pp. 195-202.

56. Lancaster, G.A. and White, M., 'The Diffusion and Adoption of Textile Chemicals and Dyestuffs within the UK Textile Industry', *Research Policy*, vol. 6, no. 4 (1977), pp. 358-73.

57. E.g. Hill, R.W. and Hillier, T.J., *Organisational Buying Behaviour* (London: Macmillan, 1977); cf. pp. 130 and 133.

58. Czepiel, J.A., 'Word-of-Mouth Processes in the Diffusion of a Major Technological Innovation', *Journal of Marketing Research*, vol. 11, no. 3 (1974), pp. 172-80. See also 'Communications Networks and Innovation in Industrial Communities' in Baker, M.J. (ed.), *Industrial Innovation* (London: Macmillan, 1979), pp. 399-416.

59. Webster, 'Informal Communication in Industrial Markets', pp. 187-8.

60. Martilla, 'Word-of-Mouth Communication in the Industrial Adoption Process', pp. 174-6.

61. See Foxall, *Marketing Behaviour*, Chapter 4.

62. E.g. Narayana, C.L. and Markin, R.J., 'Consumer Behaviour and Product Performance: An Alternative Conceptualisation', *Journal of Marketing*, vol. 39, no. 4 (1975), pp. 1-6; Mittelstaed, R.A., Grossbart, S.L., Curtis, W.W. and Devere, S.P., 'Optimal Stimulation Level and the Adoption Decision Process', *Journal of Consumer Research*, vol. 3, no. 2 (1976), pp. 84-94.

63. E.g. Rothwell, R., 'The Relationship between Technical Change and Economic Performance in Mechanical Engineering' in Baker, M.J. (ed.), *Industrial Innovation* (London: Macmillan, 1979, pp. 36-59; Turnbull, P.W. and Cunningham, M.T. (eds.), *International Marketing and Purchasing* (London: Macmillan, 1981).

64. Aylen, J., 'Innovation in the British Steel Industry' in Pavitt (ed.), *Technical Innovation and British Economic Performance*, p. 208.

# 7 INNOVATIVE BEHAVIOUR

## Innovativeness

Innovativeness is the capacity and tendency to purchase new products and services. While this appears a simple enough definition, however, there have emerged in the literature of innovation and marketing two broad understandings of innovativeness depending upon whether it is viewed primarily as a property or quality of the individual innovator *himself* or of his purchase and consumption *behaviours*. Midgley and Dowling[1] are among the chief exponents of the view that innovativeness should be conceptualised as a mediating process, internal to the individual which manifests itself in the purchase and consumption of new items. These authors claim that innovativeness consists in 'the degree to which an individual is receptive to new ideas and makes innovation decisions independently of the communicated experience of others'.[2] The theoretical evaluation of innovative buying advanced by Midgley and Dowling involves the distinction of 'innate innovativeness' from 'actualised innovativeness': the former is a personality variable assumed to be possessed by the entire population and distributed normally among its members; the latter is observed innovative behaviour.

In this model, 'innate innovativeness' is depicted as a function of the social behaviour[3] and psychological traits of the individual and is assumed to exert an influence upon innovative behaviour via the intervening factors of interest in the product category, communicated experience and the effects of situational interventions. 'Actualised innovativeness' is measured in terms of the relative time of adoption.

Although this model may appear intuitively correct to those who are steeped in the stimulus → organism → response paradigm of social psychology, it has a number of defects as far as the prediction of innovative behaviour is concerned. Since such prediction is a primary managerial objective, these difficulties cannot be avoided in this discussion. They revolve around the measurement of 'innate innovativeness' since it is this measure from which forecasts of overt innovativeness must, according to the model, be derived. Like mental attitudes, which are also believed by many psychologists and marketing researchers to prefigure overt behaviours, innate innovativeness is likely to be measured in terms of verbal responses to questionnaires or verbalised reactions to innovative products or ideas. Its measurement might further be obtained by respondents' verbal descriptions of the product or idea in terms of its 'perceived novelty', much in the way suggested by Ostlund (see Chapter 6). Ultimately, a measure on which to base predictions of future overt innovativeness (to early purchase and/or use of the item) could be obtained from respondents' verbal *intentions to innovate*, their own forecasts of the likelihood of their adopting the product. Unfortunately, as the last chapter showed, even the most rigorously-devised and employed measures of buyer intention permit behaviour to be predicted for only a very short time after the expression of the attitudes and social norms which constitute behavioural intentions. Measures of expressed behavioural intentions are, moreover, predictive of the behaviour they immediately precede only when situational correspondence between the attitude measure and the behavioural measurement is very high indeed. As Fishbein[4] states, conditions must be maximally conducive to high correlations between measures of intention and measures of behaviour in order for the latter to be predictable from the former. The longer the period between the expression of intention and the execution of the behaviour, and the smaller the situational correspondence between the focus of the intention and the opportunity to act, then the less accurate are intentions as predictors of behavioural response. Measures of intentions, customers' self-rated 'venturesomeness' or ability to discriminate novelty in new products or ideas are usually predictive of innovative adoption only under closely-specified circumstances. Just as the search for links between attitudes and behaviour have benefited from the recognition that very specific attitudinal and behavioural measures are required if high correlations are to be found, so innovation researchers may need to refine their analytical and methodological frameworks, measuring not just 'innovativeness', still less latent, covert or 'innate' innovativeness, but *overt innovative behaviour with respect to a particular new product in a given purchase and/or consumption* situation. The general findings of the prediction of behaviour from attitudes, specificity of measurement and the conceptualisation of measurements of behavioural intention as the *immediate precursors* of the behaviour to which they refer are being increasingly applied in social psychology and consumer research.[5] Research into innovativeness has yet to recognise the import of these findings.

Midgley and Downing show implicit recognition by their inclusion of situational effects between the latent or internal processes of 'innate innovativeness' and the measurement of 'overt innovativeness' in terms of observed behaviour. But the certainties of situational interventions between verbalised intentions to innovate and the presentation of opportunities to do so make any prediction of overt innovativeness which is founded upon measures of intended innovative behaviour hazardous in the area of commercial consumer research. It would be wrong to suggest that Midgley and Downing's model is automatically invalidated as a predictive device because evidence from elsewhere in consumer research and social psychology suggests it might be. Certainly the mediatory variables, 'interest in product category' and 'communicated experience' are likely to be measureable only in terms of behavioural observations or reported behaviour. In either case, behaviour in one context is being used as a predictor of *behaviour* (overt innovation) in another. Behaviourist psychologists would argue that one class of behaviour will be predictive of the other only if the consequences of the first are identical with the consequences of the second. The difficulty that neither responses to questionnaires nor observed behaviour in one setting are predictive of later behaviour in different circumstances is, of course, a perennial problem in social and market research. The view that all behavioural responses are mediated by the same underlying, latent variable ('true attitude' or 'innate innovativeness') and should, therefore, show consistency is generally unsupported by empirical evidence.[6] Rather, careful testing of the hypotheses which derive from this work is strongly indicated; before the results of such testing become available, our confidence in the capacity of their model, based upon the notion of 'innate innovativeness', whose connection with overt innovative behaviour has not been demonstrated, should not be overestimated.

The second major understanding of innovativeness frames it solely in terms of the observed innovative behaviour which Midgley and Downing make their measure of 'actualised innovativeness'. According to this view, innovativeness is a behaviour: its presence can be inferred only from direct evidence of adoption and not with any degree of certainty from measures of attitude towards adoption or intentions to innovate. Rogers and Shoemaker[7] state, for instance, that innovativeness is 'the degree to which an individual is relatively earlier in adopting an innovation than other members of his social system', while Engel and Blackwell[8] state that '*innovativeness* is usually defined as the *degree to which an individual is relatively earlier in adopting an innovation than other members in the system*'. This definition is consistent with the view that behaviour is a function of previous behaviour (and its consequences) in similar situations. As Defleur and Westie[9] put it 'A latent something interposed between attitudinal behaviour patterns and the social variables which mediate them is simply unnecessary.' Such an operational view of behaviour, in which innovativeness is defined in terms which are closely-linked with its indisputable measurement, is not unproblematical. Midgley and Downing point out difficulties in measuring overt innovativeness and in determining the exact timing of the introduction of a new idea into a social system.[10] But it remains at present the safest definition and is not likely to involve a fruitless search for the 'psychological' determinants of behaviour.[11]

The quest for innovativeness is marked not only by theoretical dispute but by differences over methodological design and the interpretation of results. While theoretical work in this area remains largely untested (and in places untestable), empirical evidence which might lead to the identification of behavioural variables in terms of which overt innovativeness can be predicted has been gathered largely without benefit of an integrated conceptual and analytical framework. Study of consumer innovativeness has generally proceeded separately from that of innovation in industrial contexts (the above discussion of innovativeness, like its sources, applies almost entirely to the former). The following account of recent evidence *vis-à-vis* the correlates and the context of consumer and industrial innovation is thus concerned with piecemeal evaluation of the evidence rather than with the testing of a viable analytical framework or theory.

## Consumer Innovation

No active field of social scientific enquiry yields conclusive, determinative answers to the problems posed by those who work in it: the study of consumer innovation is no exception. Consumer researchers must, therefore, face the fact that the search for consumer innovativeness and its correlates hardly constitutes a unified field. As the following examination of the empirical evidence attests only too well, some of the findings of applied research are mutually contradictory and the interpretation of results as a prelude to managerial decision-making is not always unequivocal. Yet it would be misleading to dwell at length upon the deficiencies of the field. Some authors[12] have emphasised the view that the available studies demonstrate 'the confused and contradictory nature of the empirical studies relating consumer innovativeness to sociodemographic, attitudinal and personality factors'; but, beyond the ostensibly inchoate volume of empirical findings which research into consumer innovativeness shares, as an area of social science, with so many other sub-disciplines, there are discernible patterns and trends which are rewarding to academic and commercial researchers alike. In particular, there are noteworthy indications of consistencies among consumer innovators in the areas of (i) their socioeconomic characteristics, (ii) social affiliations, interactions and communications, (iii) personal factors such as attitudes, perceptions and behavioural response traits, (iv) evaluations of the characteristics of new products and (v) purchase and consumption behaviours.[13]

*Economic and Socioeconomic Correlates.* Numerous studies indicate that innovators have greater income and/or wealth than either later adopters or the population as a whole. Rogers and Stanfield[14] record that a far larger proportion of empirical studies show a positive relationship between income and level of living and related characteristics like education and literacy, and innovation than show a neutral or negative association. Although their review refers to innovation studies from a wide range of disciplines, Robertson's[15] review of marketing-based investigations draws similar conclusions. Most economic and socioeconomic variables are themselves intercorrelated, of course, and there is a tendency in empirical work to report consistency among social class, occupational status, education, privilegedness'.[16] From his study of touch-tone (push button) telephones, Robertson[17] reported innovators as possessing greater discretionary income than non-innovators and a high self-perception of wealth. Innovators were less concerned about cost. While they were 'overprivileged' within their own social class, however, they did not necessarily belong to the highest class or income level. 'Privilegedness' also figures strongly as a discriminative variable in a survey of early adopters of a domestic appliance reported by Robertson and Kennedy[18], while Kegerreis, Engel and Blackwell[19] noted that fifty per cent of innovative users of an automobile diagnostic centre earned annual incomes in excess of $10,000 compared with 31 per cent of the population generally; 20 per cent of innovators earned over $15,000 per year compared with 10 per cent of the general population; innovators also had a greater chance of owning relatively newer cars than motorists generally and of using two or more cars. These authors examined a number of inter-correlated socioeconomic characteristics of innovators including occupation, education level, household income and house value and concluded that 'consumer innovators of a substantial new product or service are *very* likely to have significantly higher social status than other consumers'. These and other studies also indicate that consumer innovators tend to be upwardly socially mobile.[21]

*Social Interaction and Communications.* Numerous studies have shown innovators in a wide range of contexts to have greater or different mass media exposure, contact with change agencies, group participation, interpersonal communication, opinion-leadership and 'cosmopoliteness', than others; consumer innovators are, generally, not exceptions to the general findings, though some studies have not replicated the frequently-reported tendency towards cosmopoliteness or orientation beyond the local social system in the case of consumer innovators.[21] Bruno, Hustad and Pessemier[22] are among the investigators who have drawn attention to the quite distinctive media exposure patterns of consumer innovators: of their American sample, innovators revealed significant patterns of preference for particular television programmes and magazines while largely ignoring others. The study of innovative use of automobile diagnostic centres, mentioned above, showed tendencies for innovators to have more magazine subscriptions and greater purposeful prior knowledge of the innovation in question than the population as a whole.[23] Further, the innovators generally planned their purchases, carried out a more systematic search for information, and acquired more knowledge than others, showing themselves to be far from passive receivers of knowledge.[24] No doubt this process of information acquisition is facilitated by the greater social integration and participation which is characteristic of many consumer innovators.[25] The role of innovators as receivers and initiators of word-of-mouth communication is also well-known as is their passive and active opinion leadership; Kegerreis, Engel and Blackwell[26] report that innovators are both more frequently consulted about innovations than are members of the population at large and are more likely than non-innovators and non-adopters to pass on innovation-related information: 'In the post-trial interviews it was found that in the *first week* following their trial of the new automotive service, 90 per cent of the innovators had told someone about their new experience, and 40 per cent had told more than one person. There is no doubt that these innovators were highly diffusive.'

*Personal Characteristics.* The clear majority of empirical investigations of innovativeness indicate that the earliest adopters of new products, practices and ideas tend to be more knowledgeable than others, to have a more positive attitude towards change, to show achievement motivation, educational aspirations, business orientation and empathy, and to eschew mental rigidity; nor are they noted for satisfaction with life. Several of these characteristics, along with certain other personal factors also describe consumer innovators.[27] Innovators show a greater interest in the product area to which the innovation belongs, have a positive approach to new ideas generally, have a high perception of themselves as innovators and aspire to upward social mobility for themselves and their descendents. The attempt to link specific personality traits with innovative behaviour is ambiguous, however.[28]

But the most important component characteristic of consumer innovativeness is venturesomeness itself, the capacity to cope with high levels of risk and uncertainty, to show an inner-directed approach to novel situations and, above all, independence.[29] Kegerreis, Engel and Blackwell[30] report that the innovators identified in their specific investigation were *generally* more willing than the population as a whole to experiment and to buy new products, and less likely to be influenced in their brand choice by small price or product attribute differentials. Robertson and Kennedy[31] demonstrated that venturesomeness contributes most to attempts to discriminate between innovators and non-innovators and, from his investigation of the earliest buyers of the touch-tone telephone, Robertson[32] concluded that 'Innovators are significantly higher on venturesomeness. They more readily take new product risks. This is revealed in their actual purchases of innovations, in their stated willingness to buy hypothetical innovations, and in their self-conceptions in regard to new-product purchase behaviour.' Several studies of fashion innovations confirm this tendency.[33] Donnelly[34] also adduces evidence that inner-directedness is a dominant behavioural feature of consumer innovators, i.e. their actions represent their personal values and standards rather than those common to other members of their social group. His work, which involved grocery products has been replicated for Ford Maverick automobiles.[35] The inner- (as opposed to other-) directedness of the innovator is related to Midgley's concept of innovativeness as the degree of independence which characterises innovative behaviour. Innovators emerge as individuals capable of buying in spite of high levels of objective risk and of minimising the effects of similar levels of perceived risk and uncertainty on their decisions and actions:

It is not known whether the venturesome consumer sees less risk in a new product or whether it does not concern him. There may even be purchase occasions where risk is sought, as for fashion merchandise

. . . [But] in a majority of studies it has been found that perceived risk is negatively related to innovativeness. In the nine studies testing this relationship, mostly among grocery products, five report such a negative relationship and four report a lack of relationship. The innovator, for the most part, therefore, is likely to be a risk taker and is likely to perceive less risk in purchase as well.[36]

*Product Perception and Appraisal.* Potential buyers' perceptions and evaluations of the five product characteristics listed in the Rogers and Shoemaker model play a crucial role in determining the timing of those buyers' purchases. Most investigations show a strong, positive relationship between each of relative advantage, compatibility and observability (communicability), a positive or neutral association of trialability (sometimes known as divisibility) with innovativeness, and a negative or neutral relationship between complexity and innovativeness.[37] Studies of product innovation by marketing researchers confirm the relevance of consumers' discriminating between innovations and other products in terms of these characteristics to their subsequent trial and adoption choices.[38] For instance, *relative advantage* is expected of new consumer products whether they be fast moving goods or durables, as is evidenced by the research of Davidson which was reviewed in Chapter 4 and the study of a motor diagnostic centre which has been frequently mentioned in this one. Lack of *compatibility*, which refers to the extent to which a new product harmonises with current consumption behaviour, personal expectations and preferences, and social norms, can account for the failure of numerous consumer products from instant tea, which was quickly withdrawn from the British market, though it succeeded in Germany, to the headache remedy which, in spite of manufacturers' estimates of its relative advantage, failed to impress customers because of its novel capacity to be taken without water. Provided a new product has unambiguous advantages over its rivals and is compatible in all of the senses mentioned above, its diffusion is likely to be accelerated by its conspicuousness or *communicability*, as is exemplified by numerous innovations in the fields of clothing fashions, cars and children's toys. *Trialability* is enhanced through the availability of samples, demonstrations, 'on-approval' loans and product divisibility, all of which permit relative advantage, compatibility and, where relevant, conspicuousness to be subjectively appraised by prospective buyers. Finally, the perception of product *complexity* tends to act as a deterrent to trial and adoption and, in this case, purchase and consumption of relatively continuous innovations such as new games may be impeded by their apparent demands on times and intellect while relatively discontinuous but simply operable durables like video recorders may be far more readily adopted. It is interesting to note that consumers may well judge complexity by price, however, much as price is, within certain ranges, taken as an indication of quality. The popularity of domestic computers has increased as the price has fallen, not only because this has made them financially available to more people but because affordable items are judged to be more easily useable in spite of the need to acquire comparatively complicated programming skills.

Ostlund[39] has conducted investigations into the use of perceptions of these five product characteristics and of the perceived risk associated with purchase to isolate innovators from later adopters and non-adopters. Midgley[40] notes that this methodology allows product attribute perceptions and personal characteristics to be evaluated both in their relationships with innovativeness and in terms of their inter-relatedness, for perceptions are themselves shaped by personal characteristics of personality and behaviour.

The salience of the uncomplicated Awareness → Trial → Adoption approach to the modelling of innovative buying behaviour is borne out by the empirical evidence which points to the attractiveness to consumers of trialable new products. Shoemaker and Shoaf[41], for instance, report a reduction in the quantities purchased of new consumer brands as a result of buyers' selecting smaller sizes of the new item, while subsequent purchases restored some or all of the previous levels of purchase of similar products. Trial reduces the risk associated with innovative purchase and these investigators draw the conclusion that manufacture and distribution of small sizes of new products appear vital based on consistent downward shifts in trial quantities for about two-thirds of the new brand triers.

*Purchase and Consumption Behaviour.* The buying behaviour of innovators and their patterns of product usage tend to differ from those of other buyers in a number of ways, some straightforward and predictable from the nature of innovativeness itself, others less so. Robertson[42] points out that a large majority of investigations conclude that the earliest adopters of a new product or brand are *'heavy users* of that product or similar products. The innovator for a new kind of coffee is likely to be a heavy coffee drinker. The innovator for a new telephone product is likely to have a larger monthly telephone bill. This, of course, makes it particularly crucial to secure innovator adoption since innovators may account for a disproportionate amount of product category sales.' This is borne out by a study of coffee brand innovations by Frank and Massy[43] and by Robertson's[44] own survey of the innovation patterns for push-button telephones which showed that early users of the Touch-Tone product were more likely than non-innovators to have bought such additional domestic appliances as colour television, electric toothbrushes and electric carving knives. Taylor[45] has called the tendency of consumer innovators to be heavy users a striking characteristic of early adopters. His study, which concerned fast moving consumer goods and fairly continuous innovations, demonstrates that there is a strong relationship between usage quantities and innovative trial: 'in 10 of 11 instances, those households that purchased more of the product class over the whole year tried the new products in the first quarter and their usage of the product class was substantially greater than that of later triers'. In the eleventh product category, the heaviest users tended to try the new product, a personal care item, in the second quarter, a result which does nothing to detract from the overall conclusion; in fact, Taylor's results also provide indirect confirmation of the tendency for consumer innovators to exhibit low levels of brand loyalty.[46]

## Patterns and Problems

While some personal behavioural characteristics of innovators apply across the various categories of consumer product types, there is unmistakeable evidence to the effect that the dominant characteristics of consumer innovators vary with the degree of discontinuity involved in the innovation. The profile of the innovator which emerges from the foregoing review is, typically, that of the domestic appliance innovator whom Robertson[47] characterises as rather likely to be younger, with higher education, income and occupational status, usually involved to a greater degree in social activities, more likely to be an opinion leader with respect to home appliances, more of a risk-bearer, with a more positive attitude towards innovation and more probably owning other domestic durables. Furthermore, a consistent synthesis of the findings of investigations of consumer durable innovation may be made: 'The innovator is a competent and self-assured person, intelligent and educated enough to set his/her own standards, and to evaluate innovations against these criteria.' Taken together, the conclusions of the studies which have been discussed point to consumer innovators who 'can comprehend the abstract implications of adopting major innovations' — Kegerreis, Engel and Blackwell drew particular attention to the capacity of innovators to calculate and plan — 'and furthermore have the financial resources to experiment. Above all else the innovators favour change and are willing to take risks. Thus they are inner-directed and do not need the experience, attitudes and values of others to mould their decisions for them'.[48]

Midgley[49] notes that, although the ability to cope with risk, attraction to change, and inner-direction appear to be present in all consumer innovators' personal profiles — and, indeed, these factors are almost by definition, the essence of innovativeness — various categories of potential consumer innovator may be distinguished on the basis of other, correlative social, demographic, psychological and economic characteristics. Innovators for (i) consumer durables, (ii) fashion items and (iii) supermarket products respectively differ significantly from one another. While relatively high educational levels, income and occupational status are, on *a priori* grounds, relevant to the innovative purchase of a consumer durable, with all the risks and inflexibilities it entails and the facilitating conditions such as discretionary income it demands, these factors are far less relevant to the purchase of fast moving consumer products, as several writers have pointed out. The lower the salience of price and other economic factors in the purchase decision and the greater the familiarity of buyers generally with the product class, the less likely it is that the major factors associated with the earliest adopters of comparatively discontinuous innovations will be encountered. Fashion innovators conform to some of the patterns found among each of these categories but are deviant in other respects; they exhibit more social integration, mobility and mass media exposure, calculative planning and higher usage rates for the relevant product category, but the position with respect to education appears, at least, ambiguous while one study indicates that fashion adopters derive from lower socioeconomic classes.[50]

If the evidence for distinct categories of consumer innovators is not clearcut and the need for routine replicative research enormous, this is quite consistent with most other themes in consumer adoption research. The difficulties of properly classifying innovations, accurately labelling types of buyer in behavioural terms, and of interpreting the results of empirical investigations are evident in a recent study of 'a major automotive innovation', the rotary-engined Mazda car. The examination of the backgrounds and behaviours of various classes of Mazda purchasers and nonpurchasers undertaken by Feldman and Armstrong, the comments on this investigation and presentation of apparently paradoxical results by Peat, Gentry and Brown, and Feldman and

Armstrong's rejoinder[51] illustrate well the uncertainties which can characterise innovation research. The nature of Feldman and Armstrong's research and their findings may be usefully described as a prelude to raising methodological issues in their own right.

These investigators selected the Mazda in preference to more minor consumer product innovations, describing it as 'significantly different from previous products in that it offers substantive consumer benefits such as freedom from engine noise and vibration'. Furthermore, 'its purchase requires a high degree of commitment'. The study involved an examination of the characteristics of four separate samples: (i) of the earliest Mazda adopters (innovators) in California, (ii) later Californian purchases of the Mazda, (iii) innovative Mazda buyers in the American Midwest, and (iv) Midwest Toyota purchasers. This survey design permitted three interesting hypotheses to be tested: first, that the two groups of innovators would be similar; secondly, that Mazda innovators would differ significantly from later Mazda buyers; and, thirdly, that Mazda innovators would differ significantly from buyers of the car with the more orthodox engine. The first hypothesis was generally supported: any differences between the two groups of innovators in terms of opinion leadership, product interest, venturesomeness, personal competence and perceptions of the product's relative advantage, complexity, communicability and compatability were not statistically significant; a significant difference with respect to perception of product divisibility, defined as the degree of opportunity available to minimise risk and reduce uncertainty through trial of the product, was found and the authors explain this result in terms of the availability of a manufacturer's guarantee for this essentially non-trialable product and the different lengths of times the respondents had been exposed to the product.[52]

The second hypothesis — that Californian innovators and later adopters would differ significantly — received mixed support from the data: statistically significant differences were found in opinion leadership, age, sex and family income; but measures of personal competence, product relative advantage, communicability and compatibility, and education and occupation revealed no significant differences between the samples. The final hypothesis — that Mazda and Toyota buyers would be significantly different — received strong support, however, and the authors draw encouragement from their observation that Californian innovators were shown by the results relevant to the first hypothesis to be similar in several characteristics to Midwest innovators, while the results which pertain to the third hypothesis identified different Midwest Mazda and Toyota buyers ('innovators' and 'non-innovators') on the same characteristics. With respect to the latter, Feldman and Armstrong point out that,

> . . . relative to their noninnovator counterparts, Midwest innovators are more likely to be male, older, less educated and employed as craftsmen or foremen. Higher on opinion leadership and product interest, they perceive their purchase as having greater relative advantage, being easier to understand, involving lower risk of purchase, and being more consistent with present ways of doing things. On the other hand they perceive a relatively greater difficulty in communicating the advantage of the innovation.

While these results are not entirely consistent with those of some earlier researchers, they are of considerable interest, not least because of the novel survey design employed in the investigation. Peat, Gentry and Brown, nevertheless, find three areas of difficulty in the interpretation of these results. First, they take exception to the description of the Mazda as a genuinely radical innovation: apart from its rotary-powered engine, it is similar in every way to the Toyota. Feldman and Armstrong's reply indicates that members of their Midwest samples perceived the two cars in quite different terms: Mazda purchasers mentioned the rotary engine, mechanical reliability, smoothness, better acceleration, the newness and novelty of the car and its smaller contribution to pollution as salient attributes of their chosen purchase, while Toyota buyers referred to their chosen car's fuel economy, quality of assembly and finish, and size. While this shows that the two groups had rather different perceptions of their purchases, the question remains: how far is the rotary engine a relatively discontinuous innovation from the point of view of manufacturers and how far is it genuinely discontinuous in terms of its descriptive intervention in behaviour patterns?

Peat, Gentry and Brown also reject Feldman and Armstrong's use of the term 'noninnovator' to describe Toyota buyers since nothing is known of the future Mazda-related buying behaviour. The term 'non-adopter' should be applied to current Toyota owners, they argue, since 'noninnovator' suggests later adopters of the Mazda. Finally, Peat, Gentry and Brown report different patterns of variables in terms of which innovators and noninnovators exhibit significant differences and suggest that buyers of various models of Mazda differ significantly from buyers of other variants.

The consistent picture of innovativeness and its correlates, derived largely from the study of adopters of major innovations, is rendered rather less clear by the suggestion that there might be different classes of consumer innovation according to the nature of the product under review and the inability of researchers to agree on definitions, methodological imperatives and the meaning of their results. The difficulty involved in attempts to show convincingly that there exist general patterns of innovativeness on the part of specific individuals adds to the argument that, although all consumers may possess the capacity to innovate to some degree, their manifest innovativeness is likely to be confined to a given product class, or a few related product classes.[53] However, this tendency is readily understood when the predilection among researchers to explain innovative behaviour by means of an intrapersonal trait or process, 'innovativeness' or 'venturesomeness' which mediates behaviour across situations is taken into account. As the introduction to this chapter and the discussion of adoption in Chapter 6 suggest, generalised measures and general foci of research attention are likely to go on producing incomparable results. Verbal self-ratings of 'venturesomeness', 'innovativeness' and other 'personality attitudinal variables' which *researchers* believe ought to be consistently related to innovative behaviour consist in part of reports of past behaviour with respect to new products: they do not necessarily constitute accurate predictors of future behaviour with respect to different novel products in different situations from those previously encountered. As yet, recent interest in and work on the situational context of purchasing and consumption,[54] has to catch up with the buying of innovative products.

## Industrial Buying and Innovation

Reliance upon the discovery and measurement of a personality trait or other psychological mechanism which determines (and, therefore, 'explains') innovative buying is largely absent from studies of industrial innovation. Rather, there is a stronger emphasis upon the situational context of buying. Baker[55], for instance, states that adoption is a function of *enabling conditions* (such as purchasing power), *precipitating circumstances* (e.g. a machinery breakdown), *specific cost-benefit analyses* (in terms of the cost and likely economic and technical performance of the innovation under review), and *managerial response* (including organisations' structure and 'climate'), and thereby duly stresses the environmental background of the buying process. This acts as a reminder that the innovative buying of industrial products and services — notably capital goods and processes and intermediate products— can be understood only within the overall framework of our knowledge of industrial buying in its entirety. Relatively infrequent replacement of capital equipment may always involve innovative buying as a result of the adoption of technological advances by suppliers and this reinforces the relationship between the innovative and general facets of industrial buying. Whatever the superficial similarities between industrial buying procedures, there is a constant need in all but the most frequent routine reordering processes to lay emphasis upon the influences of uniquely-composed buying centres, decision-making units, activating factors induced by environmental change, product availability and the acquisition of information.[56] Accordingly, in order to comprehend better the nature of industrial adoption, it is necessary to consider briefly the general character of organisational purchasing.[57]

## The Nature of Industrial Buying

The industrial buying process is usually contrasted with consumer purchasing, the terms of which reflect its complexity. This useful point of departure must not be accepted without qualification; some routine re-ordering processes in industry such as those involved in obtaining further supplies of office stationery doubtless involve rather less complexity as a rule than does the purchase of an infrequently-purchased home appliance such as a colour television or video recorder. Nevertheless, it cannot be overlooked that very many industrial purchases are characterised by a level of complexity and risk never encountered in domestic buying. The demand for industrial products is a derived demand and members of the organisation which purchases capital equipment and components thus have the relationship between two markets to consider in the context of their purchasing decisions. Demand is often cyclical in both the factor and the product markets in which industrial companies operate and there is frequently pressure to take buying decisions within the constraints imposed by time, costing and budgetary procedures, and the firm's bureaucratic structure which may require central approval of even minor changes in product specifications, prices or suppliers. The uncertainties and risks which surround industrial buyers' decisions processes are also far greater than is usually the case among final consumers and they increase with the comparative discontinuity of the potential purchase under review, new suppliers and the relatively unprogrammed nature of the problem (activating circumstance) which makes a purchase necessary.[58]

The complexity of industrial buying is nowhere more apparent, however, than in the observation that the decisions it entails are seldom the responsibility of an individual, still less consistently those of 'the buyer'. Rather they are diffused among the occupants of the several roles which comprise the *buying centre*, that transient group of diverse persons who influence the nature and outcomes of purchase decision processes: users, influencers, deciders and information gatekeepers as well as professional buyers.[59] Moreover, Choffray and Lilien[60] note that 'the organisational decision process can be separated into phases more easily than the consumer decision process, and different individuals are usually associated with different phases' and, while their initial observation argues for the simplicity with which the industrial buying sequence may be described, the latter is symptomatic of its complications. The three general models of buyer behaviour discussed above are relevant to the identification of the salient phases in the industrial buying process but it is also relevant to consider the similarities among the many specialised depictions of this process which are summarised in Table 7.1. The sequence of initial problem awareness, pre-purchase search and evaluation, purchase, and post-purchase appraisal is essentially identical to that usually assumed to characterise consumer buying. Complexity arises in the industrial buying context, however, as a result of differences in the composition of the buying centre at each stage in the purchase process and different patterns of buying centre composition and influence for the various types of purchase, for example, the straight rebuy, 'modified rebuy' and 'new buy' situations.[62] While buying centres follow up immutable structural pattern, Hill and Hillier[63] discern three usually important groups of roles or units: the decision-making unit (DMU), information unit and control unit. The DMU consists of those members of the organisation who are authorised to take final decisions and thus inaugurate their implementation. Information units frequently include senior managers whose decisions with respect say to the expected life of a capital good constitute a constraint on the buying process (and thus act as a control mechanism) and those organisational members such as engineers who make available specialist data about the desired nature and performance of products to be purchased. Other individuals whose behaviour affects the shape and outcome of the buying process, such as users and professional buyers, are assumed to act in an informational or control capacity and this justifies the simple, tripartite depiction of the buying centre. A generalised example of the diversity of roles involved in the composition of DMU for three types of purchase as the buying process proceeds is shown in Table 7.2. The search for information, for evaluative criteria, and the clarification of constraints which are elements in the conversion of uncertainty to risk (or, in some cases, ignorance to partial ignorance) are clearly likely to be expanded quantitatively and qualitatively as perceived uncertainty increases. The more discontinuous the product under review is considered to be by members of the buying centre, the greater is the probability that the size of the centre will be increased and that the information, control and decision units will comprise more specialists in a strategic attempt to cope with uncertainty and perceived risk. Perceived risk and the consequent need to include more individuals formally (in the case of technical personnel, for example) or informally (in the case of suppliers' salesmen) in the buying centre also increase with the novelty of the problem which initiates the decision process and this approach to the classification of buying situations, like that which categorises them as straight/modified rebuy or new buy draws attention away from the psychological background of 'the buyer' towards the precipitating circumstances which make necessary a decision response. In the case of routine problems, this response may be *relatively* programmed in order to cope automatically with problems as they arise; however, many problems which

Table 7.1: Models of Industrial Buying[61]

| | |
|---|---|
| Robinson and Farris | Problem (need) recognition → Determine characteristics → Describe characteristics → Search for sources → Acquire Proposals → Evaluate proposals → Select order routine → Performance feedback |
| Ozanne and Churchill | Awareness → Interest → Evaluation → Trial Adoption |
| Webster and Wind | Identify needs → Establish specifications → Identify alternatives → Evaluate alternatives → Select supplier |
| Sheth | Initiation of the decision to buy → Information gathering → Evaluation of alternative suppliers → Conflict resolution → Supplier/brand choice |
| Kelly | Recognise need → Information search → Evaluate alternatives → Approval of funds → Decision |
| Hill and Hillier | Precipitating decisions → Product decisions → Supplier decisions → Commitment decisions |
| Bradley | Purchase initiation → Survey of alternatives → Supplier short listing → Award contract |
| Wind | Identification of needs → Establish specifications → Search for alternatives → Establish contact → Set purchase and usage criteria → Evaluate alternatives → Budget availability → Evaluate specific alternatives → Negotiate → Buy → Use → Post-purchase evaluation |

necessitate industrial purchases are *unprogrammed* and an *ad hoc* decision procedure must be established before decisions which are closely related to *product* choice (e.g. the selection of a relatively continuous or discontinuous item) can be made.[64]

Understanding and modelling complex industrial buying remains problematical, however. Theoretical frameworks are certainly capable of specifying that a DMU must exist but empiricists often ignore it in practice and concentrate for their data upon the verbal reports of just one member of this unit.[65] In spite of the vast volume of research which has been conducted over the last decade in this area, Bonoma[66] has still recently had to pose the question, 'Who really does the buying?' Bonoma, Zattman and Johnston[67] concluded a recent literature review by stating that 'The complex, vague, and often changing composition of the buying centre makes it difficult to ascertain empirically just who is involved in organisational buying;' while Silk and Kalwani[68] state that 'Among the most basic problems to be resolved is that of establishing a workable method for delineating the composition of buying centres.' Yet buying decisions are made by somebody. What is known of their behaviour?

The academic representation of industrial buying can easily confer upon it an artificial air of rationality which obscures the realities of purchasing under conditions of uncertainty. Professional purchasers and other DMU members may well exhibit the awareness, alertness and energy to identify and pursue all of the necessary sources of information required to make decisions on the basis of the fullest available information: their behaviour may thus, on occasion, approximate to the taking of decisions under circumstances of *bounded rationality* which is the closest human managers are likely to come to the orthodox economist's idea of rational action.[69] There is, nevertheless, much empirical evidence to confirm the common-sense observation that industrial buyers satisfice as a result of the non-economic influences which surround their decision processes. The risks involved in industrial buying are not only those which involve the organisation directly; they incude also the personal risks borne by the buyers themselves. It is not surprising, therefore, that 'fear is one of the major influences in industrial buying. Fear of displeasing the boss. Fear of making a wrong decision . . . Fear of losing status. Fear indeed, in extreme cases, of losing one's job.'[70] While further replicative studies must precede generalisations, there is evidence that some industrial buyers evince fear of authority and compliance and that they rely more upon their personal risk-reducing preconceptions than adequate knowledge.

Table 7.2: DMU Members by Type of Purchase

| Stage in the purchase process | New purchases | Change in supplies | Repeat purchase |
|---|---|---|---|
| Recognition of need to purchase | Board, general management | Buyer | Stock control system |
| Determination of product characteristics | Technical personnel | As specified when new purchase | As specified |
| Description of product characteristics | Technical personnel | As specified | As specified |
| Search for suppliers | Technical personnel | Buyer | Approved suppliers |
| Assessing Qualifications of suppliers | Technical personnel | Technical personnel and buyer | Approved suppliers |
| Acquisition of proposals | Buyer and technical personnel | Buyer | Purchasing staff |
| Evaluation of proposals | Technical personnel | Buyer | Purchasing staff |
| Selection of supplier | Technical personnel, General Management, Buyer | Buyer | Purchasing staff |
| Selection of order routine | Buyer | Buyer | Purchasing staff |
| Performance feedback and evaluation | Technical personnel and Buyer (informal) | Buyer (informal) System (formal) | Buyer (informal) System (formal) |

Source: Brand, G.T., *The Industrial Buying Decision* (London: Cassell/Associated Business Programmes, 1972), p. 71. Used by permission.

Certainly, there have been repeated observations of very limited pre-purchase search behaviour and the conclusion that buyers' behaviour is characterised by inertia as they retain known suppliers rather than actively seek out alternatives. The greater uncertainty, greater perceived risk and greater anxiety which naturally result from unprogrammed buying situations and knowledge of the availability of relatively discontinuous solutions *may* precipitate greater informational search within the bounds of subjective rationality: they may, however, result in recourse to the perceived safety of further inertia.[71] It should come as no surprise to recognise that buyers, like other people, are influenced by non-task rewards (e.g. status enhanced), that they are involved in political manoeuvring, that they form habits and that their behaviour reflects their personality traits, national stereotypes and personal backgrounds.[72] Indeed, even if supernormally consistent and economic rationality were a commonly-encountered feature of industrial buying procedures, situational interventions would still influence the implementation of decisions; as Sheth realistically points out in the context of his own model of industrial buyer behaviour:

> . . . there is ample empirical evidence in the literature to suggest that at least some of the industrial buying decisions are determined by *ad hoc situational factors* and not by any systematic decision-making process. In other words, similar to consumer behaviour, the industrial buyers often decide on factors other than rational or realistic criteria . . . [S]ituational factors which often intervene between the actual choice and any prior decision-making process . . . include: temporary economic conditions, such as price controls, recession or foreign trade; internal strikes, walkouts, machine breakdowns, and other production-related events; organisational changes such as merger or acquisition; and *ad hoc* changes in the market place, such as promotional efforts, new product introduction, price changes, and so on, in the supplier industries.

The task of modellers of industrial buying is to balance the various economic and non-economic explanatory variables in their models, selecting and sifting those which are relevant to their explicative and predictive purposes from among the multitude of descriptive labels available.

The salient point for students of the purchase of industrial innovation is that organisational buyers are likely to be *adapters* rather than *innovators*. Kirton[74] argues that 'everyone can be located over a continuum ranging from an ability to "do things better" to an ability to "do things differently", and the ends of this continuum are labeled *adaptive* and *innovative*, respectively'. Both are creative in their separate ways but their personality (behavioural response) traits are different, albeit potentially complementary as well as conflicting. Their essential characteristics are shown in Table 7.3. Not all members of a buying centre are likely to be adaptive rather than innovative, of course: these terms are, in any case, relative; effective buying requires a combination of the creative virtues offered by both patterns of behaviour and the research which is currently underway in this area[75] promises to provide interesting leads for innovation research in terms of the varied roles of adaptors and innovators in the communication of

technical information, problem-solving, inter-organisational relationships, the adoption and execution of reactive or proactive strategies
and joint behaviour/decision-making. However, it is already apparent
that companies marketing new products are by no means necessarily
dealing with personal innovators when they contact buyers. How then
may innovative companies be identified?

## Table 7.3: Behaviour Descriptions of Adaptors and Innovators

| Adaptor | Innovator |
|---|---|
| Characterised by precision, reliability efficiency, methodicalness, prudence, discipline, conformity. | Seen as undisciplined, thinking tangentially, approaching tasks from unsuspected angles. |
| Concerned with resolving problems rather than finding them. | Could be said to discover problems and discover avenues of solution. |
| Seeks solutions to problems in tried and understood ways. | Queries problems' concomitant assumptions; manipulates problems. |
| Reduces problems by improvement and greater efficiency, with maximum of continuity and stability. | Is catalyst to settled groups, irreverent of their consensual views; seen as abrasive, creating dissonance. |
| Seen as sound, conforming, safe, dependable. | Seen as unsound, impractical; often shocks his opposite. |
| Liable to make goals of means. | In pursuit of goals treats accepted means with little regard. |
| Seems impervious to boredom, seems able to maintain high accuracy in long spells of detailed work. | Capable of detailed routine (system maintenance) work for only short bursts. Quick to delegate routine tasks. |
| Is an authority within given structures. | Tends to take control in unstructured situations. |
| Challenges rules rarely, cautiously, when assured of strong support. | Often challenges rules, has little respect for past custom. |
| Tends to high self-doubt. Reacts to criticism by closer outward conformity. Vulnerable to social pressure and authority; complaint. | Appears to have low self-doubt when generating ideas, not needing consensus to maintain certitude in face of opposition. |
| Is essential to the functioning of the institution all the time, but occasionally needs to be 'dug out' of his systems. | In the institution is ideal in unscheduled crises, or better still to help to avoid them, if he can be controlled. |
| *When collaborating with innovators*: supplies stability, order and continuity to the partnership. | *When collaborating with adaptors*: supplies the task orientations, the break with the past and accepted theory. |
| Sensitive to people, maintains group cohesion and cooperation. | Insensitive to people, often threatens group cohesion and cooperation. |
| Provides a safe base for the innovator's riskier operations. | Provides the dynamics to bring about periodic radical change, without which institutions tend to ossify. |

Source: Kirton, M.J., 'Adaptors and Innovators: A Description and Measure',
*Journal of Applied Psychology*, vol. 61, no. 5 (1976), p. 623. Copyright 1976,
by the American Psychological Association. Reprinted by permission of the
author and APA.

## Innovative Adoption in Industry

The level of uncertainty and risk involved in the purchase of new industrial products makes some sort of attempt at economic appraisal of the probable costs and benefits associated with innovative adoption not only desirable but predictable. Indeed, it is in the area of 'economic motivations' that consumer and industrial buying have been most sharply dichotomised. One theorist writes, for example, that

> Innovations are adopted because of their potential rewards to the adopter. In the consumer sector, the rewards may be convenience, social prestige, or even the inherent value of 'newness' itself. In the industrial sector, the reward is better measured in monetary terms. In either sector there is risk in adopting — both functional and psychological risk forms. The decision to adopt involves weighing potential rewards and costs. In the industrial sector, this decision lingers more on economic than personal-satisfaction considerations.[76]

It is almost as if the identical economic motives so frequently ascribed by economists (and some other investigators) to producer innovators could simply be reversed in the case of innovative purchasers. Mansfield[77] has suggested that the former should assess the likely rate of return from the introduction of the innovation from estimates of required capital investment expenditures, sales forecasts, production costs and the effects of innovation on the current product portfolio. These are, he notes, contingent upon the pricing strategy of the firm (in fact, they depend upon its use of the entire marketing mix) and managerial estimation of the risks of innovation. Turning this round to cover the rationale of innovative industrial purchasing, customers may be expected to balance initially the costs of introducing a new product into their productive processes, the risks inherent in such a venture and the benefits in terms of the consequent enhancement of their own sales and profits. Mansfield[78] has himself concluded from a number of *ex post* studies of industrial innovation that there is a direct relationship between the rate at which new products and processes are adopted and the innovation's contribution to profitability; he found also an inverse relationship between that rate and the magnitude of investment demanded by adoption.

The assumption of relatively purposeful buying in industrial markets makes these economic considerations a logical starting point for discussions of the factors which influence innovative adoption. Webster[79] summarises the results of a large number of empirical examinations of the adoption and diffusion of innovations in industrial contexts by noting that the earliest purchasers of new items tend to be the largest companies in the relevant industries, especially when the innovations involved are relatively expensive. Such firms can afford the necessary investment and bear the associated risks far more readily than others. Echoing Mansfield's conclusions, he writes that 'The earlier adopters are also consistently those for whom the innovation offers the highest potential return on investment, or profitability . . . [while] higher price means lower profitability for potential adopters.'

It would be inaccurate and misleading to deny these statements: the empirical work to which reference has been made is strongly supportive of a generalised economic influence on adoption and diffusion and attention will later be drawn to this. Not to qualify these conclusions would, however, attribute a spuriously high degree of economic rationality to the process in which industrial innovations are purchased. Two important caveats must be entered. First, economic influences are by no means the sole forces which impinge upon and shape industrial innovative buying; there is a considerable amount of evidence to support the contention that behavioural and organisational influences are far-reaching and may be decisive. Secondly, it is invalid to represent that economic decision-making which does precede industrial innovation as entirely logical, rational and consistent — as though it were possible to carry out an *ex ante* objective cost-benefit analysis which quantifies exactly the consequences of adoption.

Although several authors have long hinted that organisational and managerial factors might provide extra-economic influences upon the adoption of innovators, the empirical identification of these factors and the estimation of their explanatory power compared with that of the strictly economic criteria mentioned above are of comparatively recent origin. Furthermore, the sources of this empirical evidence are relatively few. Baker,[80] in particular, has employed measures of 'organisational climate' as explanatory variables to account for patterns of industrial adoption. The notion of organisational climate represents something of a latent variable conveying recognition that the individual's perception of the organisational rules, operating procedures, managerial attitudes and, perhaps above all, the situational context of organisational behaviour, fundamentally affect individual and group action. But if organisational climate is a slippery concept, it certainly points to the need to appreciate the effects on individual and group behaviour of organisational structure and managerial style. Burns and Stalker's[81] seminal work, which differentiated two broad structural forms, the organic and the mechanistic, also stressed that there were appropriate responses to the situations presented by the firm's technology, its product portfolio and its market environment. An organic organisational structure denotes flexibility, network communications and task-based groupings of employees and is appropriate to corporate effectiveness when technological and marketing conditions are rapidly dynamic, say in the context of a pharmaceutical firm. Effective organisation is contingent upon a quite different structural response when technology is relatively unchanging and market needs relatively stable, say in school furniture (*relatively* being the operative word), where a more mechanistic structure involving hierarchical command and communication and functional groupings of employees (rather as in the case of the classic Weberian model of bureaucracy) would usually reflect more appropriately the firm's situational context. Contingency theory, as this approach has become known, thus posits rather different styles of organisational capacity and behaviour for comparatively organic and comparatively mechanistic firms and it is these to which the idea of organisational climate points. (See also Chapter 11.)

From his studies of the adoptors of two American innovations, one a machine tool, the other a machine employed in the manufacture of shoes, Baker[82] reports that organisational behavioural variables explained about half of the variance in adoption patterns under investigation. These variables were size (15.47 per cent of variance in the case of machine tool users, 14.52 in the case of shoe machine users), organisational formality (6.79 and 8.99), business functions (6.46 and 4.91), conflict resolution by problem solving (5.89 and 7.25), departmental performance review procedure (4.92 and nil), conflict resolution by smoothing (4.65 and 4.29) and importance accorded new products/ R&D (4.26 and 6.08). Subsequent replication of these studies in the UK earthmoving industry[83] and the carpet industry 'lend weight to the strengthening conviction that adoption decisions are very much situation-related'. Abu-Ismail[84], in an investigation of the adoption of fibrous backing materials by carpet manufacturers concluded that innovativeness, defined in terms of elapsed time since the new product's launch, was explained in terms of *economic and performance variables* ('the ability of attributes of the innovation to cope with the existing economic and technological situation in prospective markets'), *organisational variables* (especially organisational organicism,' progressiveness of personnel policies, marketing-orientation and size), and the *identity of the decision-making group* (e.g. opinion leadership, characteristics of decision-makers, their professionalism and creativity). Further analysis revealed that the principal behavioural and organisational variables which explain innovativeness are company size, inter-departmental communication and integration, past performance in the appraisal of innovations on technical and economic grounds, and opinion leadership.

It is not possible to mention all of the studies which are broadly corroborative of Baker's work: Fisher[85] for instance, in research into the purchase of computers for UK industrial process control convincingly draws attention to situational 'facilitating circumstances'; Mahajan and Schoeman[86] show that, in American hospitals, 'adopters and nonadopters of the use of computers are found to be significantly different in terms of . . . 32 indicators measuring the characteristics of the hospital, the environment in which the hospital operates, and the hospital administrators' background and training'; Hayward[87] in studies of the adoption of innovations by British flourmillers, emphasises the effects of plant size, perceived characteristics of the innovations and opinion leadership influences; and Kennedy[88] provides a useful review of other studies.

All of these investigations indicate, however, that there are good grounds for supposing that non-economic factors (or, at least, factors which are not directly related to the assessment of post-adoption profitability) account for patterns of industrial adoption as much as do narrowly-defined economic criteria. This is not to rule out the relevance of the latter, to deny that companies attempt to justify adoption decisions on economic grounds or to claim that behavioural, organisational and situational influences never reflect economic concerns: it is only to show how far recent empirical research suggests stress should be placed upon factors which early investigators intuitively recognised as having the potential to shape industrial purchasing decisions actually impinge upon the decision processes involved and determine their outcomes. What is particularly interesting is the identification of the organisational structural type – of predominantly organic features – which facilitates early adoption and the suggestion that managerial process variables associated with this form of organisation might also be consistently associated with innovativeness. This has close parallels in the development of thought among some organisation theorists, notably Child,[89] who have pointed out that organisations' structures are not deterministically shaped by their environments but that managers may fail to perceive, misperceive or fail to acknowledge the significance of environmental factors, that managers can influence and modify the contexts in which their firms operate, that product and factor markets do not rigidly constrain firms and that there may be more than one appropriate form for a given set of contingencies. There is evidently much scope here for further empirical work on the nature and role of managerial awareness and response to situational and contextual factors in the adoption of innovative products and processes, a theme to which the organisation theorists do not appear to have addressed themselves.

Not only are economic criteria not the sole grounds upon which the decision to adopt an innovative product or process rests: the question of the extent to which and the manner in which economic factors influence the outcomes of adoption decision processes must be approached with circumspection. The commonplace conclusion of *ex post* investigations of industrial adoption to the effect that the prepurchase opportunity to increase profitability (or, at least, the perception of such an apparent opportunity) explains and justifies the decision to adopt has been challenged as unenlightening and tautological by Gold[90] Any actions of a profit-seeking organisation may be subsequently 'explained' as profitable; the behaviour of managers acting rationally or even within the confines of bounded rationality must be deemed to be motivated in accordance with the purposes of the organisations they serve. In practice, most innovations are rejected by most organisations upon which they might confer benefit and one reason for this is the lack of authoritative information upon which *ex ante* purchase decisions would be rationally taken. Gold's observations are entirely consistent with what has been said of the essential nature of industrial buying in general and with the difficulties inherent in the forecasting of costs, sales and risks. Other economists have also pointed to the inevitably subjective nature of estimates of costs. Littlechild[91] for instance, notes that, in the final analysis, all costs are opportunity costs (the value to the decision-maker of the best rejected alternative) and argues persuasively that

> . . . the opportunity cost to each person depends upon that person's own perceptions of the alternatives open to him, upon his own forecasts of the consequences of each alternative and upon his own preferences for these consequences. Thus, opportunity cost is subjective — it depends upon the person making the decision . . . Cost cannot be measured directly by an outside observer. It is measured in terms of the utility of the chooser . . .

and, what is true of costs, applies equally to the predecisional estimation of risks and streams of future benefit such as sales and profits.

It is natural, in view of the evidence which has been brought forward and the arguments based upon it, to enquire of the actual nature and purpose of economic analysis in the industrial adoption process. One response is to the effect that, while behavioural and organisational distortion undoubtedly intervene betwixt the intention to undertake objective economic appraisals of potential purchases, these intentions are themselves rational enough; managers may be prevented from undertaking entirely economically-rational appraisals and decisions but this implies what Simon calls 'bounded rationality' rather than irrationality or non-rationality. Gold[92] suggests an alternative understanding of the uses which are made of economic appraisal and reasoning while, at the same time, re-emphasising the need to understand better managerial and organisational effects: economic appraisal and reasoning are, he argues, part of a managerial rationale of decisions previously taken on the basis of engineering assessments. In a passage which ties together the various strands of his argument, he states that

> Because decisions involving commitments for future activities must always be made on the basis of serious informational inadequacies and consequent uncertainties, they tend to be based in large measure . . . on the value orientations of influential management personnel, which are rooted in turn on their past training and experience. Indeed, our detailed intraplant studies suggest that a surprisingly high frequency of technological adoption decisions seem to be based essentially on engineering evaluations of expected physical input-output improvements with parallel economic benefits simply being assumed. As might be expected, technologically oriented executives tend to be more responsive to such approaches than those with backgrounds oriented primarily to marketing and finance. Hence, managerial attitudes are not merely one of the factors to be included casually along with ostensibly more important quantitative determinants. On the contrary, such subjective judgements probably overshadow the latter in shaping most major capital decisions, although the growing obeisance to seemingly objective decision-making often entails repeated revisions of formal capital budgeting estimates by staff specialists until they accord with the judgement-influenced conclusions of senior management.

The clear indication is that, far from even ostensibly fulfilling the rationally-perceived objectives of the enterprise, economic and accounting procedures may well be instrumental in justifying decisions which have been made on separate grounds. Such rationalisations may be consciously or unconsciously pursued by managers – it is arguable which is the more misleading and dangerous – but the point that academic researchers seeking *ex post* explanations of the criteria upon which adoption decisions have been made are asking to be deceived cannot be evaded.[93]

## Conclusion

Reviewers of social scientific and managerial literature so frequently conclude by referring to 'the need for further research' that this remark has become a platitude. But, in spite of the considerable deficiencies in our knowledge of innovative buying, the prospects that, in this case, additional research will provide useful data for practical decision-making and applied research models are evident enough. Already, the value of the categories of 'awareness', 'trial' and 'repeat buying'/'adoption' is clear from their use in marketing management, especially in the forecasting of probable adoption levels prior to product launch.[94]

## Notes

1. Midgley, D.F. and Downing, G.R., 'Innovativeness: The Concept and its Measurement', *Journal of Consumer Research*, vol. 4, no. 4 (1978), pp. 229-42.

2. Ibid., p. 236.

3. Midgley and Downing refer to 'Sociological traits'. As 'sociological' is an adjective that properly qualifies 'Sociology', i.e. an academic discipline, the term 'social behaviour' seems preferable.

4. Fishbein, M., 'The Prediction of Behaviour from Attitudinal Variables' in Mortenson, C.D. (ed.), *Advances in Communications Research* (New York: Harper and Row, 1973), pp. 3-31.

5. Ajzen, I. and Fishbein, M., 'Attitudes and Normative Beliefs as Factors Influencing Behavioural Intentions', *Journal of Personality and Social Psychology*, vol. 21 (1972), pp. 1-9. For a discussion of recent research and its applications to research in marketing and consumer behaviour, see Foxall, G.R., *The Treatment of 'Attitude' in Consumer Research*, University of Birmingham, Faculty of Commerce and Social Science, Discussion Paper No. B77 (1981).

6. Foxall, F.R., *Consumer Choice* (London: Macmillan, 1983).

7. Rogers, E.M. and Shoemaker, F.F., *Communication of Innovations* (New York: The Free Press, 1971), p. 27.

8. Engel, J.F. and Blackwell, R.D., *Consumer Behaviour*, fourth edn (Hindsdale, Illinois: Dryden, 1982), p. 392.

9. DeFleur M. and Westie, F., ' "Attitude" as a Scientific Concept', *Social Forces*, vol. 42, no. 1 (1963), pp. 17-31.

10. Though the latter should be fairly easy to discover in the case of a new product.

11. Midgley and Downing are reticent about the way in which psychological traits and past behaviour and experience induce or shape 'innate innovativeness'. Cf. Hirschman, E.C., 'Innovativeness, Novelty Seeking, and Consumer Creativity', *Journal of Consumer Research*, vol. 7, no. 3 (1980), pp. 283-95.

12. Midgley and Downing, 'Innovativeness', p. 229.

13. The following is a discussion of salient outcomes rather than an exhaustive account. For a recent review, see Engel and Blackwell, *Consumer Behaviour*, Chapter 13.

14. Rogers, E.M. and Stanfield, J.D., 'Adoption and Diffusion of New Products: Emerging Generalisations and Hypotheses' in Bass, F.M., King, C.W. and Pessemier, E.A. (eds.), *Applications of The Sciences in Marketing Management* (New York: Wiley, 1968), pp. 228-40.

15. Robertson, T.S., *Innovative Behaviour and Communication* (New York: Holt, Rinehart and Winston, 1971), pp. 100-4.

16. E.G. Bell, W.E., 'Consumer Innovators' in Greyser, S.A. (ed.), *Toward Scientific Marketing* (Chicago: American Marketing Association, 1963), pp. 83-95; Coleman, R.P., 'The Significance of Social Class in Selling' in Bell, M.C. (ed.), *Proceedings of the AMA* (Chicago: American Marketing Association, 1960), pp. 171-84.

17. Robertson, T.S., 'Consumer Innovators: The Key to New Product Success', *California Management Review*, vol. 10 (1967). See also: 'The Touch-Tone Telephone: Diffusion of an Innovation' in Blackwell, R.D., Engel, J.F. and Talavzyk, W.W., *Contemporary Cases in Consumer Behaviour* (Hindsdale, Illinois: Dryden, 1977), pp. 257-67.

18. Robertson, T.S. and Kennedy, J.N., 'Prediction of Consumer Innovators: Application of Multiple Discriminant Analysis', *Journal of Marketing Research*, vol. 5, no. 1 (1969), pp. 64-9.

19. Kegerreis, R.J., Engel, J.R. and Blackwell, R.D., 'Innovativeness and Diffusiveness: A Marketing View of the Characteristics of Earliest Adopters' in Kollat, D.T., Blackwell, R.D. and Engel, J.R. (eds.), *Research in Consumer Behaviour* (New York: Holt, Rinehart and Winston, 1970), pp. 671-89.

20. Opinion Research Centre, *America's Tastemakers* (Princeton, NJ: ORC, 1959); Robertson, 'Consumer Innovators'; Robertson and Kennedy *Predictions of Consumer Innovators*; Robertson, *Innovative Behaviour and Communication*. Further evidence of a direct relationship between social class and innovativeness is provided by Boone, L.E., 'The Search for the Consumer Innovator', *Journal of Business*, vol. 48, no. 2 (1970), pp. 135-40.

21. Rogers and Stanfield, p. 242; Robertson, *Innovative Behaviour*, pp. 101-6; Robertson, 'Consumer Innovators'; Robertson and Kennedy, *Prediction of Consumer Innovators*; cf. Katz, E., *Human Organisation*, vol. 20 (1961), pp. 70-82.

22. Bruno, A.V., Hustad, T.P. and Pessemier, E.A. 'Media Approaches to Segmentation', *Journal of Advertising Research*, vol. 13, no. 2 (1973) pp. 35-42. See also Foxall, G.R., *Strategic Marketing Management* (London: Croom Helm and New York: Wiley, 1981), pp. 118-23; Summers, J.O. 'Media Exposure Patterns of Consumer Innovators', *Journal of Marketing*, vol. 36, no. 1 (1972), pp. 43-9.

23. Kegerreis, Engel and Blackwell, 'Innovativeness and Diffusiveness', pp. 681-4.

24. And thus showing closer correspondence to the model of consumer communication behaviour and effects advanced by Cox, D.F., 'The Audience as Communicators' in Greyser, *Toward Scientific Marketing*, pp. 58-72. See also

Foxall, *Strategic Marketing Management*, Chapter 5; Foxall, G.R., *Consumer Behaviour* (London: Croom Helm and New York: Wiley, 1980), Chapter 6.

25. Robertson, 'Consumer Innovators'; Robertson and Kennedy, *Prediction of Consumer Innovators*.

26. Kegerreis, Engel and Blackwell, 'Innovativeness and Diffusiveness', p. 688. See also, *inter alia*; Whyte, W. 'The Web and Word-of-Mouth', *Fortune*, vol. 50 (1964), pp. 140-5; Arndt, J. 'Product Related Conversation in the Diffusion of a New Product', *Journal of Marketing Research*, vol. 4, no. 3 (1967), pp. 291-5. Cf. Summers, J.O., 'Generalised Change Agents and Innovativeness', *Journal of Marketing Research*, vol. 8, no. 3 (1971), pp. 313-16.

27. Rogers and Stanfield, *Adoption and Diffusion of New Products*, p. 241; Robertson, *Innovative Behaviour and Communication*, pp. 101-8.

28. Zaltman, G., *Marketing: Contributions from the Behavioural Sciences* (New York: Harcourt, Brace, Janovich, 1965); Whyte, 'The Web of Word-of-Mouth'; Robertson, *Innovative Behaviour and Communication*, pp. 101-3; Pizam, A., 'Psychological Characteristics of Innovators', *European Journal of Marketing*, vol. 6, no. 3 (1972), pp. 203-10. Cf. Jacoby, J., 'Personality and Innovation Proneness', *Journal of Marketing Research*, vol. 8, no. 2 (1971), pp. 244-7; Coney, K.A., 'Dogmatism and Innovation: A Replication', *Journal of Marketing Research*, vol. 9, no. 4 (1972), pp. 453-5; Blake, B., Perloff, R. and Heslin, R., 'Dogmatism and Acceptance of New Products', *Journal of Marketing Research*, vol. 7, no. 4 (1970), pp. 483-6. Robertson, *Innovative Behaviour and Communication*, pp. 107-8.

29. Robertson, *Innovative Behaviour and Communication*, p. 108; Midgley, *Innovation and New Product Marketing*, pp. 56-64.

30. Kegerreis, Engel and Blackwell, 'Innovativeness and Diffusiveness', pp. 687; 8.

31. Robertson and Kennedy, *Prediction of Consumer Innovators*.

32. Robertson, 'Consumer Innovators'.

33. Baumgarten, S.A., 'The Diffusion of Fashion Innovators among US College Students' (Amsterdam: ESOMAR, 1974); Midgley, D.F. 'Innovation in the Male Fashion Market' (Amsterdam: ESOMAR, 1974).

34. Donnelly, J.H., 'Social Character and Acceptance of New Products', *Journal of Marketing Research*, vol. 7, no. 1 (1970), pp. 111-13.

35. Donnelly, J.H. and Ivancevich, J.M., 'A Methodology for Identifying Innovator Characteristics of New Brand Purchasers', *Journal of Marketing Research*, vol. 11, no. 3 (1974), pp. 331-4.

36. Robertson, *Innovative Behaviour and Communication*, p. 107.

37. Rogers and Stanfield, *Adoption and Diffusion of New Products*, p. 243.

38. Ostlund, L.E., 'Perceived Innovation Attributes as Predictors of Innovativeness', *Journal of Consumer Research*, vol. 1, no. 3 (1974), pp. 23-9.

39. Ibid.

40. Midgley, D.F., *Innovation and New Product Marketing* (London: Croom Helm, 1977), pp. 65-70.

41. Schoemaker, R.W. and Shoaf, F.R., 'Behaviour Changes in the Trial of New Products', *Journal of Consumer Research*, vol. 2, no. 1 (1975), pp. 104-9. Cf. Mittelstaed, Crossbart and Curtis, 'Optimal Stimulation Level and the Adoption Decision Process'.

42. *Innovative Behaviour and Communication*, p. 100.

43. Frank, R.E. and Massy, W.F., 'Innovation and Brand Choice', *Proceedings of AMA Conference* (Chicago: American Marketing Association, 1963), pp. 96-107.

44. Robertson, 'Consumer Innovators'.

45. Taylor, J.W. 'A Striking Characteristic of Innovators', *Journal of Marketing Research*, vol. 14, no. 1 (1977), pp. 104-7.

46. Robertson, *Innovative Behaviour and Communication*, p. 109.

47. Robertson, T.S., 'New Product Diffusion' in Kassarjian, H.H. and Robertson, T.S., *Perspectives in Consumer Behaviour* (Glenview, Illinois: Scott, Foresman, 1981), pp. 254-5.

48. Midgley, *Innovation and New Product Marketing*, p. 60.

49. Ibid., p. 62.

50. Ibid., p. 60, citing Baumgarten (note 33); Darden, W.R. and Reynolds, F.D., 'Backward Profiling of Male Innovators', *Journal of Marketing Research*, vol. 11, no. 1 (1974), pp. 78-85; and Midgley, 'Innovation in the Male Fashion Market'.

51. Feldman, L.P. and Armstrong, G.M., 'Identifying Buyers of a Major Auto-mative Innovation', *Journal of Marketing*, vol. 39, no. 4 (1975), pp. 61-2; Feldman, L.P. and Armstrong, G.M., 'Reply to Peat, Gentry and Brown', *Journal of Marketing*, vol. 39 (1975), pp. 63-4.

52. Demographic differences between the samples involved in testing the first hypothesis, i.e. between Californian and Midwest innovators, were not considered valid points of comparison because of 'cross-regional differences'.

53. Robertson, T.S. and Myers, J.H., 'Personality correlates of Opinion Leadership and Innovative Buying Behaviour', *Journal of Marketing Research*, vol. 6, no. 2 (1969), pp. 164-8; Summers, J.O., 'Generalised Change Agents and Innovativeness', *Journal of Marketing Research*, vol. 8, no. 3 (1971), pp. 313-16. Arndt, J., 'New Product Diffusion' in Sheth, *Models of Buyer Behaviour*, pp. 327-35.

54. E.g. Belk, R.W., 'Situational Variable and Consumer Behaviour', *Journal of Consumer Research*, vol. 2, no. 3 (1975), pp. 157-64. A recent review is pro-vided by Kakkar, P. and Lutz, R.J., 'Situational Influence on Consumer Behaviour' in Kassarjian and Robertson, *Perspectives in Consumer Behaviour*, pp. 204-14.

55. Baker, *Marketing New Industrial Products*, Chapter 4.

56. E.g. Ozanne, O.B. and Churchill, G.A., 'Five Dimensions of the Industrial Adoption Process', *Journal of Marketing Research*, vol. 8, no. 3 (1971), pp. 322-8.

57. Useful reviews can be found in Hill, R.W. and Hillier, R.T., *Organisational Buying Behaviour* (London: Macmillan, 1977); Wind, Y. and Thomas, R.J., 'Conceptual and Methodological Issues in Organisational Buying Behaviour', *European Journal of Marketing*, vol. 14, nos. 5/6 (1980), pp. 239-64. Kennedy, A., *Buyer Behaviour — Review and Discussion* (Paper presented at the MEG/ SSRC Marketing Theory Seminar, Ross Priory, Scotland, 1981).

58. Foxall, *Marketing Behaviour*, Chapter 4.

59. Webster, F.E. and Wind, Y., *Organisational Buying Behaviour* (Englewood Cliffs, NJ: Prentice-Hall, 1972), p. 132; cf. Klass, B., 'What Factors Affect Indus-trial Buying Decisions?', *Industrial Marketing* (May 1961), p. 33.

60. Choffray, J.M. and Lilien, G.L., 'Methodology for Investigating Differences in Evaluation Criteria Among Industrial Buying Influences', Working Paper No. 975-78, Massachusetts Institute of Technology (1978), p. 3.

61. This table represents an adaptation and expansion of Table II in Wind and Thomas' 'Conceptual and Methodological Issues in Organisational Buying Behaviour', p. 243. The references cited are: Robinson, P.J. and Faris, C.W. (eds), *Industrial Buying and Creative Marketing* (Boston, Mass.: Allyn and Bacon, 1967); Ozanne, U.B. and Churchill, G.A., 'Five Dimensions of the Industrial Adoption Process', *Journal of Marketing Research*, vol. 10, no. 3 (1973), pp. 322-8; Webster and Wind, *Organisational Buying Behaviour*; Kelly, P., 'Functions Performed in Industrial Purchase Decisions with Implications for Marketing Strategy', *Journal of Business Research*, vol. 2, no. 4 (1967), pp. 421-33; Hill and Hillier, *Organisational Buying Behaviour*, p. 45; Bradley, M.F. 'Buying Behaviour in Ireland's Public Sector', *Industrial Marketing Manage-ment*, vol. 6, no. 4 (1977), pp. 251-8; Wind, Y., 'The Boundaries of Buying

Decision Centres', *Journal of Purchasing and Materials Management*, vol. 14, Summer (1978), pp. 23-9.

62. Robinson and Faris, *Industrial Buying and Creative Marketing*.

63. Hill and Hillier, *Organisational Buying Behaviour*, pp. 62-6.

64. Foxall, *Marketing Behaviour*, Chapter 14.

65. Moriarty, R.T. and Bateson, J.E.G., 'Exploring Complex Decision Making Units: A New Approach', *Journal of Marketing Research*, vol. 19, no. 2 (1982), p. 182.

66. Bonoma, T.V., 'Major Sales: Who Really Does the Buying?', *Harvard Business Review*, vol. 60, no. 3 (1982), pp. 111-19.

67. Bonoma, T.V., Zaltman, G. and Johnston, W.J., 'Industrial Buying Behaviour', Report No. 77-117 (Cambridge, Mass.: Marketing Science Institute). Cited by Silk and Kalwani (see Next note).

68. Silk. A.J. and Kalwani, M.U., 'Measuring Influence in Organisational Purchase Decisions', *Journal of Marketing Research*, vol. 19, no. 2 (1982), pp. 165-81.

69. Simon, H.A., *Administrative Behaviour* (New York: Free Press, 1957).

70. Lazo, H., 'Emotional Aspects of Industrial Buying' in Hancock, R.S. (ed.), *Proceedings of the A.M.A.* (Chicago: American Marketing Association, 1960), p. 265. Cited by Robertson, T.S., *Consumer Behaviour* (Glenview, Illinois: Scott, Foresman, 1970), pp. 23-4.

71. See Hill and Hillier, *Organisational Buying Behaviour*, pp. 80-6; Kennedy, S.H., *The Rationality of the Industrial Buyer* (unpublished dissertation, University of Bradford, 1970); Cunningham, M.T. and White, J.G., 'The Behaviour of Industrial Buyers in their Search for Suppliers of Machine Tools', *Journal of Management Studies*, vol. 11, no. 2 (1974), pp. 115-28.

72. It is unfair to single out buyers for their human behaviour; managers and other industrial employees also satisfice and are influenced by 'non-rational' factors. The purpose of this discussion is simply to qualify the notion of rational buying which is sometimes assumed as a result of the satisficing inertia of marketing academics. For discussion and evidence of the factors mentioned in this paragraph, see, *inter alia*, James, B.G.S., *Integrated Marketing* (London: Penguin 1972), pp. 378-83; Petigrew, A.M. 'The Industrial Purchasing Decision as a Political Process', *European Journal of Marketing*, vol. 9, (1975), pp. 4-19; White, P.D. and Cundiff, E.W., 'Assessing the Quality of Industrial Products', *Journal of Marketing*, vol. 42, no. 1 (1978), pp. 80-6; Haksansson, H. and Wootz, B., 'Risk Reduction and the Industrial Purchaser', *European Journal of Marketing*, vol. 9, (1975), pp. 35-51.

73. Sheth, J.N., 'A Model of Industrial Buyer Behaviour', *Journal of Marketing*, vol. 37, no. 4 (1973), pp. 50-6.

74. Kirton, M., 'Adaptors and Innovators: A Description and Measure', *Journal of Applied Psychology*, vol. 61, no. 5 (1976), pp. 622-9.

75. Kirton, M., 'Adaptors and Innovators: The Way People Approach Problems', *Planned Innovation*, vol. 3, no. 2 (1980), p. 53.

76. Robertson, *Consumer Behaviour*, p. 138.

77. Mansfield, E., *The Economics of Technological Change*, (New York: Norton, 1968).

78. Mansfield, E., *Industrial Research and Technological Innovation* (New York: Norton, 1968).

79. Webster, F.E., *Industrial Marketing Strategy* (New York: John Wiley, 1979), p. 119.

80. Baker, *Marketing New Industrial Products*; see especially Chapters 5 and 6.

81. Burns, T. and Stalker, G.M., *The Management of Innovation*, 2nd edn (London: Tavistock, 1966). See also Lawrence, P.R. and Lorsch, J.W.,

'Differentiation and Integration in Complex Organisations', *Administrative Science Quarterly*, vol. 12, no. 1 (1967), pp. 1-47; *Organisation and Environment* (Homewood, Illinois: Irwin, 1969); Child, J., *Organisation: A Guide to Problems and Practice* (London: Harper and Row, 1977), especially Chapter 1.

82. A useful summary is found in Baker, M.J., 'Industrial Buying Behaviour and the Adoption of Innovations' in Baker, M.J. (ed.), *Industrial Innovation* (London: Macmillan, 1979), pp. 345-66. See *Marketing New Industrial Products*, however, for full details of method, hypothesis and conclusions.

83. Baker, M.J. and Parkinson, S.T., *Predicting the Adoption and Diffusion of Industrial Innovation*, Report to the Social Science Research Council (1976) (cited by Baker in 'Industrial Buying Behaviour and the Adoption of Innovations').

84. Baker, M.J. and Abu-Ismail, F., 'The Diffusion of Innovation in Industrial Markets' in Baker, M.J. (ed.), *Buyer Behaviour* (Proceedings of the MEG Annual Conference, 1976), pp. 329-48.

85. Fisher, L.V., 'The Adoption of the Digital Computer in Process Control' in Weir, A. (ed.), *Proceedings of the MEG Conference* (Hull, 1978), pp. 331-76.

86. Mahajan, V. and Schoeman, M.E.F., 'The Use of Computers in Hospitals: An analysis of Adopters and Nonadopters', *Interfaces*, vol. 7, no. 3 (1977), pp. 95-107.

87. Hayward, G., 'Market Adoption of New Industrial Products', *Industrial Marketing Management*, vol. 7, no. 3 (1978), pp. 193-8.

88. Kennedy, A.M., 'Industrial Innovation and Marketing Strategy', paper tabled at the 1981 MEG Conference, Dublin.

89. E.g. Child, J., 'Culture, Contingency and Capitalism in the cross-national study of organisations' in Cummings, L.L. and Straw, B.M. (eds), *Research in Organisational Behaviour* (Greenwich, Connecticut: JAI Press, 1981); 'Organisational Design and Performance: Contingency Theory and Beyond', *Organisation and Administrative Sciences* (Summer/Fall, 1977), pp. 169-83. Budge, A., Child, J., Francis, A. and Kieser, A., 'Corporate Goals, Managerial Objectives and Organisational Structures in British and West German Companies', *Organisation Studies*, vol. 3, no. 1 (1982), pp. 1-32.

90. Gold, B., 'Technological Diffusion in Industry: Research Needs and Shortcomings', *Journal of Industrial Economics*, vol. 29, no. 3 (1981), pp. 247-68.

91. Littlechild, S.C., *Social Cost — A Subjectivist View* (University of Birmingham, Faculty of Commerce and Social Science, Discussion Paper No. B39, 1976). See also: Wiseman, J., 'Costs and Decisions' in Curtis, D.A. and Peters, W. (eds), *Contemporary Economic Analysis* (London: Croom Helm, 1980).

92. 'Technological Diffusion in Industry', pp. 259-60.

93. An interesting case for treating the reasons given by businessmen for *not* adopting innovations is provided by Carter, who argues that behind such standard reasons as lack of awareness, cost, timing and finance lie more fundamental economic problems such as an unfavourable environment for new product and process adoption, an adverse social and educational atmosphere, lack of state support and inadequate management. See Carter, C., 'Reasons for Not Innovating' in Carter (ed.), *Industrial Policy and Innovation*, pp. 21-31.

94. See Part Three, particularly Chapter 10. For some interesting evidence on awareness and trial, see Narayana, C.L. and Markin, R.J., 'Consumer Behaviour and Product Performance: An Alternative Conceptualisation', *Journal of Marketing*, vol. 39, no. 4 (1975), pp. 1-6; Olson, J.C. and Dover, P.A., 'Disconfirmation of Consumer Expectations Through Product Trial', *Journal of Applied Psychology*, vol. 64, no. 2 (1979), pp. 979-89.

PART THREE

NEW PRODUCT DEVELOPMENT

# 8 INTRODUCTION TO PART THREE

## Uncertainty and Its Reduction

In the world of perfectly competitive markets depicted in the neo-classical microeconomic model, new product development would be a straightforward affair. This is because the theory of perfect competition credits businessmen with total knowledge – of competitors, consumers and costs – and portrays both firm and industry in a state of imperturbable equilibrium. Lack of information on the part of those managers who are responsible for new product development is the single, ultimate reason for innovative failure in the world of experience: into this reason devolve all the causes of ineffective new product development identified in Chapter 4. High product failure rates are probably an inevitable consequence of competitive, market-based, customer-oriented economies simply because of the impossibility of reducing uncertainty sufficiently for there to be any other outcome. Where consumer sovereignty exists and is valued, product failure is inevitable, just as unsuccessful political campaigns are an essential feature of political democracies. Industrial innovation consists in the production and marketing of variety as each company competes to satisfy customers more completely than do its rivals: the proliferation of product offerings and the evolution of intricate and expensive product testing procedures are inescapable consequences of making variety available. Far from being content to maintain an equilibrium position, most managements are compelled to innovate, incurring the costs of this risk-laden process as well as receiving its promise of financial gain. As Tauber[1] notes, 'to test-market a loser may cost several hundred thousand dollars out-of-pocket, while the opportunity cost (or foregone profit) of failing to market a big winner can amount to millions over many years . . . It is cheaper to have a lot of market failures than it is to avoid the loss and miss a big sales winner.' As product life cycles and spans of diffusion become increasingly short,[2] this problem is going to remain a feature of the innovative scene.

Nevertheless, some companies have exceeded the average level of new product success for their industry as a result of improvements in the management and organisation of innovative development. One measure of their effectiveness is the reduction in the number of new product

163

ideas required to yield a successful new product: in the original Booz, Allen and Hamilton[3] survey reported in 1965, some 58 new ideas or concepts were required for each success; by 1981 this number had fallen to seven. Rockwell and Particelli[4] ascribe this change to the increased sophistication of companies' new product development procedures. Their conclusion is borne out by the finding that a smaller proportion of investment in new products is nowadays directed towards products which eventually fail; furthermore, more money is today spent on the initial stages of new product development (i.e. research into the location and evaluation of ideas and preliminary business analysis) and less on market testing and commercialisation.

While some degree of product failure is inevitable in a society which values choice, the fundamental ingredients of effective innovation are capable of greater managerial control than is often realised. The various stages of the new product development process — from the location and screening of ideas, through their commercial evaluation, product design, development and trial, to the launch of the innovation — are always capable of reflecting more closely user needs, purchase propensities and consumption behaviours; in short, of fulfilling more fully the objectives of the company by fulfilling more fully the objectives of customers and users. The pursuit of greater innovative effectiveness is pointless, however, unless it is preceded by the establishment of a sound strategic foundation for new product development — corporate self-assessment, policy-making, the setting of feasible objectives which act both as targets for action and criteria for control, and so on. This is borne out by the recent research into corporate innovation reported by Rockwell and Particelli:[5]

Companies that have successfully launched new products — a success being a product which met or exceeded its objectives — are more likely to have had a formal new product process in place for a longer period of time. They are also more likely to have a strategic plan, and be committed to growing through internally developed new products. The new product strategy links corporate objectives to the new product effort, and provides direction for the new product process. The step identifies the strategic roles to be played by new products — roles that depend on the type of product itself and the industry. It also helps set the formal financial criteria to be used in measuring new product performance and in screening and evaluating new product ideas.

The use of information to reduce uncertainty is an important theme of Part Three which seeks to understand the nature of new product development in the firm.

## The Nature of New Product Development

Successful new product development depends upon many favourable coincidences. The identification of market need is not, on its own, a sufficient starting point for the corporate innovative process; nor does technological breakthrough alone provide a viable justification for investing in changes to a company's product portfolio. Many technical managers and some marketing executives show signs of 'technological determinism', a belief that whatever is technically feasible will inevitably be successfully marketed. It is certainly possible to find examples of discontinuous inventions such as television and computers which in their time had considerably disruptive impacts upon buyer behaviour but which were widely accepted and succeeded in commercial terms. But the tendency to concentrate upon successes overlooks the large number of failures, even in the case of fairly continuous innovations such as a new brand of cigarettes or toothpaste.

If technological change is to be effective, there must be a coincidence in time and place of three factors:[6] '(1) a technical concept capable of being developed to the stage of achieving (2) an *advantage* over alternative technical concepts, and (3) the capability of developing (1) to the stage of achieving (2)'. In other words, technological advance is relevant to corporate innovation only if it offers the firm a competitive advantage and if the firm has the resource capacity to exploit that advantage commercially. Many new products have a sound technological base but lack advantages which consumers detect — compare *J.-Cloths*, the Gilette *Techmatic* and Birds Eye frozen foods, which successfully increased consumers' perceptions of value-added with *Cheer* detergent, *Nestea* (an instant tea product) and *Corfam* which failed to do so.

In seeking to understand the capacity of business organisations to innovate successfully, it is important to maintain a balanced view of two competing impressions of the management of new product development. The first emphasises the complex nature of corporate innovation and and consequent need for its serious planning. This approach is also likely to stress the range of managerial decision techniques, especially those which involve quantitative modelling, and to give the impression that business innovation is becoming or can become a deterministic process. The alternative impression is that innovation is more often than not unplanned, the result of chance occurrences or unbounded managerial insights. The view developed in Part Three is that, while successful innovation generally occurs within a viable strategic framework, this should not become so restrictive as to exclude entrepreneurial alertness and the organisational and managerial flexibility it requires. Successful innovation is often achieved, moreover, in the absence of widespread use of advanced quantitative methods, though this fact should not be used to rationalise managerial unfamiliarity with and comprehension of genuine means of reducing uncertainty through their use.

Although effective innovation depends upon the 'coincidence' of external (market) opportunities and internal (resource) capacities, it is far from being an unplanned phenomenon which occurs by chance. Successful new product development is usually the result of a deliberate sequential process involving

(1) the generation and evaluation of product ideas;
(2) business analysis and preliminary market assessment; and
(3) development, market testing and launch.

Another recurring theme in the following chapters is the need for corporate strategy to be clearly defined before serious new product planning occurs. If the constraints laid by explicit strategy upon the corporate innovative process are known, then the problems encountered in the planning and development of marketing-oriented innovative strategy — can be the more easily solved. In other words, the development of those new product concepts which are adopted, and the scope and methods of market exploration which produce them, must be fitted to the strategic framework consciously constructed by the highest levels of management. Indeed, even at the point at which new ideas are generated, some evaluation or screening is often inevitable. The pressing managerial task is to ensure that potentially useful ideas are not arbitrarily discarded at this stage nor unsuitable ideas passed for expensive development at the next more formal phase of screening. And so on throughout the new product development sequence: explicit strategy and the accommodation of product development to the demands of a known strategic framework are prerequisites of effective innovation.

Undertaken within the appropriate strategic framework and properly accommodated to its requirements, the new product development process is capable of reducing the uncertainty which surrounds and permeates corporate innovation. Yet, while there exists the possibility of informing more adequately the development process, it cannot be supposed that corporate innovation can ever become an entirely rational, orderly and systematised procedure. Abstract accounts may assume some of these qualities in order to clarify and generalise the process they describe, but actual managerial problems are always much 'squishier' than this in the sense that they lack 'well-defined formulation'.[7] New product development resembles an art or craft more than a science and, although the quality and quantity of recent research make some generalisation possible, techniques and solutions remain appropriate to particular instances rather than providing universal guidelines.

Mention has been made of the phases of the new product development process which have been assumed in the organisation of the following chapters. They are based upon the findings and conclusions of applied research but categorisations such as 'exploration', 'screening', 'business analysis', 'development', 'testing' and 'commercialisation',[8] may, in any particular investigation, prove arbitrary. The actual stages are not always so easy to unravel as the model suggests. In order to emphasise the flexibility of new product development, Chapter 9 is concerned primarily with the *initiation* of the development process, i.e. the location and evaluation of new product ideas as part of the pre-commitment phase, while Chapter 10 deals with the design, development and testing of new products which follows initial commitment.

## Notes

1. Tauber, E.M., 'Forecasting Sales Prior to Test Market', *Journal of Marketing* vol. 41, no. 1 (1977), p. 84.

2. Olshavsky, R.W., 'Time and the Rate of Adoption of Innovations', *Journal of Consumer Research*, vol. 6, no. 4 (1980), pp. 425-8.

3. *The Management of New Products*, Booz, Allen and Hamilton (New York: 1965 and 1968).

4. Rockwell and Particelli, 'New Product Strategy'.

5. Ibid., p. 50.

6. Langrish, J., 'The Effects of Technological Change' in Baker (ed.), *Industrial Innovation*, p. 453.

7. Strauch, B.E., ' "Squishy" Problems and Quantitative Methods', *Policy Sciences*, vol. 6, no. 3 (1975), p. 177.

8. *The Management of New Products* (New York: Booz, Allen and Hamilton).

# 9 THE LOCATION AND EVALUATION OF MARKETING OPPORTUNITIES

## The Location of Marketing Opportunities

The origins of entrepreneurial insight form a favourite theme in accounts of corporate innovation. Various classifications of the relevant sources of new product concepts are to be found in the marketing literature, from those in which the genesis of innovation inheres in the creative genius of an individual 'prime mover' to those which seem to assume that ideas for successful new products are so elusive as to require strenuous generation by experimental techniques such as brainstorming. Another type of classification of the sources of new product ideas dwells upon their location: those sources which are internal to the company — such as the analysis of marketing intelligence data, R&D personnel, venture committees and employee suggestion schemes — are distinguished from such external sources as competitors, customers, patients, consultants and agents. On occasion, idea-deficient situations arise in which these environments must be carefully monitored lest important concepts for effective innovation are overlooked. However, the strategic problem faced by most firms at the early stages of the new product development process is not that too few potentially-workable ideas exist but that the means of discriminating between appropriate and inappropriate ideas are lacking. The strategic need is for ways of ensuring that those ideas selected for development harmonise sufficiently with corporate capabilities and with genuine market opportunities to contribute adequately or better to the fulfilment of business objectives.

Much academic and semi-academic wisdom consists in the provision of prescriptions for *formal* screening procedures in which specific criteria — often in the form of checklists — are thought to increase managerial assurance that selected products will enhance corporate profitability sufficiently for investment in them to have been justified. But, in reality, managerial awareness of potential new products and market opportunities often goes hand in hand with much more *informal* screening procedures in which an effective match between the firm's policy and strategic frameworks including objectives and assessments of corporate strengths and weaknesses on the one hand and

168

feasible innovative projects on the other, is effected almost spontaneously well before formal screening methods are enacted.

Both formal and informal screening processes ought ideally to express overall strategic awareness and commitment. These factors in turn are closely associated with the most appropriate (i.e. profitable) sources of new product ideas. For instance, the proactive, marketing-oriented organisation can be expected to balance technology-push and market-pull influences on innovation in order to ensure that neither source of innovation dominates product development in such a way that the necessary confirmation and support of the other is neglected. Such balance between intra-firm capacity for the well-executed exploitation of a technical comparative advantage and the capacity of the market environment to absorb the new product is essential to effective innovation. Yet its achievement remains one of the most difficult tasks of entrepreneurial management. The reason for this is that, as Pessemier[1] points out, most industries tend to have an apparently inherent tendency towards either a *market-orientation* or an *R&D orientation* to new product development.

'Market-orientation', as used in this context, is not synonymous with marketing-oriented management, though it is true that industries and firms characterised by market-orientation rely heavily upon opportunities offered by demand factors. The significance of this category of company is that firms within it tend to rely upon relatively stable technological bases while their product innovation programmes reflect primarily changes in customer tastes and patterns of usage. Their use of technological knowledge in R&D and production may well be immense but, at the idea stage of the innovative process, they are likely only to use changes in technology available to them rather than search for new product ideas among the advanced literatures of technical breakthrough. In such firms, external sources of product ideas are pre-eminent. The polar extreme of the market-oriented industry is represented by companies which cater to the supermarket grocery and personal care markets: these industries are characterised by both market-based generation of innovative possibilities and relatively easily-targeted, already-existing technical capabilities. Consumer electronics industries, which are involved in the production of such products as colour televisions, video equipment and personal computers also tend to be market-oriented, though the difficulties of technical product development are often of a much higher order of magnitude. The innovative process in such industries is generally inaugurated by consideration of the behaviours of consumers and competitors on the assumption that current technological capacities are sufficient to make product development feasible. Specific technical development is likely to be brought to bear upon the process only after extensive testing in the marketplace has refined the initial idea sufficiently to produce a viable product concept. While many consumer products exemplify this pattern, market-orientation is also encountered in certain industries which supply standard industrial components and capital equipment as well as those involved in the marketing of industrial electronics-based products.

In R&D-oriented industries, the specific product development process is often inaugurated by technological advances, albeit in many cases the work of technical creation is undertaken and guided by a relatively vague and amorphous awareness of the possibility of market need for which no product solution is available. Industrial chemicals and consumer pharmaceutical industries are typical of those which adopt this style of product innovation in which developmental programmes are initiated by remotely market-based intelligence but constantly updated by the direct impact of technological progress. Yet this particular pattern is not the only one which falls into the R&D-oriented category. There is a spectrum of R&D-oriented industries from those which produce breakthroughs in polymer and medicinal chemistry and which are predominently science-based to those which involve the application of technical expertise to a given difficulty — e.g. the production of metals with pre-specified qualities — which are accordingly designated 'problem-based'. Thus, just as market-oriented companies differ one from another in terms of the magnitude of technological invention demanded by the innovative projects they undertake, so R&D oriented firms make differential use of market signals in the inaugural stages of the new product development process. Also like market-orientation, R&D-orientation is relevant to companies operating in consumer markets as well as to whose which supply industrial products and services.

In summary, Pessemier's classification of industries emphasises that the fundamental sources of innovative opportunity are two-fold: advances in technological/productive capability and changes in purchase and consumption behaviours. Successful new product development incorporates effective corporate responses to both of these environments, of course, and even in Pessemier's largely dichotomous model, technological and market influences are shown to be mutually contingent at the various stages of new product development, so much so that in some specific cases it proves difficult to unravel the dominant source of innovative response. The fact that the 'technology push' and 'market pull' dichotomy is not entirely unambiguous should not, however, obscure the valuable clues it provides in the location and evaluation of ideas for new product development. Just as formal screening procedures should incorporate criteria which allow product ideas to be rejected or retained on the basis of an objective estimate of the extent to which they fit into the firm's strategic framework, so the most appropriate source of effective new product ideas is predictable from the extent to which the firm's general strategic response is best described as 'reactive' or 'proactive'.

As noted in Chapter 3, reactive firms tend to wait for innovative opportunities to become available or for the need to innovate to be forced upon them, say by competitors' 'actions'; they are imitative, or second-(to market)-but-better, or passively responsive to customers' product ideas. Proactive firms are aggressively innovative, actively seeking opportunities to develop new products through their marketing-orientation and expertise, technological capabilities and entrepreneurial spirit. Companies, divisions, plants or other 'strategic business units' display relatively reactive or proactive strategies, sometimes temporarily, sometimes as their dominant strategic mode of responding to their internal and external environments. The four broad possibilities for the location of product ideas and the identification of corresponding market opportunities are shown in Table 9.1.

Table 9.1: Strategically-relevant Sources of Innovative Opportunity

| Relative strategic response | Nature of source of innovative opportunity | Locus and direction of entrepreneurship |
| --- | --- | --- |
| Reactive | 1. Producer innovates only when forced to do so in order to survive or protect strategic business unit. | Competitors. From external environment to producer. |
| | 2. User needs identified *for* producer. | Buyers and/or users. From external environment to producer. |
| | 3. User needs identified *by* producer. | Producer. From customer-oriented search. |
| | 4. Relatively unhampered exploration. | Producer. From creative product-market search and entrepreneurial alertness to opportunity. |
| Proactive | | |

Since the fourth type of source is open only to the largest, most successful companies, it is treated in the following discussion as a special case of market location and identification by producers.

## Competitor-dominated Reactive Innovation

Regardless of their general strategic mode, the majority of companies are influenced in some way by the actual or expected actions of their competitors. Habitually-reactive firms tend, by definition, to obtain their product development cues from other industry members. In the case of production-oriented reactive companies, mere observation and imitation of rivals' market offerings suffices, but even more customer-oriented companies may show essentially reactive responses to their environments and can therefore be expected to approach new product development by monitoring and attempting to supersede their competitors' efforts. Indeed, even the most progressive and generally proactive companies exhibit reactive behaviour on occasion. During the 1970s, the British foods and confectionery manufacturer, Cadbury, enjoyed distribution levels for its *Dairy Milk* chocolate bar of little under one hundred per cent for confectionery, tobacco and newsagency outlets and probably well in excess of ninety per cent for groceries, figures which indicate a very high level of general marketing effectiveness and, in particular, of distributive presence based upon consumers' positive behaviour. However, in the face of rising costs, the company reduced the size of this product, retaining as large as possible a surface area but making a thinner bar. Its rival, Rowntree, capitalised on its marketing intelligence reports which indicated that chocolate consumers preferred a thicker, chunkier bar by introducing and skilfully promoting the *Yorkie* product which by early 1978 equalled the *Dairy Milk* brand in terms of market coverage. Sales of the latter were also affected to a significant degree by *Yorkie*'s success. Cadbury's reactive relaunch of a thicker *Dairy Milk* product was essentially a well-executed reactive move to recapture sales. It was not entirely imitative but depended upon new consumer research data and a strongly consumer-oriented campaign.

Even the most progressive companies are forced on occasion to engage in purely reactive strategies of innovation, perhaps because of blunders or omissions in their marketing information systems but also because no single firm can be expected always to gather the most suitable market intelligence or to have complete knowledge of market opportunities. Nor is entrepreneurial awareness which bridges the gap between whatever market knowledge is available and the perception of profitable opportunities always available within the company.

Companies which have been market leaders not infrequently become followers temporarily or for extended periods. Some, relatively few, companies enjoy a comparative advantage in being second-but-better, which may be based upon small size, flexible organisation, adaptive or more productive technology or superior use of a neglected element of the marketing mix, say price or distribution levels. But the habitual use of competitors as uncontested sources of innovative opportunity is notoriously dangerous in dynamic markets. The monitoring of other companies' new market offerings is no guide to the soundness of the resulting ideas or to their capacity to match the strategic capabilities and needs of the initiator. It is unwise to rely mechanically upon rivals' readings of customers' needs: competitors might be wrong or ignore aspects of demand which the following firm is actually well-placed to meet but of which it remains unaware because of the tunnel vision produced by its restricted search for new products. Less extreme, though essentially reactive strategies include the search for new markets for existing products (market development) which is prone to high levels of customer rejection as the quantity of consumer and industrial goods which have failed to cross the Atlantic attests, and the use of ideas developed by companies in other industries or countries, perhaps through licensing agreements. The successful pursuit of a reactive strategy towards innovation depends upon the company's having the requisite resources in abundance: the uncertainties and risks associated with this approach are obviously considerable.

## User-initiated Idea Location

Market development is not the most reactive of strategies for it at least looks towards the customer or user as the source of innovation. The observation and assessment of buyers' behaviour is, of course, central to any marketing-oriented strategy and management and, in market development, the company is responsive directly to the wants of the ultimate customer rather than as they are perceived by competitors. For such responsive firms, the origin of the new product development process is frequently the customer who suggests specific innovations to the manufacturer; the hallmarks of their reaction are an unwillingness to seek actively for market opportunities before they have been identified and assessed by customers, but a willingness, once the initial uncertainties have been reduced, to adopt and exploit the idea. In consumer markets, swift and appropriate response to revealed consumer wants is a frequent source of innovation, as is evidenced by the 'chopper' bicycle for children, 'egg' shampoos, many fashion products (as the parallel diffusion hypothesis[2] predicts) and non-stick coatings for cookware.[3] But it is within the context of industrial products and processes that the theme of buyer-instigated innovation has recently received attention.

On the basis of a review of several recent studies of buyer-seller interactions in industrial markets, von Hippel[4] concludes that 'Users seem often to be the most frequent "sources" of new product and process innovations − designing, building and using a home-made version of a given innovation *before* a commercial version is available from any manufacturer.' The case of user-initiated innovation was noted in Chapter 3 and, from his own researches, von Hippel estimates that more than two-thirds of innovative process machines employed within semiconductor industries were developed by users as were four-fifths of innovative scientific industries subsequently made by specialist manufacturers.

By limiting his review to studies which indicate that the first working model of the innovation was entirely produced by the customer, von Hippel arrives at only the most conservative estimates of customer-led innovation since simple *requests* for new products and processes are excluded from his analysis on the grounds of the ambiguity and unreliability of retrospective research findings. His thesis is, moreover, well-supported by the results of several other investigations.[5] That thesis is summed up in the 'customer active paradigm' (CAP) of industrial new product development which he contrasts with the prevailing 'manufacturer active paradigm' (MAP). The MAP conception conforms to the conventional marketing textbook notion of the role of marketing research, intelligence and planning in the innovative process: manufacturers survey customers' attitudes and usage patterns and are then instrumental in developing new product concepts on the basis of the perceived needs and wants of buyers and users. The prescribed role of the buyer and/or user is essentially responsive rather than initiatory as the consumer is intended to accept the product which has been shaped to his assumed requirements. This approach, which is at the heart of the marketing concept continues to be widely applicable but it is not universally relevant. By contrast the CAP portrays the customer as generating the new product idea, selecting his target supplier and initiating the corporate innovative process, while the manufacturer assumes the relatively passive role, becoming comparatively active only at the point of screening the new product idea for commercialisation in accordance with criteria derived from his own strategic requirements and capacities.[6]

Because neither the CAP nor the MAP is of universal applicability, it becomes of strategic importance for manufacturers to be able to predict the locus of innovation and entrepreneurship in order that manufacturer-customer relationships and the division of innovative labour can be appropriately planned in specific industrial marketing situations. Two promising hypotheses enjoy a measure of empirical support and may permit manufacturers to predict the behaviour of their customer-entrepreneurs more accurately. First, in line with Utterback and Abernathy's conceptualisation of the process of innovation, it is contended that the earliest developments of new products and processes in industry are bound to be controlled by those parties who have the detailed, relevant knowledge of the desired performance characteristics of the innovation: these people are often likely to be users, especially in the case of relatively radical or discontinuous innovations. As more continuous, incrementally-modified products come on stream in later stages of the product diffusion process, the locus of innovation moves from user to manufacturer.[7] The second hypothesis relates the locus of innovation to the clarity of perception of benefit from the development process: where users have high expectations of the economic rate of return which will accrue to them as a result of successful adoption of the innovation, they are likely to invest directly in process innovation and only later to involve outside firms in the development of the item as a generally-available product innovation.[8] It is also probable that users who are uncertain about the feasibility of a new idea will experiment rather than make an immediate approach to a manufacturer and that other factors such as the nature and strength of competition among firms in the industry will help determine the identity of the innovator. Thus 'manufacturers may be aware of a need but consider the market too small or too risky to justify the investment required. If, in these circumstances, users need the product enough to justify developing it themselves, they will do so later, when some of these products turn out to serve or build markets that *are* of commercial interest, manufacturers will get into the act and market the products.' Users' desire to retain for themselves the benefits of their inventions also leads, on occasion, to their hiding their new process from potential manufacturers and thereby from competitors.[9] (The two hypotheses are clearly related; the second provides part explanation of the first.)

Figure 9.1 portrays the circumstances in which either the CAP or the MAP is of relevance in terms of two factors: (i) the customers' alertness to his need of the innovation, which is a prerequisite of the CAP and (ii) the accessibility of the new product or market opportunity to 'manufacture managed action', which is a fundamental assumption of the MAP approach.

Figure 9.1: Manufacturer and Customer Initiation of Innovation

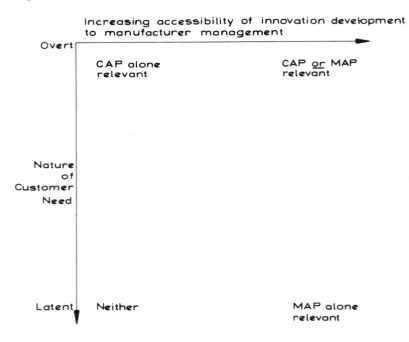

Source: Derived from von Hippel, E., 'A Customer-active Paradigm for Industrial Idea Generation' in Baker, M.J. (ed.), *Industrial Innovation* (London: Macmillan, 1979), p. 99.

Although it is predictable that users facing these industrial conditions are likely to develop their own innovative products and processes, the strategic issue is whether manufacturers can make use of this process or stimulate its inauguration. The use of incentives to customers for their devising new ideas is suggested by von Hippel[10] as a means of stimulating user-initiated innovation. For this method to work effectively, it is necessary to specify the required product in some detail and to make available to users criteria for screening their ideas (which has the advantage of eliminating inappropriate concepts at an early stage and thus reducing the manufacturers' screening burden). It is necessary, however, to provide suitable rewards for this form of externally-administered suggestion scheme and to ensure confidentiality by careful selection of companies approached. An alternative approach is to monitor carefully customers' behaviour and to be alert to their internal innovative development, offering where appropriate to progress them further.

The CAP, therefore, has radical implications *for marketing research* — which would be targeted upon (i) locating and providing the data to appraise customers' creation and use of in-house prototypes and (ii) the subsequent assessment of their market potential and possible strategic contribution to the manufacturer; for personal selling — which would be involved with the acquisition as well as the dispersal of information; and for R&D — which would be concerned with the engineering-based advancement of user-built prototypes rather than the comprehensive design and development of new products on the basis of experimentally-tested product concepts under the auspices of the firm's marketing and/or marketing research functions.

### Producer-dominated Innovation

Where the CAP is relevant, it evidently points to new areas of manufacturer vigilance, especially when user-led innovation represents a deviation from the usual procedure. But for many companies, operating in dynamic markets, *reliance* upon a system in which user needs are identified *for* the supplier rather than directly by the supplier may become a dangerous strategy. Customers' awareness of the probability that they will benefit significantly from the development of the innovation is, as noted above, an essential ingredient of user-initiated innovation. What is evident to one customer is likely to be obvious to others; an idea which one user is able to take to a manufacturer may become available to that manufacturer's competitors through the efforts of another user. The entrepreneurial alertness implied by the marketing-oriented approach to corporate management is highly relevant even where the CAP provides the most accurate description of the new product development sequence. It also remains the case that in the majority of cases of industrial and consumer product innovation, the ideas and concepts upon which development depends are formulated and refined principally through the actions of producers.

Market exploration is an essential component of the formulation of such product concepts whether the underlying idea is identified as a result of routine market research procedures or suggested by members of the firm (or its consultants) and only later tested by means of external research. Even the most technologically-based ('R&D-oriented') companies require a sound market foundation for effective product development and one of the arts of proactive managerial strategy is the *integration* of marketing, R&D design, production and other functional areas by means of a customer-oriented perspective. Such co-ordinated use of R&D and marketing has been shown in detailed investigations of the factors which distinguish successful from unsuccessful new product development to be a *sine qua non* of effective innovation. General Electric Laboratories exemplify this integration in that R&D resources are directed to the solution of problems which arise *after* the location of market needs which are relevant to the company's policy and strategic frameworks. Technical breakthroughs are channelled to the fulfilment of measureable market needs rather than being used to develop products which might prove only superficially appropriate to consumer behaviour and requirements. R&D scientists and managers are not excluded from the process in which new product ideas are located, however; entrepreneurial responsibility is so diffused throughout the company that R&D personnel actively alert marketing staff to the likelihood of forthcoming technical breakthroughs in order that market opinion can be tested at an early stage.[11]

## Technological Forecasting

While it is usually dangerous to vest complete responsibility for new product ideas' generation among the members of the R&D function, it is evident that technological factors often provide the source of a company's comparative advantage upon which successful innovation depends. *Technological forecasting* represents the broadest managerial perspective for the pursuit of this source of competitive superiority. Bright[12] defines technological forecasting as 'a quantified statement of the timing, the character or the degree of change in technical parameters and attributes in the design and application of devices, materials and processes, arrived at through a specified system of reasoning'. Delphi forecasting is a widely-used method of predicting technological development which involves the estimation by a group of experts, acting separately, of the most probable date at which technical methods, processes and related practices will emerge and/or become generally available.

Reiterations of this procedure, interspersed by feedback to the panel of data generated in previous rounds, continue until the desired level of agreement is arrived at.[13] Technological forecasting has been successfully employed in such ostensibly disparate spheres as construction, textiles, microelectronics, biotechnology, energy, materials technology and community health. In spite of the procedural difficulties which inhere in this type of forecasting, it can provide valuable insights — which may be otherwise unavailable to the proactive company — for the targeting of R&D efforts, especially if it is accompanied by the long term forecasting of customer needs. There is danger, however, in an overenthusiastic approach to long term prediction which is not closely related to corporate needs and the strategic modes to which the enterprise is suited. Indeed, the unchannelled pursuit of technical novelty may well impede the development of the necessary awareness of the requirements of the market.[14]

## Gap Analysis and Product-market Positioning

Technological sophistication as manifested in both managerial vision and specific design and productive competence is clearly essential to the effective development of even the most continuous innovations. But the necessity of *guiding* the exploitation of technical strengths towards the profitable satisfaction of users' needs is also indicated by recent research into the innovative process which substantiates the commonsense tenets of the marketing philosophy. As Rothwell[15] notes, it is the customer or user who must eventually decide the appropriateness of technologically-based product attributes. Innovation involves the matching of invention with need and demands that both specific expertise and general customer-orientation be well-developed features of the producer company's outlook and practice. Market search by means of segmentation analysis[16] enables gaps in existing generic markets to be located by means of buyers' and users' definitions of wants and needs. A popular technique for the identification of such gaps and the construction of product concepts and realities is *multi-dimensional scaling* by which unsupplied market needs can be located and the capacity of apparent marketing opportunities to sustain a profitable differentiated segmental marketing programme can be ascertained. Figure 9.2 shows how the perceptual mapping of the market for eight makes of machine tool in terms of two salient dimensions (quality and size of machine) can be used to position existing and potential brands. In this example, the results of attitude scaling research are depicted in such a way as to fix makes (brands) in terms of customers' judgements of the performance of these two dominant attitudes with the result that the bases of consumers' discrimination between brands can be determined. Non-existent, 'ideal' or preferred brands can also be shown by reference to their possession of unique combinations

Figure 9.2: Positioning Industrial Products Using Attitudinal Data

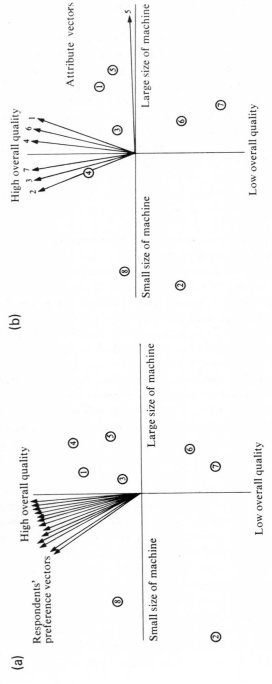

(a) Respondents' Perceptions and Preferences for the eight makes using M-D-Scal and PREFMAP Programmes
(b) Position of the eight makes on the basis of scores achieved on Prespecified Attribute Vectors using the MD-PREF Programme

Source: Johne, A., 'Positioning an Industrial Product Using Attitudinal Data', *Quarterly Review of Marketing,* vol. 2, no. 1 (1977), p. 4. Used by permission.

of the attributes represented by the selected dimensions. Because the future market is defined in terms of the attributes of existing brands, the resulting product-development is likely to result in comparatively continuous innovations (or, in this case in repositioning extant makes) and, although attempts have been made to produce models that incorporate multidimensional scaling techniques which offer predictive as well as diagnostic utility, Green[17] notes that the major uses of the technique in marketing have been essentially diagnostic. Thus they have been extensively employed to

- identify the dominant dimensions of the product class in terms of which its members are distinguished one from the rest and appraised;
- establish groups of brands whose members are similarly perceived (perceived as direct substitutes);
- identify customers' most salient perceptual viewpoints;
- suggest new brand opportunities;
- locate ideal points in terms of new configurations of the most salient attribute dimensions; and
- evaluate advertising and other promotional claims and slogans by reference to customers' brand perceptions.[18]

Gap analysis based upon multi-dimensional scaling is capable of identifying needs for new products, brands or segments but is only the beginning of market exploration. Novel configurations of the attributes in terms of which customers define members of the product class must be tested in the market place perhaps by means of *conjoint* analysis (which is discussed later).

*Brainstorming*

Not all companies face the need or possess the capacity to undertake unconstrained explorations of the potential requirements of customers which may lead to the development and marketing of discontinuous innovations. For them, gap analysis based upon multi-dimensional scaling represents an appropriate approach to the location of new product ideas. But many proactive marketing-oriented businesses attempt to break free from prevailing definitions of the markets they serve in order to locate and satisfy previously unsuspected needs. Two types of idea-generating techniques exist for this purpose: (i) essentially problem-*solving* devices and (ii) problem-*creating* procedures.

The problem-solving technique which has produced the widest recent impact is brainstorming, introduced by Osborn,[19] in which the quality of ideas for overcoming a given difficulty or impasse is viewed as a function of the quantity of ideas generated. The amassing of ideas is encouraged by the postponement of evaluation until the generating session is completed. Brainstorming teams are thus encouraged (i) to suggest as many ideas as possible in the absence of critical comment: participants are not inhibited from advancing apparently zany ideas which may prove feasible solutions if immediate adverse criticism is withheld; (ii) to improve and extend each other's ideas in an unrestricted manner; and (iii) to welcome the proliferation of ideas. Variants of this basic theme encourage a wider spectrum of ideas to be put forward by the injection into the session of keywords or phrases − such as 'Adapt', 'Modify' and 'Put to other uses' − (the checklist approach), more radical ideas, and the coercion of group members into suggesting associations of apparently separate issues and subjects.[20]

In spite of the popularity of brainstorming as a means of finding creative solutions to known problems, it has recently been pointed out that the rule that criticism should be deferred is more difficult to operationalise than is generally realised, that individuals acting alone may produce more ideas than interactive groups and that the quality of ideas is not necessarily determined by the quantity aggregated. Furthermore, although refinements of the brainstorming approach such as synectics[21] have attempted to overcome such difficulties as there are they remain relevant to the solution of managerially-perceived problems rather than the generation of customer-perceived problems whose resolution may be within the capacity of the company. In order to overcome this, Tauber[22] suggests the technique of *problem inventory analysis* in which customers are presented with a list of problems (which could itself be generated by customer survey employing repertory grid or similar measurements)[23] and asked to which products or brands each problem specifically relates. Examples used in his study of the food industry include

'My husband/children refuse to eat . . .',

to which the reported responses were

liver (18 per cent), vegetables (5 per cent), and spinach (4 per cent);
'The packet of . . . doesn't fit well on the shelf:'

cereal (49 per cent) and flour (6 per cent);

and

'I wish my husband/child could take . . . in a carried lunch:'
hot meal (11 per cent), soup (9 per cent) and ice cream (4 per cent).
On occasion, consumers' complaints are not sufficiently serious to

warrant managerial action: the redesign of cereal packets by General Foods, based upon the reported answers, produced no change in consumers' brand choice. The validity of complaints must, therefore, be carefully determined by more probing research before managerial decisions are taken. As long as the customer attaches sufficient importance to the stated problem, problem inventory analysis is capable of initiating viable product modifications. The term 'modifications' signals that relatively continuous product innovations are likely to result from this methodology but, in the case of so many consumer goods, modifications which offer substantial improvements over other brands are precisely what consumers desire. More radical product changes might be forthcoming in the case of problem inventory analyses in the area of consumer durables and industrial products.

Less constrained market exploration requires the use of long range market need research and/or technological forecasting. Christopher[24] provides an example of general forecasting of consumer behaviour in his essay on the 'existential consumer of 2001' but comparatively disaggregated market forecasting, focusing upon the interests of a particular industry or sector, is also possible. The forecasting of needs must be accompanied by knowledge of how these needs may be satisfied and the controlled use of technological forecasting is valuable in this regard.

## Limited Strategic Innovation

The location and initial evaluation of new product ideas are, therefore, managerial responsibilities which may be simplified and rendered more appropriate to the resource capabilities of the firm if they are allied to the dominant strategic mode of the business. As noted above, the more reactive strategies are bound to produce continuous innovations because these are the new products which the business is most fitted to produce and market. Idea generation *for* the producer is also likely to produce continuous and, occasionally dynamically-continuous new products. Idea generation by companies may be consistent with either of these as well as with discontinuous innovations. The important point is that the initiation of new product development should occur in a strategically-appropriate manner. Incremental development, product modification, may be as relevant to and demanding of the corporate capacity and effort from which it emerges as more radical innovation is suited to the capabilities of the companies which produce it. Both may be equally effective in terms of the customer behaviour they provoke.

As it is generally conceived, however, innovation requires the development of not just a novel physical product or a service but an entirely new marketing mix. According to this view, price, promotions and distribution in addition to the product or service demand individual creative attention based upon primary market intelligence, new and comprehensive analyses of consumer behaviour and radical uses of technology. Innovation, both in much macro-economic literature and in some managerial writings, comprises a complete reconceptualisation of the company's overall marketing offering and its technical and commercial bases. New product marketing, in this light, is the fulfilment of an entirely new need by a completely new product and service.

Many companies appear, however, to pursue far more limited strategies of innovation. For example: (1) The spectacular growth of the Carnation Company during the ten year period to the early 1970s was firmly based upon the use of existing technology, reputation and distribution network to devise and launch additional milk products: *Instant Breakfast*, *Slender* and *Coffee Mate* – into existing markets.[25] (2) Much of the success of the ZX81 personal computer derives from the decision of Sinclair Research Ltd to distribute their product through established high-reputation retailers in addition to their original mail order approach. (3) Several European passenger transport operations have introduced monthly season tickets based upon substantial price reductions for existing services. Because of the low price elasticity of demand for these 'Travelcards', as fares have risen, a greater element of stability has been introduced into cash flow than is the case for passenger transport operations based solely upon single ticket sales. (White[26] calculates that demand elasticity for Travelcards is such that a ten per cent price increase would be unlikely to reduce demand by more than three per cent.) (4) These examples extend the frequently-quoted examples of firms which have increased their revenue by advertising their existing products, distribution channels and prices to novel market segments by suggesting that any element of the marketing mix can be employed in pursuit of limited innovation.

None of these innovations follows the grand pattern of a revolutionary marketing mix suggested by the popular image of new product development which is based upon the comparatively rare emergence of discontinuous innovation. Each of the developments illustrated above certainly depended upon the design of a novel marketing mix but one which deviated principally in respect of a single major element from a currently successful marketing offering. Beyond that deviation, the innovative marketing mix relied steadfastly upon existing proven elements. This is of strategic significance for several reasons.

First, effective innovation depends vitally upon presenting prospective consumers with a distinct advantage in terms of price or performance and a noticeable difference from competitors' products, and upon early market entry.[27] Consumers' limited capacity to process new information[28] confines radically-new innovations founded upon comprehensively novel marketing mixes to a small initial market. Furthermore, the diffusion of innovations depends upon innovative consumers experimenting with the new item and acting as influencers of the later buyers: this is often a slow process. Where it is appropriate, the strategy of limited marketing mix innovation facilitates the process in which consumers of the new product compare it with its predecessors, makes clear to the consumer the advantages of the new mix (which can often be expressed simply as a 'unique selling proposition'), simplifies and brings forward the timing of market entry and thus speeds the diffusion of the innovation through its market. Secondly, the process of limited innovation directs attention from the production-oriented assumption that a single product variant can fulfil all of the needs of the market. It also avoids market segmentation based upon uncritical product differentiation. Carnation's success was established upon the identification of consumer needs which competitors' products satisfied only poorly and upon the company's technical capacity to solve customers' problems more effectively. The instant meal could be more quickly prepared and consumed than the traditional breakfast but provided equivalent nourishment. *Slender* replaced the somewhat unpleasant tasting sterilised milk in which other slimming aids were based with fresh milk. *Coffee Mate* can be added to hot coffee and is less fattening than milk.[29]

Sinclair's innovation also reflects interest in an untapped need — that of prospective owners of personal computers who regard specialist suppliers of electronic equipment as catering for another type of person and who are suspicious of mail order or cannot wait three or four weeks for delivery. Their purchase probably involves a greater degree of impulsiveness than those of other buyers.

And Travelcard represents an attempt to cater to a section of the travelling community who would otherwise not be attracted to public transport: car owners whose commuting costs are substantially reduced by the season ticket. But successful limited innovation is not simply a case of rejigging the marketing mix for immediate tactical gain — spending more on promotion for a period or engaging in short term price battles. Rather it is the identification of market segments which are not served by available marketing mixes because one or other mix element is not suited to the members of that segment. The accessibility of market segments to the marketing efforts of the firm has long been recognised as a centrally-important criterion in the planning and implementation of differentiated marketing programmes.[30] But accessibility has all too often been defined in terms of vulnerability to marketing communications since there is little point in basing a segmentation strategy on a group of consumers whose members have, say, a specific personality trait unless individuals with that trait have common media preferences. But the strategy of limited innovation lays emphasis upon the accessibility of consumer groups to each and every marketing mix element.

But there is another sense in which limited strategic innovation is more than market segmentation under a new name. It is vitally concerned with the integration of innovative marketing mixes into the existing marketing portfolio and, because the company is highly familiar with most of the elements of the new mix — their resource implications and contributions to cash flow or profit — its officers can the more easily estimate those implications and contributions in the case of proposed innovations and thus make better informed investment decisions and plans than when innovation involves more radical departures from corporate experience. Stepwise concentration upon one significant element of the mix at a time eliminates the need to juggle with an entirely new marketing mix and removes the need to integrate four major elements and their subcomponents with the elements and images created by the members of the current marketing portfolio. Where innovation strategy depends upon the construction of a derived marketing mix (one based upon a deviation in respect of a single novel mix element from an existing successful mix) the integration of the innovation with the existing array of marketing offerings made available by the company becomes *comparatively* easy.

The strategic use of limited innovation also takes care of tactical planning to some extent. Having established its new distribution network, Sinclair Research reduced the price of its already-inexpensive personal computer by some twenty-nine per cent. In doing so, the company warded off a competitive threat from Binatone which intended to introduce an inexpensive personal computer on to the British market and, thereby, conserved its major planning and strategic resources for the launch of the Sinclair Spectrum range of more powerful and more expensive computers aimed at a rather different market segment from that which forms the target of the ZX81 mix.

## Limited Strategic Innovation: Summing-up

The concept of limited innovation may appear less exciting than that of introducing the radically-novel products with which the term 'innovation' is usually associated. But such product breakthroughs are few and far between. The opportunities to develop and market the resulting products and services are usually taken by those proactive businesses which have the appropriate strategic outlook, mode and resources to invest in technological advance and to bear the risks of marketing discontinuous products in an environment marked by severe inter-industrial competition. Most companies are not of this kin. Their product development takes place, as a rule, after a dominant product design has been accepted by the relevant industry (something which generally occurs several years after the initial breakthrough)[31] and their competitive advantages derive from the capacity to add value to that dominant product pattern by catering to previously-unsupplied market segments, by offering unique product modifications or price differentials. This is especially so in the case of consumer products where failure rates for innovations are often of the order of seventy to ninety per cent.

Most companies which experience failure in introducing new products do so because they have entered product-markets with whose requirements they are relatively unfamiliar. Their concept of innovation implies that new product development must invariably involve new products and/or new markets but few organisations possess the marketing intelligence and planning capabilities to fulfil completely new customer needs effectively with new or substantially-new products. Effective innovation depends upon the exercise of considerable expertise in the areas of design and production efficiency, consumer-orientation and marketing execution, and product superiority. Successful companies build up such expertise and orientation over long time periods in ways which become increasingly appropriate for their overall strengths and strategic capacities. Limited strategic innovation facilitates the search for new products and market opportunities by allying it to previously-established patterns of effective new product development. Thereby it eases the fundamental strategic problem by reducing the risks inherent in the management of what would otherwise be rather diverse product portfolios. Nevertheless, even the relatively continuous ideas obtained from marketing portfolio analysis require careful assessment.

## The Evaluation of Marketing Opportunities

The relatively informal appraisal of new product ideas is inevitable if the new product development process takes place within a context of strategic awareness since the guiding tenets of formalised business policy and the strategic options made available by the firm's environments act as criteria by which 'legitimate' ideas are recognised. Depending upon the nature of the search for new products and the volume of ideas advanced for consideration some ideas may be withdrawn prior to formal and detailed screening – the process in which this occurs is sometimes known as *coarse* screening – because comparatively superficial examination shows their lack of feasibility: legal strictures on marketing might be too costly to surmount, for instance. Relatively formal evaluation on the basis of objective criteria is necessary because product ideas which ostensibly satisfy equally well the general requirements of strategy may yet make distinct demands upon resources or promise rather different financial contributions. Much of the conventional marketing literature suggests that from the point at which formal screening is contemplated and planned, the company is attempting to make surrogate estimates of the rate of return on investment which will be forthcoming if a specific product idea is selected for full development and commercialisation. But early evaluation, even of the most formal kind, cannot provide such forecasts with any degree of accuracy. Screening may, however, provide a rough and ready check upon product-market/company compatibility. Indeed, the manifest function of screening is essentially negative: the elimination of ideas which provide no apparent basis for the creation of products which are appropriate to the company's strategic requirements.

Various criteria have been suggested as the bases of the formal screening to which those ideas which survive initial evaluation are subjected. Most attempt to quantify the match between product and company on the basis of objectively available measures, but subjective factors cannot be entirely eliminated. The best that can be hoped is that formal criteria are set in advance of screening and that the attempt is made to apply them even-handedly to each idea in turn. The criteria summarised in Table 9.2 belong to methods of screening which require that each new idea be rated (dichotomously or on a point scale) and that the resulting figure be multiplied by a weighting factor which reflects the importance of each criterion in the overall system. An overall score for each idea is then obtained by the summation of the individual scores for each criterion. Except in the case of the most continuous of products, the resulting estimates of projected perform-ance are necessarily crude because they are based upon notions of corporate capacity or industry attractiveness which can have no abso-lutely firm basis. Obvious incompatibilities between the projected idea of the finalised product and the company can, however, be identified. Scores obtained through the use of such procedures allow comparison of new product ideas to be undertaken on a basis which is more satis-factory than an entirely subjective appraisal but these scores remain more or less arbitrary since scales are not necessarily equally sensitive in the case of each criterion; the criteria overlap and thus distort ideal scores; and they have no absolute meaning — it may be the case that *all* ideas should be rejected but the comparative nature of the exercise tends to save some.

Table 9.2: Screening Criteria — Some Examples

| 1. Kotler | 2. Wilson |
|---|---|
| Company competence in terms of: | *Position*: ease of development of manu-facturing process (2); value-added by in-company processing (1); exclusive or favoured purchasing position (1); effect on purchasing position (1); availability of raw materials within company (2); effect on negotiating position (1). |
| Company personality and goodwill (.20); | |
| Marketing (.20); | *R&D*: utilisation of existing knowhow (1); relationship to future development planning (2); utilisation of existing laboratory or pilot plant equipment (1); availability of R&D personnel (1). |
| R&D (.20); | |
| Personnel (.15); | *Engineering*: reliability of process or knowhow (2); utilisation of standard-ised equipment (1); availability of engineering personnel (2). |
| Finance (.10); | *Stability*: durability of the market (3); breadth of the market (2); possibility of captive market (1); difficulty in copying (1); stability in depressions (2); stability in wartime (1). |
| Production (.05); | |
| Location and facilities (.05); | *Growth*: unique character of product or process (2); demand-supply ratio (3); rate of technical change (1); export possibilities (1); improved opportuni-ties for management personnel (2). |
| Purchasing and supplies (.05); | |
| | *Marketability*: relationship to existing markets (2); company's image in allied fields (1); ease of market penetration (1); ability to provide technical services (2); competition with customer's prod-ucts (2); user stratification (1); few variations required (1); freedom from seasonal fluctuations (2). |

Table 9.2 Cont'd.

| 1. Kotler | 2. Wilson |
|---|---|

**2. Wilson**

*Production*: utilisation of idle equipment (1); utilisation of surplus energy etc. (1); utilisation and upgrading of by-products (1); utilisation of process familiar to company personnel (1); availability of production and maintenance workers (2); plant maintenance requirements (1); ability to cope with waste disposal (1); ability to cope with hazardous operating conditions (1).

**3. Krausher**

*Growth*: sales trend (3); volume trend (4); long-term prospects (6).

*Market*: current market size (3); buying by social class (3); age group characteristics (2); are profile (1).

*Stability*: economic factors (5); seasonality (3).

*Marketing skills*: penetration of branding (3); companies in the market (5); marketing/sales ratio (3); product differentiation (5).

*Image*: company (2); brand (4).

*Production*: technology (5); buying resources (3).

*Selling and Distribution*: sales force (6); distribution (5).

**4. O'Meara**

*Marketability*: relation to present distribution channels, relation to present product lines, quantity-price relationship, number of sizes and grades, merchandisability, effects on sales of present products.

*Productive ability*: equipment necessary, production knowledge and personnel necessary, raw materials availability.

*Growth potential*: place in market, expected competitive situation, expected availability of final users.

*Durability*: stability, breadth of market, resistance to cyclical fluctuations, resistance to seasonal fluctuations, exclusiveness of design.

*Profitability*: short-term, long-term.

---

Sources: Kotler, P., *Marketing Management* (Englewood Cliffs, NJ: Prentice-Hall, 1980), p. 320; Wilson, A. 'Selecting New Products for Development', *Scientific Business* (November 1963) after the outline provided by Baker, M.J. and McTavish, R., *Product Policy and Management* (London: Macmillan, 1976) pp. 11-13; Kraushar, P.M., *New Products and Diversification*, (London: Business Books, 1977), pp. 69-71; O'Meara, J.T., 'Selecting Profitable Products', *Harvard Business Review*, vol. 39, no. 1 (1961), pp. 83-9. Figures in brackets refer to weighting factors.

In an attempt to overcome some of these difficulties, Roberto and Pinson[32] have advanced a form of compatibility analysis for screening. Having decided upon the minimum acceptable level of performance on each of the selected criteria – this can only be done by reference to previous innovative launches and thus the procedure applies specifically to continuous products — the company can proceed to rate each of the ideas under scrutiny in terms of those criteria. The criteria employed by these authors are those suggested by O'Meara (see Table 9.2) which are ranked by those responsible for screening in terms of their separate importance — so productive ability might be sixth, short-term profitability fifth, and so on. The available product ideas are rated by a scaling method (5 = very good . . . 1 = very poor) and the deficient ideas can be eliminated according to their failure to reach the minimum prespecified standard on the most important criterion. Those which survive this test can be judged in terms of the second criterion, and so on. This method, like many other screening techniques, does not obviate managerial judgement, especially in the setting of evaluative criteria and minimum acceptable levels, and even in the case of the most continuous of products there may be grounds for deviating from past experience. No mechanical screening methods can remove the need for careful managerial appraisal and human choice.

The most effective, commercially-applicable screening devices are not likely to be published during their useful lifetime. In any case, more important than the promulgation of a single method which at best can have proved advantageous in peculiar circumstances, is the identification of the implications for screening of the strategic requirements of the company. Kotler[33] notes a number of instances in which product ideas subsequently adopted and successfully-implemented by other companies were initially rejected by other firms which considered them. He draws attention to IBM and Eastman Kodak's failure to develop the idea of a copying machine as did Xerox, and RCA's seizing the opportunity to produce radio receivers while the Victor Talking Machine Company failed to discern it. But there is another interpretation of the failure to recognise new product opportunities such as these. Companies' screening procedures have relevance only within the frame of reference of their overall corporate purposes and strategies; some ideas which are appropriate to other firms are inevitably rejected by those organisations which generated them first because they do not prove compatible with strategic capabilities and needs. Each company must decide upon its own areas of business on the basis of the most suitable means at its disposal to satisfy customers' wants. Screening may lead to the rejection of innovative ideas which might have proved appropriate had more time and information been available for these early appraisals. But it may also quite reasonably lead to the elimination from the firm's agenda of ideas which are right — but for other companies.

One of the concerns of Project NewProd (see Chapter 4) has been the formulation of guidelines for idea screening and product development. Checklist and rating scale methods of assessing ideas have been criticised by Cooper[34] on the grounds that they tend to emphasise variables which are known to exist at the time of screening and necessarily exclude the factors which are under managerial control and upon the manipulation of which success usually depends. From the earlier discussion of this research project it emerged that product, market and technical superiority factors served to discriminate between successful and unsuccessful innovators. Cooper suggests that insofar as product characteristics are concerned screening techniques should select for development ideas which promise significant and unique user benefits, particularly economic advantages which reduce buyers' costs. Much as Davidson pointed out in the case of consumer products, he advises against the development of expensive products which do not offer clearly identifiable benefits of this kind and which thereby fly in the face of customers' ability to discern value for money. With respect to the market factors and the firm's marketing proficiency, he draws attention to the need for screening criteria to reflect the advantages of product development rather than market development, i.e. expansion within known markets, and to identify product/company compatibility in such a way as to ensure that the product portfolio will be balanced after the introduction of the new item. In view of the discussion of the Marketing Portfolio concept introduced earlier, the complexity of this operation must be reckoned immense. Screening should discourage the attempt to enter markets which are highly competitive or in which customer tastes and requirements change quickly. In short, existing markets and cognate opportunities should be emphasised – especially if they exhibit a high rate of predictable growth and substantial unsatisfied customer needs – and the aim of product development should be to fulfil those needs more effectively than previously. Discontinuous products and market scenarios which include new competitors and unfamiliar customers should be very carefully evaluated before a decision to continue development is taken. Such advice appears to contradict the exhortations to accept risk and attempt to conquer new markets which are all-too-frequently made to marketing managers regardless of their strategic needs and the environments in which they operate. The emphasis in this book is upon adopting the strategically-appropriate approach to innovation: there are companies which have the capacity to bear high levels of risk but many do not. The important factor is that this capacity should be assessed before idea generation and screening occur and that suitable methods for both should be devised in the light of this analysis. Nevertheless, *all* businesses should find good reason before ignoring Cooper's warning that unfamiliarity with customers and their needs is a very frequent source of unsuccessful innovation.

Finally, screening should eliminate product ideas which promise low or negative synergy in technical and production areas between the product and the company. Production synergy is the most difficult to realise; while expected financial and marketing synergies are often achieved, technical and production synergies are, contrary to the expectations of many engineers and microeconomists, far more elusive. Above all, the company should rate itself in relation to each new product idea in terms of its capacity to obtain and act upon information regarding the technical and marketing aspects of new product development and its ability to develop internally or buy in the required expertise for the programme of innovation envisaged. These are notoriously difficult areas in which to carry out corporate self-assessment and the successful execution of such intra-firm appraisal depends considerably upon the prior installation of an effective management and marketing information system. If objectivity cannot be guaranteed, however, the advice of external consultants should be sought.

Although the results of Project NewProd stress the need for screening procedures to be flexible and to reflect general issues, the need to evaluate competing product ideas in consistent terms by emphasising similar criteria in each case remains as important as ever. The use of techniques to appraise strengths and weaknesses, opportunities and threats retains an important place in the initiation of product development and checklist screening, for all its deficiencies, at least ensures that the initial assessment of ideas is relatively quick and consistent. Furthermore, it places upon managers the responsibility and the discipline of defining product acceptability and of conceptualising current prospective marketing portfolios. The essential points are that rigid adherence to checklists is seldom sufficient, that elimination scores must be creatively interpreted in the context of the overall effect of the marketing portfolio and that *no* screening method can act as an efficient forecasting device. The financial information available at this stage is too lacking in detail and too scant to enable valid economic projections to be made. Screening is concerned with the identification of obvious losers rather than of winners and it provides only a general picture of product-company-portfolio compatibility over time rather than hard financial appraisal. Calantone and Cooper[35] have nine new product scenarios on the basis of their analysis of the progress made by industrial innovations, each of which has a unique pattern of product, market and technical requirements and associations which are amenable to evaluation at the screening stage. The development of such scenarios at an early stage in the innovative process of the firm allows some prediction of the likely outcome of turning ideas into marketable products and services. However, its value decreases with the discontinuity of the product idea.

## Business Analysis

Screening can provide useful information but is of no help in formulating hard predictions of financial returns, largely because it is concerned with somewhat nebulous *ideas* rather than with the more refined product *concepts* to which consumers can respond more effectively. Business analysis is clearly concerned with making predictions about putative products' financial performance and, although such forecasts are fraught with uncertainties at so early a stage in the product development process, the evolution and testing of specific product concepts permits a more concrete foundation for calculations of returns on capital investment. In order to understand the role of product concepts in the development of innovations, it is necessary to explore three areas: the generation of product concepts, the rationale of concept testing and the limitations of product concept testing. This discussion of business analysis concludes with a short account of discounted cash flow procedures as a means of comparing the likely outcomes of investing in projects based upon refined and tested product concepts.

### Generating Product Concepts

A single idea may give rise to the generation of a number of specific product concepts: the idea is usually conceived in terms of a novel set of product attributes, while each concept represents a definite combination of those attributes which promises a special range of consumer benefits. The generation of product concepts may be a relatively informal occurrence based upon knowledge gained through experience or customer research, customers' own ideas for new products or, in the case of what we have called limited strategic innovation, the observation that the development of one or another element of the marketing mix would provide an innovating combination of attributes which is capable of fulfilling untapped customer needs. Such informal concept generation is of declining importance in new product development: especially in consumer goods markets, it may provide the inauguration of innovative development but depends upon more formal methods of identifying markets such as gap analysis via perceptual mapping which was mentioned in the context of idea location, and conjoint analysis in which the utilities to customers of different combinations of product attributes are compared.

*Perceptual Mapping.* The development of attitudinal measures in marketing research has been largely bound up with the recording of customers' reactions to products and brands in terms of attributes which are salient to their purchase or use. The last twenty years have seen dramatic progress in the ability of firms to describe markets by reference to measures of dominant product attributes in terms of which buyers discriminate among brand models and makes. The technique of multi-dimensional scaling has contributed significantly to this trend. Figure 9.2 (above) indicates the positioning of products in terms of two important dimensions; although computerised methods of analysis can cope with multi-dimensional configurations of markets, they can often be described by two especially salient variables identified by factor analysis and with which other dimensions correlate highly. Perceptual maps of this kind allow a firm's existing and proposed brands to be compared both with one another and with buyers' ideal brands expressed as preferences for novel combinations of product attributes. The distance between existing and ideal brands can be used as a measure of the attractiveness of the ideal to the customer and its feasibility to the firm. Even the repositioning of an existing brand may constitute worthwhile innovation. It is important to bear in mind, however, that gaps may exist in perceptual maps not only because competitors have been myopic in their market exploration or tardy in developing appropriate new products. Though either of these might be the case, it is also possible for a gap to exist because there is not sufficient demand for an item with the attribute mix indicated. Furthermore, the techniques by which perceptual maps are drawn involve the averaging of customers' perceptions and stated preferences, whereas it is widely known that customers rarely constitute an homogeneous group; it is necessary therefore to employ a method such as cluster analysis to discover whether a single perceptual map conceals a variety of product possibilities by aggregating the perceptions and preferences of several potential market segments. These means of analysis apply as much to services and to industrial products as to fast-moving consumer products. In the case of industrial product marketing, the mapping of buyers' perceptions and preferences does not always prove efficient and alternative means of describing markets and locating segments are generally available.

*Conjoint Analysis.* Most planned new products involve a large number of attributes which research and experience have shown to be important to customers. The most appropriate combination of these attributes is that which stimulates the highest possible rate of trial among buyers, who may subsequently become satisfied users and thus repeat purchasers. Often the number of possible combinations is so vast that their comparative testing would be an enormous task; but conjoint analysis uses orthogonal arrays of variables which allow the sensitivity of potential buyers to each attribute factor to be assessed from tests involving a much smaller selection of the theoretical total of combinations.[36] The *utility* of each attribute to the customer can be judged by this method and a variety of concepts derived from a single new product idea can be compared in order that the company can judge the advisability of extending its portfolio to include the new item, the number of versions of the basic product required, and so on. Conjoint analysis is not without practical and conceptual limitations but it has been successfully employed in the development of numerous new products and services because it is able to reduce what might otherwise be so unacceptable a level of uncertainty that product development would be arrested. Conjoint analysis thus assists the generation of concepts from ideas as well as enabling the relative merits of concepts to be directly tested in the market-place.

## Concept Testing

Concept testing involves the measurement of customers' responses to verbal descriptions (and, occasionally, simple mock-ups) of potential products. Its most frequent justification derives from the need to check customers' understanding of the product concept which has been generated within the firm or through previous marketing research and to gauge the extent to which customers would be likely to derive positive benefits from the product. Respondents may also suggest improvements to the concepts such as the addition of particular features or the recombination of attributes. New segments of the market might be identified. Various aspects of customer behaviour can be assessed from such testing including the extent to which the prospective product harmonises with current purchase and usage patterns, i.e. the buyer's judgement of the relative continuity of the innovation, the uses to which the item will be put and the associations evoked by the concept (perhaps in comparison with existing brands). The fundamental principle is that concept testing can form the basis of reliable decisions with respect to future development. In particular, the possibility that intentions to buy the product expressed during concept testing can be employed as valid means of predicting actual purchase behaviour is often presented as a justification for the practice of this phase of marketing research.[37] This is overoptimistic for several reasons. The Awareness — Trial — Reinforcement model of buyer behaviour developed by Ehrenberg and described in an earlier chapter depicts repeat buying as a function of successful trial outcomes which cannot be predicted at so early a stage in the intra-firm innovative process. The forecasting of purchase behaviour from intentions fails to take the intervention of situational variables into account: there will certainly be many alterations in intent as a result of such interventions as changes in purchasing power, perceived need, the availability of competing products and so on between the time at which the intention is expressed in the course of concept testing and the launch of a specific product months or years later.[38] Concept testing is, moreover, able to convey an accurate idea of the prospective product only in the case of relatively continuous products; its accuracy and trustworthiness as a means of appraising present reactions and future purchasing declines as more discontinuous concepts are put before the respondents who may or may not turn out to be buyers and users.

Two recent examples illustrate the unreliability of interpreting mechanistically the results of concept testing.[39] In the first, customers' reactions were sought with respect to the value of a lipstain concept: the intended product would be used at monthly intervals and thereby render the use of lipsticks unnecessary. Reactions at the concept testing stage were positive but subsequent probing indicated that most respondents believed that the product was suitable for other women, not themselves; as a result they were unlikely actually to purchase it. The second example concerns reactions to instant potato mixes and skimmed milk powder, both of which evoked negative reactions at the concept stage but both of which became successful products for Cadbury Limited.

Concept testing, whether conducted through home interviews, focus groups at a central location or other means takes place in a highly artificial atmosphere and relies substantially upon the imagination of the respondents. The results may reflect copywriters' persuasiveness as well as genuinely useful innovative ideas and may be misleading if they are uncritically interpreted. There are, however, three ways in which concept testing is of value at this stage of the development process in reducing the uncertainty faced by the firm.[40] First, concept testing permits the analysis of markets defined in terms of customer-based needs and perceptions of product attributes thus facilitating the identification of genuine markets and segments which the company is capable of supplying. Thus marketing analysis makes a substantial contribution to the fundamental strategic problem faced by the firm. Secondly, concepts may be compared with each other and the most promising attribute combinations selected as the basis for further development. Thirdly, while the prediction of long term adoption is a particularly intractable problem at this stage, confidence that a diffusion process for the innovation is probable can be increased by the selective investigation of *innovative* buyers' reactions to the product concept since it is upon their initial trial and repeat buying behaviour that the socio-economic process which inaugurates the product life cycle is dependent. This final point requires elaboration in order to demonstrate the connection between the analysis of customer behaviour in Part Two and managerial decision-making.

*Innovative Buyers and Diffusion.* It is common practice to test new product concepts upon samples of potential consumers which are selected on the basis of their being representative of the population or prospective market as a whole. Midgley[41] argues against this practice on the grounds that prelaunch testing should concentrate upon the acceptability of the concept or product to the earliest buyers and adopters who are crucial to the initiation of the diffusion process. This is not to say that non-innovators should not be sampled since there will be no diffusion without them either; however, since it is known that the first buyers of many products have distinctive media preferences and act upon market-dominated communications which are likely to be ignored by later adopters, it is sensible to plan the initial marketing mix for a new product with innovators especially in mind. Admittedly, only when innovators are prominent opinion leaders and the probability that their reference group influence will rapidly and significantly enhance the company's cash flow is high, is it worthwhile seeking out innovators within target segments, monitoring their opinions and responses from this point forwards in the development process, and devising a differential marketing programme appealing specifically to them. The procedure is likely to be of use only for the more continuous of innovations, too, since innovators can be identified only on the basis of their reactions to and purchases of previously launched, basically-similar products.

Opinion leadership, nevertheless, manifests itself in so many ways in addition to the word-of-mouth influence which is a central component of the two-step communications theory — Robertson[42] notes that such leadership may be expressed visually or verbally, as a one-way or two-way process, source-initiated or recipient-initiated, giving eight feasible patterns of opinion dissemination — that the cases where some form of interpersonal influence is not important must be comparatively rare. Even where such influence is weak, as in certain industrial buying situations where competitive market structures impede the flow of information among firms, the distinctive purchase and consumption characteristics of innovative buyers are worth examining: even if these buyers are not crucial to the inauguration of the diffusion process itself, since they form a primary market, they are likely to be valuable to the company which requires rapid sales and immediate returns.

## Concept Testing: Practical Limitations

Some of the limitations of concept testing have been mentioned already but there remains a frequently-encountered difficulty: managerial expectations of concept testing are often more demanding of the available methodologies than is warranted by the evidence of their efficacy. Conceptualisations of concept testing are usually such that the tester's verbal description acts as a stimulus $(S)$ which elicits the respondent's assessment of the imagined product in use, which verbal assessment is assumed to be indicative of the underlying psychological attitude or other intervening process or cause within the individual (or organism, $O$) which will, in turn, elicit or cause a behavioural response $(R)$. Furthermore, the response is assumed to be directly predictable once the intervening variable has been measured. The acute problem for consumer researchers steeped in the tenets of the familiar $S - [O] - R$ paradigm is that consumers' verbal statements of purchase intention are rarely predictive of behaviour with respect to the general purchase of the product in question. As was discussed in Chapter 6, behavioural intentions are predictive of behaviour only when the situational correspondence between the verbal and the overt behaviours is very high and the former is the immediate precursor of the latter.

Thus it is hardly surprising that the empirical evidence for concept testing as a predictor of actual consumer behaviour in the new product market place is disappointing to those engaged in managerial decision-making with respect to innovative marketing. Tauber[43] is highly critical of those researchers who pay little attention to the predictive validity of their measuring instruments. Commenting upon a study by Taylor, Houlahan and Gabriel[44] which draws over-optimistic conclusions from correlations of respondents' stated intentions and self-reported behaviour with respect to purchase, he writes:[45]

> A number of companies, my own [Carnation] included, have conducted many of the same types of studies relating both pretrial and posttrial purchase intentions to later behaviour. Correlations do exist in all cases to date. Unfortunately, what Taylor and his colleagues could not have known is that there is no reliability in the probabilistic relationships of these intentions to behaviour. Having conducted only one test, Taylor found that 35 per cent of the 'definitely buy' and 'probably buy' group did, in fact, later purchase. Had he conducted a second and third test using different products, he probably would have found that in these other cases only 20 per cent of the positive purchase intention group did purchase, or 50 per cent, or 10 per cent. Thus, while correlation is an encouraging finding, prediction cannot take place unless the probabilistic relationships relating intention to behaviour are relatively constant. It is one thing to conclude that attitudes or intentions relate to later behaviour; it is another to be able to predict the level of that behaviour from the earlier intentions. Even if one could predict that accurately, this would not be enough. The key to new product success rests with predicting continued repeat [buying].

These conclusions are certainly borne out by the experience of companies which have attempted to forecast buyer behaviour on the basis of concept test results. In his own researches into the relationship between concept test data and consumers' purchase patterns for six new food products which employed brand concept testing, Tauber[46] found that 'for triers of the six test marketed products, purchase intent at concept did not differentiate between those who had made repeat purchases and those who had not'. More recent concept testing methodologies based upon multi-attribute procedures are still at the experimental stage; however, the work of Ajzen and Fishbein[47] suggests that behavioural intentions data gained in the use of such models are predictive of behaviour only in the closely-defined circumstances mentioned above (and in Part Two). Accordingly, Shocker and Srinivason[48] identify the needs of consumer situations (i) to define the product-market contexts of consumer choice and product use and (ii) to investigate more thoroughly the *situational determinants* of buyer behaviours generally. The slightly better impression of concept testing as a means of differentiating triers from non-triers on the basis of expressed purchase intentions which is gained from Tauber's empirical work, enhances the credibility of Midgley's belief that intial purchasers (customer innovators) should provide the focus of a significant proportion of market testing at this stage.

The limitations of social science in the area of forecasting human behaviour from verbal statements of intention underscore the requirement that marketing managers, academics and consultants understand that 'the general purpose of concept testing is to screen out losers at the idea stage through some form of consumer evaluation'.[49] Assuming the basic $A \rightarrow T \rightarrow R$ depiction of consumer behaviour, Tauber[50] notes further that

> Concept testing and product testing relate to trial behaviour and early repeat behaviour; but if new product success is determined by the adoption level and frequency of purchase, we must find tools to accurately measure these dimensions. There may be a way to predict this adoption behaviour with some type of early measurements. Or, we may be forced to accept that the only predictor of long-term behaviour is the long-term behaviour itself.

Concept testing (and much of the product testing considered below) is no more positive a device than suggested here. But the consequences of a more behaviourally-based perspective for consumer research are of immense interest.[51]

## Financial Appraisal[52]

Concept testing, like screening, is not then a technique which can unequivocally identify winners; at best it contributes to the elimination of *some* losers. Even when potential innovators respond positively to concepts, their reactions provide first and foremost guidelines for product development. When it is used in industrial marketing contexts, concept testing often provides very detailed information with respect to customer and user needs and thus directly shapes development; concept testing here may be more informal, may result from customer-initiated ideas and concept refinement. Many consumer product innovations rely heavily upon the reconfiguration of existing product attributes and less confidence can be placed in prospective buyers' reactions to a verbally-described, hypothetical, novel mélange of well-known characteristics: people simply do not know how they would react to the resulting product in the market place.

Concept testing is nevertheless capable of contributing to the formulation and/or refinement of calculations of return on investment in two ways. First, it assists the development of an integrated marketing mix by confirming the probable characteristics of members of target market segments and permits the costing of product development and marketing investments. While it is unlikely to help much in establishing the *size* of segments, concept testing may confirm their existence and measureability of suspected segments and identify their relative accessibility and responsiveness to particular elements of the marketing mix. Rough estimates of costs or magnitudes of cost can then be made. Secondly, concept testing allows assessment of the level of confidence which should be placed in the assumptions and projections upon which discounted cash flow (and other means of investment appraisal such as simple return on investment and payback methods) depend. At the very least, this means that DCF projections for product concepts which are competing for development funds can be more precisely appraised and interpreted.

### Net Present Value

While exceedingly sophisticated means of financial analysis have been applied to new product planning,[53] it is important that their results can be presented in a form which is capable of universal comprehension; in any case, at this stage of preliminary financial evaluation, the available data are not sufficiently detailed and valid to permit other than the simplest of calculations. Financial evaluation depends upon indications of market size, capital and operational costs and market share which will be attained in each of a series of years adjudged to represent the life of the project. These factors depend in turn upon estimates of buyer response, competitive reactions, the behaviour of factor markets and other sources of uncertainty. Only in the case of the most continuous products are these factors genuinely capable of reasonable forecast.

Kraushar[54] describes a simple means of comparing projects which is based upon the logic of discounted cash flow methodology. This net present value approach takes into consideration the need to express future cash flows in terms of their present value in order to establish the true internal rate of return attributable to specific investments. Given a certain stated rate of return which is the minimum acceptable for each product, it is possible to compare the projected cash flows of different product possibilities. A zero net present value indicates that the project will produce the desired rate of return if the assumptions upon which cash flow projects are made prove correct. Though this is unlikely to be exactly the case, broadly similar factors may be expected to affect cash flows of each product considered and the method thus allows at least a form of comparison by which potentially disappointing projects may be eliminated.

Much of the market-oriented side of product development is concerned with gathering the data upon which this kind of calculation is based and there is clearly a trade-off between the earlier timing of financial analyses and their usefulness for predictive purposes. The temptation to make forecasts for the cash flow implications of selecting particular product ideas and concepts for project development is understandable; it is not a dangerous activity unless confidence is placed unduly in the resulting prognostications. Only after concept testing (or some other exercise designed to assess market response) has been conducted can realistic preliminary comparisons based upon financial estimates be made. Even at this stage — and indeed beyond it — the most reasonable use of the available data would involve the calculation of a range of discounted cash flows for each project, based upon different assumptions about market shares, costs and competition and the assignment to each estimate of a range of probabilities based upon past experience, technological and market forecasts and marketing intelligence. Again, it is clear that continuous products are more likely to be based upon such information than discontinuous innovations. The use of sensitivity analysis, which involves the identification of the consequences of changes in each variable in the cash flow calculation, leads to the assessment of the range within which each variable can be allowed to diverge from expectations before affecting the viability of the entire project.[55] The interpretation of the output of DCF calculations must nevertheless be undertaken with great care especially by marketing specialists. Derivatives of DCF such as the net present value and internal rate of return methods carry a variety of assumptions with respect to the reinvestment of intermediate cash flows which may affect the meaning of comparisons founded upon time.[56]

White[57] sums up the nature of financial analysis thus:
The aim of a financial evaluation is to find out whether the company is justified in spending its money on a specific project (as against investing the money, for example) or to discover which of a number of competing projects offers the best financial return to the company.

This is *not* a decision process: it is an attempt to provide financial guidance on which a decision can be based. Management still has to decide whether a less profitable involvement would be preferred because it carries less risk, opens up a new and potentially valuable sector of the market, or avoids the risk of antagonising the firm's existing customers.

In other words, those responsible for the management of the marketing portfolio must be directly concerned with the decision to develop a new product and their decision depends upon the nature of the existing and planned portfolios as overall entities rather than upon simple financial projections.

## *The Role of Business Analysis*

The measurement of market response and the financial calculations which comprise the first business analysis of the development process thus emerge as essential exercises; despite their inevitability, however, they provide negative rather than positive criteria for the 'go/no go' decision upon which further project development relies. Nevertheless, there is good reason for making the hurdles presented by this business analysis high: the probability of cancelling a project declines as its lifetime increases on account of the accumulation and entrenchment of vested interests, time pressures, absorption in the new venture and the other impediments to successful innovation mentioned in Chapter 4. While models and textbook accounts of this process usually allow for the termination of adversely evaluated projects at this stage, the reality of intra-organisational politics and the limitations of human behaviours constantly militate against abandonment. The first detailed business analysis of the project may be the last chance of eliminating potential dogs before the market place proves them to be such.

## Conclusion

The location and evaluation of new product ideas inflicts considerable costs upon the company which undertakes these operations with care. Nevertheless, the proper appraisal of such ideas is an essentially negative procedure, involved with removing those ideas which clearly cannot produce winning products. There is simply too little information for more accurate, positive vetting at this stage of the intra-firm innovative process. Up until the end of business analysis, the firm should feel no commitment to any given product idea; no earlier decision made with respect to what can be no more than an *apparent* marketing opportunity should be considered irrevocable.

Explicit corporate strategy assists the management of the early stages of the new product development process by shaping the search for new product ideas and by suggesting criteria for both crude and formal screening procedures. Ready-made, checklist methods of screening are far from universally applicable and each company's new product managers should be responsible for the establishment and use of pertinent criteria, developed within their organisation's strategic framework, for each programme of search for opportunities. As Twiss[58] points out:

> The commercial desirability of a proposed technological innovation cannot be divorced from the organisation within which it arises. Companies which may at first sight appear to be directly comparable will on closer examination reveal fundamental differences in their business and managerial characteristics. Considerable variations in business objectives, attitudes to risk and innovation, and value systems will emerge.

And what is true of separate companies on the same occasion is true of the same company during different periods of time.

The relationship between a compaany's dominant strategic mode and its managerial orientation is usually complex. Except for the most reactive firms, any company can be customer-oriented in the sense that its internal productive and marketing capacities are appropriately matched to the requirements of its markets. Proactive companies are, nevertheless, more concerned with dynamic markets and geared to serve them not only by dint of their internal physical capacities but as a result of the entrepreneurial alertness of their managements (and, on occasion, the buyers and users of their products).

The product development process cannot be deemed to have begun in earnest, however, when the preliminary financial analysis of a hypothetical innovation proves sufficiently encouraging to keep the relevant concept alive. The techniques simply do not exist which can identify those products which will succeed given the information available at this pre-commitment stage. The managerial problem of deciding which development projects to keep alive remains well beyond this stage and along with it the concomitant difficulty of allocating limited resources among those competing projects which have not yet suffered euthanasia. Mansfield and his associates[59] note the variety of capital budgeting techniques which have themselves enjoyed the status of successful innovations during the last two decades:

> Judging from our sample of nineteen industrial laboratories in the chemical, drug, petroleum, and electronics industries, about three-quarters of the laboratories use such techniques to allocate funds. However, it is important to note that many of these firms use these techniques in only a limited way: intuition and hunch continue to play an important role.

Yet they are sceptical about the value of contemporary means of estimating pay-back periods and rates of return:

> [T]hese estimates are subject to errors that are large and variable. In addition, these techniques usually are based on estimates of the probability of commercial success, the size of the market, and the capital-facility requirements of the project . . . Thus, if the laboratories in our sample are at all representative, these techniques rely heavily on estimates that, by practically any standard, are very poor.

The danger is that many new product managers appear to attribute unjustified levels of validity and reliability to such methodologies and, while their use may have the positive benefit of encouraging those responsible to think about the factors involved, unduly credulous acceptance may lead to the use of crude estimates as political weapons, i.e. to persuade top management to support ventures in which new product managers have vested interests. Evidently, the new product development process, a series of information gathering and analytical procedures, is far from over.

## Notes

1. Pessemier, E.A., 'Managing Product Innovation' in Baker (ed.), *Industrial Innovation*, pp. 326-42. The following two paragraphs draw particularly upon this source.

2. Midgley and Wills, 'The Management of Fashion', pp. 132-4.

3. Urban and Hauser, *Design and Marketing of New Products*, p. 123.

4. von Hippel, E., *Industrial Innovation by Users: Evidence, Explanatory Hypotheses and Implications*, Working Paper No. 953-77 (Cambridge, Mass.: Massachussets Institute of Technology, 1977), p. 4.

5. von Hippel, E., 'Transferring Process Equipment Innovations from User-

Innovators to Equipment Manufacturing Firm's, *R&D Management*, vol. 8, no. 1 (October 1977); 'The Dominant Role of Users in the Scientific Instrument Innovation Process', *Research Policy*, vol. 5, no. 4 (1976), pp. 212-39; 'The Dominant Role of the User in Semiconductor Subassembly Process Innovation', *IEEE Transactions on Engineering Management*, (May 1977); Meadows, D., 'Estimate Accuracy and Project Selection Models in Industrial Research', *Industrial Management Review*, Spring 1969; Peplow, M.E., 'Design Acceptance' in Gregory, S.A. (ed.), *The Design Method* (London: Butterworth, 1960); Berger, A., *Factors Influencing the Locus of Innovation Activity*, Thesis, Sloan School of Management, Massachussets Institute of Technology (1975); Boydon, J., *A Study of the Innovation Process in the Plastics Additives Industry*, Thesis, Sloan School of Management, Massachussets Institute of Technology (1976). Utterback, J., 'The Process of Innovation', *IEEE Transactions on Engineering Management* (November 1971); Robinson, P.J., Farris, C.W. and Wind, Y., *Industrial Buying and Creative Marketing* (Boston: Allyn and Bacon, 1967); Isenson, R., 'Project Hindsight' in Gruber, W. and Marquis, D. (eds), *Factors in the Transfer of Technology* (Cambridge, Mass.: Massachussets Institute of Technology Press, 1969); Materials Advisory Board, *Report of Ad Hoc Committee on Principles of Research-Engineering Interaction* (Washington, DC: National Academy of Sciences/National Research Council, 1966.)

6. von Hippel, E., 'Successful Industrial Products from Customer Ideas', *Journal of Marketing*, vol. 42, no. 1 (1978) pp. 39-49. See also von Hippel, E., 'A Customer-active Paradigm for Industrial Product Idea Generation' in Baker, M.J. (ed.), *Industrial Innovation*, pp. 82-110.

7. Evidence cited by von Hippel stems from: Knight, K., *A Study of Technological Innovation* (Thesis, Pittsburgh, Penn.: Carnegie Institute of Technology, 1963); Utterback, J. and Abernathy, B., 'A Dynamic Model of Process and Product Innovation', *OMEGA*, vol. 3, no. 6 (1975), pp. 643 and 646; von Hippel, 'The Dominant Role of the User in Semiconductor and Electronic Subassembly Process Innovation' and 'The Dominant Role of Users in the Scientific Instrument Innovation Process'.

8. von Hippel, 'Industrial Innovation by Users', pp. 14-18.

9. von Hippel, 'Get New Products from Customers', *Harvard Business Review*, vol. 60, no. 2 (1982), pp. 117-22.

10. Ibid., pp. 120-1.

11. See also Chapter 4.

12. Bright, J.R., 'Technology Forecasting as an Influence on Technological Innovation' in Baker (ed.), *Industrial Innovation*, p. 235. See also Bright, J.R., 'Some Management Lessons from Technological Innovation Research', *Long Range Planning*, vol. 2, no. 1 (1969).

13. Wills, G., *Technological Forecasting* (London: Penguin, 1972), Chapters 2-4.

14. Little, B., 'New Technology and the Role of Marketing' in Baker (ed.), *Industrial Innovation*, pp. 258-68.

15. Rothwell, R., 'The Relationship between Technical Change and Economic Performance in Mechanical Engineering' in Baker (ed.), *Industrial Innovation*, pp. 35-56.

16. Foxall, G.R., *Strategic Marketing Management* (London: Croom Helm, and New York: Wiley, 1981), Chapter 8.

17. Green, R.E., 'Marketing Applications of MDS: Assessment and Outlook', *Journal of Marketing*, vol. 39, no. 1 (1975), pp. 24-31.

18. Ibid.

19. Osborn, A.F., *Applied Imagination* (New York: Scribner's, 1963).

20. Rickards, T. and Freedman, B.L., 'Procedures for Managers in Idea-

deficient situations: An Examination of Brainstorming Approaches', *Journal of Management Studies*, vol. 15, no. 1 (1978), pp. 43-55; and 'Procedures for Managers in Idea-deficient Situations: A Note on Perceptions of Brainstorming Users Obtained from a Cross-Cultural Pilot Study', *Journal of Management Studies*, vol. 15, no. 3 (1978), pp. 347-9. For a wider discussion of creative techniques than is possible in this chapter, see Whitfield, P.R., *Creativity in Industry* (London: Penguin, 1976), esp. Chapter 4.

21. Gordon, W.J.J., *Synectics* (New York: Harper and Row, 1961).

22. Tauber, E.M., 'Discovering New Product Opportunities with Problem Inventory Analysis', *Journal of Marketing*, vol. 39, no. 1 (1975) pp. 67-70.

23. Kelly, G.A., *The Pscyhology of Personal Constructs*, vols. 1 and 2 (New York: Norton, 1955).

24. Christopher, M., '2001 – The Existential Consumer', *British Journal of Marketing*, vol. 2, no. 2 (1971).

25. Davidson, J.H., *Offensive Marketing* (London: Penguin, 1975), pp. 129-30.

26. White, P.R., ' "Travelcard" Tickets in Urban Public Transport', *Journal of Transport Economics and Policy* (January 1981), pp. 17-34.

27. Davidson, *Offensive Marketing*, pp. 249-59.

28. Foxall, G.R., *Consumer Choice* (London: Macmillan, 1983), Chapter 4.

29. Davidson, *Offensive Marketing*, pp. 129-30.

30. Kotler, P., *Marketing Management: Analysis, Planning and Control* (Englewood Cliffs, NJ: Prentice-Hall, 1980), pp. 205-6.

31. As was discussed in Chapter 2. See Abernathy and Utterback, 'Patterns of Industrial Innovation'.

32. Roberts, E. and Pinson, C., 'Compatibility Analysis for the Screening of New Products', *European Journal of Marketing*, vol. 6, no. 3 (1972), pp. 182-9.

33. Kotler, *Marketing Management*, p. 319.

34. Cooper, 'Project NewProd', pp. 287-9.

35. Calantone, R. and Cooper, R.G., 'New Product Scenarios: Prospects for Success', *Journal of Marketing*, vol. 45, no. 2 (1981), pp. 48-60.

36. Green, P.E. and Wind, Y., 'New Way to Measure Consumers' Judgements', *Harvard Business Review*, vol. 53, no. 4 (1975), pp. 107-17; Green, P.E. and Srinivasan, V., 'Conjoint Analysis in Consumer Research', *Journal of Consumer Research*, vol. 5, no. 2 (1978), pp. 103-23.

37. Kotler, P. and Zaltman, G., 'Targeting Prospects for a New Product', *Journal of Advertising Research*, vol. 16, no. 7 (1976), pp. 7-18.

38. Tauber, E.M., 'Reduce New Product Failures: Measure Needs as Well as Purchase Interest', *Journal of Marketing*, vol. 37, no. 3 (1973), pp. 61-4.

39. See Sands, S., 'Test Marketing: Can it be Defended?', *Quarterly Review of Marketing*, vol. 5, no. 3 (1980), pp. 1-10. The original reports are found in: Tauber, E.M., 'What is Measured by Concept Testing?', *Journal of Advertising Research*, vol. 12, no. 6 (1972), p. 35, and Cadbury, N.D., 'When, Where, and How to Test Market', *Harvard Business Review*, vol. 53, no. 3 (1975), p. 101.

40. Sands, 'Test Marketing'. Description of the concept testing techniques themselves is beyond the scope of the present book. Urban and Hauser, *Design and Marketing of New Products*, presenting an up-to-date review in Chapter 9. For accounts of the use of MDS and perceptual mapping in marketing see, *inter alia*, Wind, Y., 'The Perception of a Firm's Competitive Position' in Nicosia, F.M. and Wind, Y. (eds), *Behavioural Models for Market Analysis* (Hindsdale, Illinois: Dryden, 1977) pp. 163-81; Johnson, R.M., 'Market Segmentation: A Strategic Management Tool', *Journal of Marketing Research*, vol. 8, no. 1 (1971) pp. 13-18; Green, P.E., 'Marketing Applications of MDS'. See also, for example, Assael, H. and Lipstein, B., 'Recent Advances in Marketing Research' in Zaltman, G. and Bonoma, T.V. (eds.), *Review of Marketing 1978* (Chicago: American Marketing

Association, 1978), pp. 328-30; McCullough, J. and Best, R., 'Conjoint Measurement: Temporal Stability and Structural Reliability', *Journal of Marketing Research*, vol. 16, no. 1 (1979), pp. 26-31.

41. Midgley, *Innovation and New Product Marketing*, p. 225.

42. Robertson, T.S., 'Diffusion Theory and the Concept of Personal Influence' in Davies, H.L. and Silk, A.J. (eds), *Behavioural and Management Science in Marketing* (New York: John Wiley and Sons, 1978), pp. 214-36, esp. pp. 215-18.

43. Tauber, E.M., 'Why Concept and Product Tests Fail to Predict New Product Results', *Journal of Marketing*, vol. 39, no. 3 (1975), pp. 69-71.

44. Taulor, J.W., Houlakan, J.J. and Gabriel, A.C., 'The Purchase Intention Question in New Product Development: A Field Test', *Journal of Marketing*, vol. 39, no. 1 (1975), pp. 90-2.

45. Tauber, 'Why Concept and Product Tests . . .', p. 70.

46. Tauber, E.M., 'Predictive Validity in Consumer Research', *Journal of Advertising Research*, vol. 15, no. 5 (1975), pp. 59-64. The quotation is from the author's later discussion of his results in 'Utilization of Concept Testing for New-Product Forecasting: Traditional versus Multiattribute Approaches' in Wind, Y., Mahajan, V. and Cardozo, R.N. (eds), *New-Product Forecasting* (Lexington, Mass.: D.C. Heath, 1981), p. 174.

47. Ajzen, I. and Fishbein, M., 'Attitude – Behaviour Relations', *Psychological Bulletin*, vol. 84 (1977), pp. 888-918.

48. Shocker, A.S. and Srinivason, 'Multiattribute Approaches for Product Concept Evaluation and Generation: A Critical Review', *Journal of Marketing Research*, vol. 16, no. 3 (1979), pp. 159-80.

49. Tauber, 'Utilisation of Concept Testing', p. 169.

50. Tauber, 'Why Concept and Product Tests . . .', p. 71.

51. Foxall, G.R., *Consumer Choice* (London: Macmillan, 1983).

52. The techniques alluded to here are described in a profession of basic texts, e.g. Wright, M.G., *Discounted Cash Flow* (Maidenhead: McGraw-Hill, 1967). See also, White, *Consumer Product Development*, Chapter 4; Kraushar, *New Products and Diversification*, Chapter 10; and Sizer, J., *An Insight into Management Accounting* (London: Penguin, 1979), Chapter 8.

53. For discussion of some problems see van Horne, J.C., *Financial Management and Policy* (Englewood Cliffs, NJ: Prentice-Hall, 1975), and Keane, S.M., 'The Internal Rate of Return and the Disinvestment Fallacy', *ABACUS*, vol. 15, no. 1 (1979), pp. 48-55.

54. Kraushar, *New Products and Diversification*, pp. 107-11.

55. Ibid., pp. 111-12. White, *Consumer Product Development*, pp. 78, 234.

56. Keef, S., *Discounted Cash Flow and the Reinvestment Assumption* Birmingham University of Aston Management Centre Working Paper No. 204, 1981).

57. White, *Consumer Product Development*, p. 73.

58. Twiss, B., *Managing Technological Innovation* (London: Longman, 1980), p. 9.

59. Mansfield, E., Rapoport, J., Schnee, J., Wagner, S. and Hamburger, M., *Research and Innovation in the Modern Corporation* (London: Macmillan, 1971), pp. 219-20.

# 10 THE DEVELOPMENT AND TESTING OF NEW PRODUCTS

## The Design Dilemma

The statement that product designs which satisfy users' requirements are the result of customer-oriented management is a truism. It is a specific version of the tautology which expresses the whole philosophy of marketing-orientation to the effect that corporate success depends upon customers' acceptance of business activities and offerings. The questions which arise naturally from this are: how far is such customer-orientation the result of conscious managerial effort directed towards the end of satisfying buyers' needs at a profit and how far does it rely upon customers' being willing to accept whatever is offered? The problem is perhaps more acutely experienced in the design of new products than elsewhere: to what extent must pre-design customer research be taken into direct consideration during the design and development stages and is it possible for good designers to interpret market wants 'intuitively' or at least without direct reference to current market intelligence reports and data? Products whose design processes represent polar extremes appear to flourish equally: the dresses worn by brides at prestigious 'society' weddings provide the designs which are copied for the mass market while customer-made industrial components reflect in detail the wants of their buyers as determined at a pre-design stage of the development sequence. Designer-created fashion items undoubtedly appeal to particular types of consumer whose other-directedness leads them to place far greater emphasis upon being *à la mode* than upon the origin of the ideas they wear; conversely, the functional imperatives of many industrial products require customer/user involvement at pre-purchase stages of product development and, as has been noted, may result in the design stage being preempted by users as the locus of innovation shifts. The differential risks and commercial uncertainties presented by these extremes are reflected in the varying patterns of trial and error in the failure rates encountered in these product-markets. Intuitively-informed designers are, moreover, usually those whose success reflects years of experience of new product creation gained by contact with customers and through close understanding of their detailed requirements and responses. Nor does the simplistic picture of the 'design dilemma' portray accurately the relationship between design and marketing-orientation. Intuition results in failure as well as success while customer-initiated innovation may lead to the production of innovations whose markets are limited.

The true picture is rendered complex, moreover, by the products and markets which fit into neither of these categories. Fast moving and durable consumer products are often subjected to the rigours of an iterative design process which is shaped and reshaped by market intelligence; some attempts at consumer-based design fail utterly — the Ford Edsel designers attempted to incorporate as many customer demands as possible in their product with the result that no particular segment was satisfied; user design and prototype manufacture of industrial products is not universal; neither is customised production of intermediate and capital goods. Many customers are unable to conceive and describe their design wants before they are presented with products which incorporate them: this does not negate the business philosophy of marketing-oriented management — though it gives the lie to the assumptions on which marketing management is sometimes practised.[1] In fact, it reflects a common tendency of human behaviour which is seen particularly in the arts, religion, democratic political choice and the selection of material non-necessities; it is unlikely for instance, that the number of people demanding Shakespearean drama would constitute a viable market segment were the plays not widely available, culturally-sanctioned and generally highly valued.

The locus of design-origin, like the locus of innovation and entrepreneurship, appears then to depend upon product-market characteristics, but this does not exclude generalisation with respect to the nature of design processes in new product development. First, it is evident that the prevailing industrial pattern with respect to the locus of design origination should usually be respected. This pattern is, of course, well-known to companies which are producing fairly continuous new products within a familiar product-market scope but presents more dangerous ground for the company which is engaging in market development or diversification. More proactive companies may, however, seek ways of modifying or exploiting better the prevailing pattern in their industries: the search for design ideas among customers may result in a competitive advantage in product-markets normally characterised by designer-influence for example. The second point follows from this: patterns of customers' past design preferences need not dominate new product development but may be consciously used in order to accelerate the diffusion process. This is particularly the case when organisational purchases of innovative products are concerned; von Hippel and Finkel-stein[2] studied the adoption of automated clinical chemistry analysers in medical laboratories (the products are used for the clinical breakdown of, for instance, blood serum samples) and concluded that

> the level of user product innovation experienced *can* differ greatly between functionally similar products. In the particular sample we have studied, it appears that the principal cause of the variation in user innovation activity observed [lies] in the ease with which a would-be-user-innovation can modify a manufacturer's product to suit his particular needs. Doubtless, this product design variable has an influence on the level of user innovation experienced by the manufacturers of many types of product in addition to clinical chemistry auto-analysers . . .

The authors relate their findings to the idea of 'reinvention' advanced by Rogers, Eveland and Klepper[3] whose investigation of the adoption of information processing equipment revealed that, in addition to (i) the acceptance of an innovation as offered and (ii) outright rejection, which are the decision outcomes appearing in most models of innovative buying, a third possibility, the alteration of the homogeneous product to fit user requirements, is also available. Von Hippel and Finkelstein conclude that

> In the work reported on here, we saw Rogers' reinvention ('user innovation' in our terminology) being carried out by some users of one firm's product — but not by users of a similar product supplied by another firm. Thus, we may perhaps contribute to the reinvention concept by suggesting that the relative frequency of reinvention vs. straightforward adoption observed can differ for 'equivalent' products, and may be controllable by the manufacturers of some products via product designs which make user reinvestment an easy or difficult task.

In addition to the possibility of designing products in such a way as to encourage further user-led innovation, there are the related possibilities for the development of product designs which encourage the purchase of complementary products (perhaps themselves related to user innovation) and those which encourage the diffusion of the product among members of other market segments such as export markets.[4]

Thirdly, whatever the locus of design origin, the need for prelaunch market testing in most cases is clear not only from a cursory examination of the implications of marketing-orientation but from business experience. If such market testing can begin with concept evaluation by potential customers, so much the better for subsequent development; even if the testing of the product in the marketplace occurs at a relatively late stage in the innovative process, it may save the company immense sums of money and its reputation. Banting[5] relates the case of the Steel Company of Canada which produced and marketed huge quantities of nails for many years without knowing its market — who bought the nails, who used them, why they used them and so on. The need for this detailed knowledge emerged when the company produced an innovative nail, brandnamed Ardox, which incorporated a number of ostensibly progressive design features — increased strength, spiral grooves which enabled it to be driven in a straight manner with less chance of splitting the wood, and better wood-holding properties. The new product was inexpensive but 'after almost two decades on the market, Ardox nails still have not reached their expected sales volumes'. What a difference product testing and, if justified, test marketing of this innovative design might have made!

Fourthly, the nature of design/marketing interactions underlines the difficulties of laying down hard and fast rules not only for design performance but for the conduct and control of the entire innovative process. Consider, the concept of 'complete design' developed by Urban and Hauser.[6] These authors emphasise that design is an iterative process in which measurements of product attributes in terms of the benefits they confer upon customers are employed on successive occasions to form eventually the 'core benefit proposition' upon which the marketing promotional strategy of the company will be based. The process of design is thus based upon the methods of assessing customer reaction to which reference was made in the last chapter, perceptual mapping, brand positioning and the prediction of market potential — not once, as in preparation for a uniquely-significant cash flow projection, but successively as different versions of the selected product concept are subjected to exposure in the marketplace. Design is thus a means to the end of conceptualising and realising benefit segmentation (differentiated marketing based upon variations in customers' perceptions of the benefits they derive from the innovation). The necessity of incorporating into product designs and development those characteristics which facilitate the extension of the product's 'sphere of influence' to export markets has been stressed by McGuinnes and Little.[7] The role of R&D and engineering is then to convert the core benefit proposition, which is based upon the product attributes demanded by customers (rather than the product *features* the company happens to be able to supply), into a physical product which is capable of supplying the required attributes and benefits. The role of marketing is the design and creation of an integrated marketing mix which delivers these benefits via an appropriately designed and engineered product, customer-service, communicated information, price and distribution. The advertising concept of 'unique selling proposition' which suggests that every campaign should stress a single customer-demanded function of the product is similar to the idea that the marketing mix must deliver a core of proposed benefits. But it is necessary to emphasise in this concept that the entire mix is involved.

Nevertheless, 'complete design' on this model is not always an essential ingredient of successful new product development. As has been pointed out, in the case of certain products — notably, though not exclusively, fashion goods — intuition apparently replaces immediate survey data while, in the development of new services, several stages in the process of conceptualisation, design and development are often telescoped. As is so often the case, comparative advantage in marketing often derives from flaunting the rules previously imagined to be of universal applicability.

### Technical Research and Development

The purpose of 'product' design and development is the creation of an entire integrated marketing mix in which the product element harmonises with and is enhanced by customer-oriented pricing, marketing communications and distribution strategies. From the selection of acceptable designs to the building of a prototype product the effective innovative process demands a symbiotic relationship between the technical and production functions of the firm and the marketing function. Not only is a physical product or the physical capacity to perform a service under development: so is the product/business portfolio itself through the far more intangible production of a separate but unified array of market offerings, perhaps accompanied by the development and testing of a novel brand strategy. It is rare for technical and marketing personnel to appreciate one another's role in this process unless the strategic management of the organisation is pervaded and guided by marketing-oriented managerial awareness. On one level of analysis, the problem is that of devising and maintaining adequate and appropriate inter-departmental communications; as Pessemier[8] says, on the basis of his empirical research,

> The essential question is, how can marketing keep informed about the progress of research activities and provide useful information? The reporting format adopted by one study company is an effective response. The leader of each programme and project regularly presents an oral report of current findings and planned future work before all interested scientists, representatives of planning and marketing functions, and general management. The outside representatives are chosen with care since they must be able to understand the relevant technical issues and to deal effectively with laboratory personnel. These meetings keep the whole organisation abreast of the real status of laboratory work and provide laboratory administrators and scientists with an appreciation of the market and financial impact of various alternative approaches. Since reports are made on projects as well as programmes [this distinction will be made clearer later], a smoother transition can be made from development to market planning and introduction.

It goes without saying, however, that such a provision can succeed only when the need for effective communication is recognised and the contribution of R&D realised. The tendency among many marketing academics and managers is to ascribe a lack of marketing-oriented responsiveness to the R&D function. This is always a possibility but it must also be borne in mind that companies often fail to include R&D in their strategic thinking and planning. Nystrom[9] points out that 'Our language influences our perception of reality, as well as our action, and the language of business administration does not include R&D as a strategic variable.' Formulation of plans in the terminologies of marketing and financial management precludes adequate consideration of R&D's role and requirements which 'in effect means that R&D activities are viewed as relatively unproblematic from an overall company planning point of view' — at least until they fail to deliver the required goods. This is indicative of a lack of marketing-orientation and appreciation of the need to *match* internal resources with external needs, not so much at the level of the R&D department as on the part of those responsible for general strategic management.

Although the general prescriptions for effective R&D require no complicated thought — 'communications between R&D and marketing personnel must be frequent, two-way and appropriate', etc. — the real need is to accommodate technical development and testing, like every other phase of new product development − to corporate strategy. A contribution to this is made by Nystrom[10] on the basis of his investigation of eleven Swedish companies; his approach and conceptual framework are significant in view of their correspondence first to those of the contingency theorists who have attempted to relate intra-organisational social structure and behaviour to such 'contextual variables' as product-market dynamics and technological change[11] and secondly to the strategic thinking developed in the present book. The contingency view of organisational behaviour and communications will be discussed further in the next chapter, but in the present context, Nystrom's work is interesting in its own right.[12]

In relating overall corporate strategy and planning and R&D strategies, Nystrom differentiates *intended* R&D strategies which derive from the statements of top management with respect to the role of R&D in their company's activities, and *realised* strategies which are inferred from actual managerial and R&D practice with respect to product development.

Each type of strategy is described in terms of three behavioural dimensions. Intended strategy reflects, first, the product-market scope of R&D effort and is measured, along a continuum whose polar extremes are *concentrated* (suggesting market penetration) and *diversified* (novel products and/or technologies and/or markets). Secondly, intended entry is measured by the initial source of new product ideas which varies from technical-to-market-orientation. Note the special sense in which the terms are employed: they refer to the environment which the company habitually searches *first* in its exploration of innovative ideas rather than its dominant managerial orientation or business philosophy. Successful companies tend to be well informed of both technical and market considerations and, indeed, to dovetail them. The third dimension of 'intended strategy' in fact emphasises this matching process since it refers to the degree of defensiveness or offensiveness which characterises the R&D activities: a *defensive* strategy implies a reactive strategic response to competitors' product development programmes, while an offensive approach is an essential feature of what has been termed a proactive company strategy in which the ambition to be first in the market with effective novel products is determinative. Intended R&D strategies, assessed in terms of these three dimensions, may be classified along a continuum from *positional* to *innovative*. Nystrom labels those R&D approaches which evince concentration, market-orientation and defensiveness, positional: their managerial outlook directs them towards the maintenance of an existing product-market position or scope. This is essentially a *reactive* strategy and in order to be consistent with the rest of the book, the following discussion will refer to it as such. Nystrom characterises as innovative R&D strategies those which are based upon diversification, technical orientation and offensiveness; the overall corporate strategy reflected by such an approach to R&D is founded upon a perceived need to exploit new technologies and new market opportunities for the enhancement of profit levels. The following discussion, again for the sake of consistency, describes this strategy as *proactive*.

An interesting finding derived from this study of Swedish companies is that the strategic differences between companies and between their corresponding R&D strategies 'appear to be partly, but not wholly related to differences in market and technological conditions prevailing in different industries . . . Innovative [proactive] companies are companies which want to take advantage of new opportunities for profit and growth, that tend to occur in environments characterised by rapid and radical changes. Positional [reactive] companies, on the other hand, mainly try to maintain and strengthen an established position, which is easiest to do in stable environments with slow and continuous changes.'[13] The most reactive R&D strategies among Nystrom's sample were found in the pharmaceutical and chemical industries, while steel and electronic companies were generally (but not exclusively) reactive.

Realised R&D strategies are assessed by the use of rather more operational criteria, the relevant variables being the (internal → external) orientation of R&D, the use of a single technology → the synergistic combination of technologies and the (fixed → responsive) nature of R&D organisation. The orientation of R&D reflects the extent to which the organisation relies upon its own scientific and technical specialists or consults specialists on idea generation and technological development external to the firm; the size of company involved correlated well with such orientation, larger companies *tending* towards an internal orientation. With regard to the use of technology, there was a tendency for steel companies' R&D to be based upon a single technological discipline, while electronics companies, on the whole, sought to combine the benefits of multiple technologies; this dichotomy appeared not to correspond to variations in company size. The organisation of R&D was categorised as fixed or responsive by Nystrom on the basis of (i) the extensiveness of the company's 'external information contact network' (its sources of new ideas, use of customers' experience, contact with universities, and so on), (ii) its 'idea and project evaluation' methods (centralised/decentralised screening, frequency, delegation and formality of screening activities), (iii) its method of conducting 'internal project work' (through the use of flexible project groups specially mobilised for the execution of limited projects or fixed groups whose composition remains static over time and projects). The classification of actual corporate R&D organisations was related to patterns of these variables such that

A wide and flexible external information and contact network, decentralised idea and project evaluation and flexible project groups are used as indications of a responsive organisation of R&D. All these factors tend to make it easier for a company to respond to changes in its internal and external environment by developing new products. Narrow and directed information networks, centralised idea and project evaluation and fixed project groups, on the other hand, should make it more difficult to respond and are therefore used as indications of a fixed organisation of R&D.[14]

While the companies in the chemical and pharmaceutical industries showed organisational patterns for R&D which tended towards the responsive pole, those encountered in electronics and steel product-markets evinced more fixed forms of R&D organisation.

Realised strategies may be classified as open or closed, according to their descriptions in terms of these dimensions; more searching, flexible and adaptive organisations are characteristic of (relatively) open strategies, appropriate for proactive firms, based as they are on greater external orientation, synergistic use of technologies and responsive R&D organisation, while the internally-oriented, mono-technical and organisationally fixed structures are more appropriate to reactive companies. Nystrom reports a correlation coefficient of 0.48 between the reactive/proactive classification of his companies and their positions on the open/closed strategic continuum, which just falls short of statistical significance (though in so small a sample the usefulness of such measures is open to question) but is indicative, along with his general argument, of an association which should attract further research attention. Nystrom's analysis of the success of the companies in his sample suggests — as a generalisation — that companies engaged in effective innovation tended to employ actual R&D activities consistent with their overall strategic mode.[15]

Both corporate strategy in general and the organisation and strategic use of R&D activities reflect managerial awareness of the uncertainties and risks facing those responsible for business policy formulation and implementation and of the likelihood of their being able to reduce these factors to manageable proportions; that is, strategic mode depends upon the perception of the need and ability to obtain appropriate information. The conceptual framework which has just been described reflects this concern with uncertainty and information at several points. Intended R&D strategy is concerned with the need for R&D to be based upon the desired product-market scope of the firm, its strengths and weaknesses with regard to the identification, evaluation and exploitation of new product ideas and its ability to compete with its competitors in terms of the speed with which its innovation programme can initiate changes in the marketplace by successfully introducing new products. The dimensions in terms of which realised R&D strategies are described also draw attention to the need to appreciate information needs and information-gathering potential: orientation, the knowledge of technological interfaces and organisational demands. As Drucker[16] claims, 'Knowledge is the business fully as much as the customer is the business. Physical goods and services are only the vehicle for the exchange of customer purchasing-power against business knowledge.' Not all managements exhibit the same degree of strategic awareness in terms of the informational imperatives facing them, nor does awareness lead to the same strategic mode. Rather the appreciation of requirements for and availability of knowledge is shown by a (relatively) reactive or proactive response as appropriate and is, of course, a crucial factor in the effective strategic matching of internal resources and capacities and external innovative opportunities.

Uncertainties also represent an important set of reasons for shelving innovative products at the developmental stage. Reekie[17] undertook research in twenty British companies which employed among them some '12 per cent of all graduate R&D personnel in UK manufacturing industry and operated in the engineering, electronic and chemical industries'. Table 10.1 indicates the principal reasons given to indicate the sources of abandonment, which fall into two broad categories, environmental and organisational. The reasons for project abandonment were, in all cases studied, commercial since all were technically feasible. The conclusions, in addition to supporting the improvement of intrafirm communications, particularly at the 'marketing: R&D interface', draws further attention to the importance of early identification of projects which deserve postponement or abandonment and to the possibility of commercialising such projects indirectly via licensing agreements or other forms of technology transfer.

Table 10.1: Reasons for Abandonment of Innovative Projects

| Environmental Factors | Electrical | Mechanical | Chemical | Total | Examples |
|---|---|---|---|---|---|
| Unattractively small market | 10 | 2 | 7 | 19 | *Acid resistant paint:* production runs could not have achieved sufficient length for R&D and other investment costs to be recovered *and* an acceptable price charged; *Moisture measuring head:* market gaps did not represent sufficiently profitable segments given required R&D expenditure; *Anti-corrosive additive:* profitable market segment existed but was inaccessible or difficult to realise. |
| Uncertainty with monopsonistic or oligopsonistic buyers | 4 | 6 | 2 | 12 | *Modulation monitor* (for microwave equipment): risks of market research validity and reliability; buyer's spokesman not sufficiently reliable for prototype development to be justified; *Polythene tobacco pouch:* monopsony buyer's 'hunch' (in the absence of market intelligence) inaccurate; *Double-headed cutter* (for coal mining): swing in fashion; *Axial feed pump* (for electricity generating boards): ditto; *Military radar:* change in government policy; *'Helium storage tank'* (pseudonym): development depends upon future government policy on nuclear power stations. |
| Unattractive level of competition | 4 | 3 | 4 | 11 | *Sucrose-based emulsifier:* competitors' defensive pricing and promotional expenditure could not be countered; *Faster-acting MOS* (metal oxide semi-conductor integrated) *circuits:* company unwilling to undertake market entry expenses; *Helium storage tank:* feeling of inferiority in terms of technical ability vis-a-vis rivals. |

| Environmental Factors | Electrical | Mechanical | Chemical | Total | Examples |
|---|---|---|---|---|---|
| Uncertainty with suppliers | 2 | 3 | 1 | 6 | *Dual-spindle twister* (for yarn): because of the high cost of ancillary equipment supplies, the price would be too high for customers or the firm would be too high for customers or the firm would be involved in complementary innovation; *Paint-coated hardboard:* producer could not agree logistics with paint suppliers. |
| Obsolescence | 2 | 1 | 0 | 3 | *High performance vacuum value:* customers knew that semi-conductors would probably displace value technology in the near future. |
| **Organisational Factors** | | | | | |
| Lack of marketing capacity or expertise | 4 | 6 | 4 | 14 | *Pile driver:* inadequate sales force; *embossed wallpaper:* sales force accustomed to selling fast moving lines rather than speciality products. |
| Lack of production capacity or expertise | 5 | 6 | 2 | 13 | *Ultrasonic development:* producer recognised that successful production and marketing required expertise in the use of machine tools which his company lacked. |
| Faulty communications with associated firms | 4 | 3 | 0 | 7 | Seven projects were abandoned as a result of inadequate communications between the national operations of multinationals. |
| R&D cost escalation | 4 | 1 | 1 | 6 | *Voltmeter:* shelved when estimated R&D costs proved unrealistically low but subsequently revised when a new market segment was discovered to have a lower price elasticity of demand. |
| Shortage of R&D resources | 0 | 4 | 0 | 4 | *Sludge remover:* opportunity costs of R&D too high. |

Source: Reekie, D., 'A Fresh Look at the Marketing:R&D Interface' in *Innovation in Marketing*, University of Strathclyde: Department of Marketing, 1973, pp. 3.2-3.10.

**Marketing Development and Market Testing**

Technical development of the new product up to the stage of prototype manufacture must be accompanied by the planning of the remainder of the marketing mix, though little if any testing (in the market context) of non-product elements is possible before a fairly clear idea of the physical 'shape' and attributes of the product is available. As and when they are produced, however, the promotional, pricing and distributional components of the overall offering can be separately tested. Product testing involves the same uncertainties as concept testing: the format certainly reflects canons of scientific judgement as far as possible but the actual procedures, whether they consist of in-home product use and evaluation or the familiar 'town hall' tests, are far removed from the experimental methods of the natural and physical sciences. The chief benefit of product testing is the isolation of obvious product defects whether they are of a functional character or concern the innovation's compatibility with customers' comprehension, expectations and life-style. The artificiality of the test situation makes extrapolation of the results of product testing to actual markets hazardous but if they are interpreted comparatively the data gained from this source may assist in the positioning of the product and the development of non-product elements of the mix.[18]

From the point of view of increasing the quality and quantity of information available for product development, the reduction of uncertainty and the evaluation of risk, product testing is usually another necessary but highly insufficient stage in the innovative process. Respondents often alter their evaluations of and preferences for comparative products in subsequent trials, let alone between the testing and commercialisation phases. Furthermore, as soon as market testing commences, the innovative producer starts to broadcast knowledge of his new product and his intentions as well as receive external evaluations and, although this problem is not as great as in test marketing, the innovation is unlikely to remain confidential once active evaluation of customer response is undertaken beyond the firm's own laboratories and/or offices. Testing in the market place is thus a means by which knowledge is disseminated as well as information gathered.

Far from being the final testing of a completed product, market testing comprises further research into customers' requirements and produces data which are inputs to the iterative design and development process. The necessity is, therefore, for product tests to identify factors which may impede customer acceptance before the product is test marketed at great expense or launched. An example of a product whose adverse characteristics did not show up in product testing is related by Kraushar:[19] 'a company testing a new snack product against an established one found that the former had a good comparative performance when a small portion of both products was eaten. The project went on to test market but there it was found that the test results had been misleading because the new product, though palatable in small doses, palled when eaten in large quantities and over a longer period.' Product tests allow the match between company and markets to be more effectively made, not only by determining whether the product is unacceptable to prospective buyers but by ensuring that the company's capacities are such that the product can be produced and distributed in forms, quantities and qualities demanded by users. Product testing is most easily conducted among consumers of fast moving final products, but the size of most homes makes it difficult to undertake the comparative testing of many consumer durables, especially 'white goods' such as refrigerators. Industrial product testing is possible when the item involved is sufficiently small and its use sufficiently undisruptive to justify comparative evaluation. The testing of prototype service innovations may be inconspicuous (e.g. the trial of new drycleaning equipment which permits a faster industrial cleaning service) or obvious to customers (the introduction of 'Travelcards', dial-a-bus services or cable television). Conspicuousness may, however, affect the results of testing since non-innovators' as well as innovators' reactions are likely to be sampled indiscriminately; the former are almost by definition unfavourable. Midgley[20] emphasises the sampling of innovators at this stage in order to ensure that the diffusion process is possible and, indeed, probable. This is sound when innovators can be identified and isolated: the controversy surrounding the Mazda automotive innovation discussed in Chapter 7 suggests that these possibilities cannot be taken for granted.

Market testing, like previous methods of testing, may lead to the elimination of prototype versions or entire projects which do not fulfil the demands of the market and which cannot, therefore, meet the requirements of marketing and corporate planning and strategies. Various attempts to obtain ideas of future purchasing behaviour are made by companies during the market testing phase but, because product tests show the same essential drawbacks as concept testing, the prediction of sales and return on investment remain exercises of dubious value because of the incompleteness of the data, the very speculative nature of purchase intentions, and the problems of interpreting the results not so much in making go/no go/redesign decisions but in the formulation of market forecasts and further development plans. There is no shortage of decision 'rules' which might be employed in this context, usually of the form: in order to justify further development, respondents should prefer the innovation in blind, comparative tests to the current market leader, a majority should strongly intend to purchase the product, and so on.[21] Baker and McTavish[22] comment that 'The more of these requirements the test satisfies and the better it satisfies them, the greater is the probability that the test product, if marketed, will not fail *because of its qualities as a product*' and their words not only emphasise the probabilistic nature of market testing but, in addition, draw attention to the factors which influence product success over which the innovative producer has no control – competitors' new products or revamped marketing mixes, shifts in buyers' tastes or requirements and so on. Although the measurement of buyer response in terms of preferences and intentions is often an inevitable part of market testing, the elimination of products or versions of prototypes on these grounds may be based upon ignorance of performance in other segments of the market or of the dynamics of diffusion. This brings Midgley's recommendation of tests among innovators again to the fore: where they are essential to the subsequent diffusion process, much of the identification and influencing of market segments upon whose purchase and use the spread of the product depends, can be left to the behavioural dynamics of this primary market. This does not absolve the innovative company from carrying out segmentation analysis but lays further emphasis upon the role of innovative purchasers: if *their* reactions during market testing are negative, it is unlikely that non-innovators will become adopters of the product even though they try it.

Refinement of the result of experimental product tests may be obtained, where appropriate, by shop tests in which the product is made available in a limited number of outlets; this requires that a number of promotional and branding tests and decisions have been taken. When the purpose of comparative shop tests is the evaluation of a nonproduct element of the mix, distribution, price or advertising, product factors must naturally be kept constant but, even here, information on product acceptability can be obtained.[23]

### Sequential Testing and Commitment

Accounts of the new product development process normally discuss technical and marketing development in the sequence adopted in this chapter; after all, so many facets of marketing development depend upon the availability of a physical product. On the basis of his analysis of three major industrial product launches, Cooper[24] argues for wider recognition that corporate innovation is a purposeful, integrated technical and marketing development process which comprises 'discrete stages, whose purpose is information acquisition'. The importance of the guiding principle that new product development consists of a series of discrete but contingent stages is borne out by the developments he investigated: 'While technical and market activities inevitably overlapped at various points, there was a marked tendency to base each progressive stage on the concrete results of previous stages.' The commitment of the company is thus to one stage of the development process at a time: not only are design and technical developments iterative, so is marketing development. The project can be aborted at any stage or put on 'hold' until the information upon which investment in the next stage of development depends is available. This approach makes easier the identification of needs and avoids the risk associated with precipitous innovation.

## Test Marketing

Testing of the various separate elements of the marketing mix proceeds within the context of the creation of an integrated marketing offering but it is only at the test marketing stage that the success of this creation as a unified whole can be assessed. The costs and benefits of test marketing can be assessed along three dimensions: information, money and time. Test marketing is indicated by the lack of information upon which to base a confident launch; first and foremost, therefore, it is part of the process of data acquisition and uncertainty reduction which characterises the entire innovative process. Test marketing is justified if the informational benefits it promises to confer are expected to exceed the costs of making available information, especially to competitors, which is an inevitable consequence of this form of marketing experimentation. Product tests, price tests, advertising tests and shop tests can be carried out fairly surreptitiously but even they inform outsiders of the firm's marketing intentions; test marketing is by its very nature, however, a public activity aimed as it is at assessing comprehensively the reaction of a portion of the population to the innovation. The information required relates to whether innovative consumers purchase the product, the rates of awareness, trial and repeat buying in the market compared with levels of promotional expenditure, distribution levels and so on. For the first time, it is possible to obtain information on how effectively the marketing *mix* operates and to take advantage of the opportunity to make forecasts of future demand based upon actual buying responses under fairly standard conditions, to compare strategies (where multiple, comparative test market areas are used) and to guage business response capacity. Information with respect to sales representatives' ability to aid distribution of the product and to intermediaries' experiences in handling it is also obtainable and this information is particularly useful if and when national distributors have to be persuaded to stock the product at a later date. Test marketing is intended also to confirm or disconfirm the validity of information gained earlier in the process of market testing and, on occasion, to avoid disasters. Sands[25] presents a striking example of test marketing as a 'disaster check':

> In 1967, General Electric thought it had developed a sure winner in a product called the Letterwriter. It was a gadget which would have enabled an individual to correspond without the chore of physically writing letters.

> Concept and product testing had revealed a high degree of consumer buying interest. Two-thirds of those questioned said they would consider buying a machine that would let them dictate letters. Three-quarters of those who had used test models had shown them to others, and nearly one half of those had wanted one themselves. But a number of problems developed during a test market which took place in Indianapolis, Indiana. It was found that it took much too long to explain to customers how to operate the letterwriter. There was not enough sales help available to explain it to customers. Salesmen who were available objected to the time-consuming job of explaining how to use the letterwriter.

> In effect, the test market revealed that buying interest was not translated into actual purchases. Customers did not pick the product off the shelves in self-service stores. Thus the letterwriter was never marketed on a national basis.

In the absence of disaster or a new product which is seriously defective and requires redesign and redevelopment, test marketing can assist the innovative process by providing information only if the data gathered during the experiment can be used to make accurate predictions of post-launch sales. Fortunately, this is an area in which the last decade has seen much useful progress.

The value of information which is promised by test marketing must, as has been noted, be discounted against the dispersal of information which is an inevitable consequence of so public an experiment. Competitors, in particular, are capable of gleaning a great deal from test markets and those whose typical strategic or merely opportunistic and temporary responses are reactive stand to benefit considerably from the availability of more proactive companies' manifest creativity and technical/marketing research. Such companies' managers do not, of course, have access to the data provided by the test or the results, and conclusions drawn from them in their decision to initiate or supersede the tested innovation might lead simply to investment in an unviable enterprise. More serious is the question of how valid the data gained from test markets is likely to be given the opportunities of rivals to influence results, say by reducing their own competitive efforts or even by arranging to purchase large quantities of the innovation.[26] Alternatively, a competitor may wait until the product under test is launched nationally before superseding it, an occurrence which illustrates how limited the information provided by naive test marketing *can* be.

The financial costs of test marketing are so high as to persuade several companies to question whether the process can be justified:[27] sums of $1m to $1.5m are frequently incurred. The managerial issue which requires a firm decision concerns the value of net informational returns discussed above in terms of the financial outlay required for the test: how far will the expenditure of resources on the test market reduce uncertainty? Within reasonable limits the increase of expenditures on test marketing will further reduce uncertainty; sensible criteria must be set for deciding when the growth of such expenditures must cease and for evaluating the information gathered: there is clearly a natural point beyond which the marginal value of information is less than the marginal expenditure of resources involved in obtaining it. Unfortunately, many companies invest too heavily in their test markets well before this inevitable point of decreasing marginal returns is reached and the result of this overinvestment is a diminution rather than an augmentation of the quality of information received. Overinvestment occurs when test markets are given greater or more specialised attention than is justified in the light of the attention the firm can reasonably be expected to provide for the subsequent national market for the innovation. All too often companies overinvest in their test market sales teams and sales management, in advertising test products, in providing incentives for distributors, in stimulating trial and repeat buying, the provision of unrealistic levels of promotional effort, and so on. Even the checks in progress among representatives and outlets conducted by zealous sales managers can cause a 'Hawthorne effect' in which excessive effort is placed on selling the product. The weighting of the various elements of the marketing mix is, indeed, a most difficult task but the aim should be not to deviate more than is possible from what can be realistically expected under the normal circumstances of marketing the product on a national basis. When test conditions diverge by more than the marginal extent which must be expected in a dynamic socio-economic system from actual marketing situations, the investment in test marketing cannot produce the most useful or favourable returns available. Once again, it is requirements and expectations about inform-ation which lie at the heart of test marketing decisions and practice.

The third dimension along which test marketing may be costed is time. Test marketing exercises require anything from several months to several years to reduce the uncertainty surrounding innovation launches to the extent that executives have sufficient confidence to assume the necessary risks. This is time which competitors will use profitably in one way or another. Nevertheless, to rush into national marketing may be unwise. The costs of test marketing have spurred the development of techniques which can improve it or even supersede it by providing in-formation which is as reliable as that which test marketing produces but faster and cheaper. The following section describes this development in greater detail.

**Quantitative Market Assessment**

There is a longstanding debate in marketing as to whether test market-ing constitutes the final stage of product development or the initial phase of launch. Of course, it may be either or both. The opportunity to assess the entire new marketing mix as a single entity is obviously taken as part of the development sequence: a 'no go' decision can still be taken and for consumer products is about as probable as a 'go' de-cision. But the popularity of the roll-out launch, in which product availability is gradually extended region by region until the innovation has national scope, suggests that the initial test market is but the first step in the process of promoting product diffusion. The two viewpoints merge if test marketing is seen as an extension into the market place (with all the consequences for long term customer reaction that entails sequential development and commitment). Debate also rages over whether test marketing is necessary, sensible or viable. Its chief dis-advantages lie in its being expensive (often amounting to millions of pounds or dollars), public and a slow means of obtaining information

(*Head and Shoulders* shampoo was in test market for five years; *Bold* washing powder for three).[28] Furthermore, test marketing may be a wholly inappropriate means of obtaining information — in the case of industrial products or services — and there are always instances in which immediate national launch is more appropriate for consumer products — competitive prowess and progress, technological superiority, and so on. Timing and market peculiarities may also preclude test marketing even in industries which traditionally rely upon it; thus

> Festival, the twist-wrapped chocolate assortment launched by Rowntree in September 1981, was unusual in that it went national as a major brand without a test market. The reason was that in its particular market segment the seasonal peaks at Christmas and Easter are more important than they are for count lines. It is always difficult to persuade retail chains to accept test products, and Rowntree knew they would be even more reluctant to take on a seasonal brand. What also swayed the decision was that results for a seasonal test were likely to be unreliable.[29]

### Pre-Test Market Forecasting

Test marketing will always exist either because it provides the most effective means by which information can be obtained and uncertainty reduced in specific instances or because it is the beginning of a phased launch. But, whereas the reasons for avoiding test marketing have often in the past relied upon intuition or guesswork ('this *might* alert competitors', 'we *think* we have a winner'), the test/no test decision can nowadays frequently be made with the aid of quantitative decision tools. These sales forecasting devices may alternatively be used to determine whether a product in development should be aborted or should proceed to test market.

The inability of concept tests to predict adoption levels/rates and purchase frequencies has already been noted; their value is limited to the prediction of trial and initial repeat buying behaviours and then only for continuous and dynamically-continuous products. Product tests are subject to similar limitations.[30] Market forecasting models which take the form of regression equations fitted to data for similar products to that being developed necessarily perform well only for the most continuous of products, line extensions and me-too brands. The argument developed in Part Two of this book suggests that potential buyers' verbal behaviour in the market research situation, their stated 'intentions to buy', provide little guidance as to their subsequent overt buying behaviours in purchase situations. It is not surprising, therefore, that attempts at predicting future sales which are based upon the observed purchase behaviour of customers provides rather more valid conclusions but, again, these apply most accurately to trial and critical repeat behaviours.[31] Tauber[32] sums up their effectiveness by providing the following example:

> Employing one laboratory method to test four products which were simultaneously introduced into the marketplace provided some interesting insights. Laboratory sales prediction vs. market results revealed: (a) product A was predicted to be a loser, *but* in the market it reached over $40 million in annual sales; (b) product B was predicted to be a winner, *but* market performance went from marginal to defunct; (c) products C and D were predicted to be losers, *and* proved to be so when they were marketed. Thus, this technique had a poor track record — two correct out of four.

Laboratory tests have generally been concerned with the sales which occur on one test occasion after the showing of a brand advertisement. Clearly, from what is known of the social and economic dynamics of adoption and diffusion, it is more probable that relatively accurate sales forecasts will result from tests which simulate more closely the opportunities consumers have to repeat their initial purchase. Sales wave experiments which have been used for fast-moving consumer products extend concept and home-based product tests by involving several repeat purchase opportunities which allow the pattern of consumer response over time to be plotted and measured. This technique is most firmly based upon the understanding of consumer behaviour over time developed earlier. The collection and analysis of data may take several months but Tauber notes — without, however, providing detailed evidence — that 'our experiences to date have been quite positive'.

Several examples of pre-test market assessment models are available[33] but ASSESSOR, described by Silk and Urban[34] illustrates well the fundamental procedures. ASSESSOR is based upon measures of trial and repeat behaviour and consumers' *post-usage* product attitudes (verbal ratings of product attributes and brand preference). Table 10.2 portrays the test procedure and types of measurement employed. The model attempts to predict brand market share: Table 10.3 indicates the pre-test market predictions for a number of products and compares them with the actual market share achieved in subsequent test marketing.[35]

Table 10.2: ASSESSOR: Research Design and Development

| Design | Procedure | Measurement |
|--------|-----------|-------------|
| $Q_1$ | Respondent Screening and Recruitment (personal interview) | Criteria for Target Group Identification (e.g. product class usage) |
| $Q_2$ | Premeasurement for Established Brands (self-administered questionnaire) | Composition of 'Relevant Set' of Established Brands, Attribute Weights and Ratings, and Preferences |
| $X_1$ | Exposure to Advertising for Established Brands and New Brand | |
| $[Q_3]$ | Measurement of Reactions to the Advertising Materials (self-administered questionnaire) | Optional, e.g. Likeability and Believability Ratings of Advertising Materials |
| $X_2$ | Stimulated Shopping Trip and Exposure to Display of New and Established Brands | |
| $Q_4$ | Purchase Opportunity (choice recorded by research personnel) | Brand(s) Purchased |
| $X_3$ | Home Use/Consumption of New Brand | |
| $Q_5$ | Post-Usage Measurement (telephone interview) | New Brand Usage Rate, Satisfaction Ratings, and Repeat Purchase Propensity; Attribute Ratings and Preference for 'Relevant Set' of Established Brands Plus the New Brand |

Note: Q = Measurement
X = Advertising
Source: Silk, A.J. and Urban, G.L., 'Pre-Test-Market Evaluation of New Packaged Goods: A Model and Measurement Methodology', *Journal of Marketing Research*, vol. 15, no. 2 (1978), p. 177. Reproduced by kind permission of the American Marketing Association.

Urban and Hauser[36] note of ASSESSOR that 'Of the approximately 120 new packaged goods studied to date, 60 per cent failed to meet the established pretest standards for a positive test market decision. These standards were expressed as a required minimum longrun share objective. A number of these failures were improved and retested so that eventually 60 per cent of the products went to test market.' The probability of a successful test market can be gauged from the extent to which the market share predicted by the model exceeds the minimum share required by the company and there is no doubt that models such as ASSESSOR can reduce the uncertainty inherent in the new product development process for those products for which it is suitable.

Table 10.3: ASSESSOR: Predicted and Observed Market Shares

| Product description | Initial | Adjusted | Actual | Deviation (initial-actual) | Deviation (adjusted actual) |
|---|---|---|---|---|---|
| Deodorant | 13.3 | 11.0 | 10.4 | 2.9 | 0.6 |
| Antacid | 9.6 | 10.0 | 10.5 | −0.9 | −0.5 |
| Shampoo | 3.0 | 3.0 | 3.2 | −0.2 | −0.2 |
| Shampoo | 1.8 | 1.8 | 1.9 | −0.1 | −0.1 |
| Cleaner | 12.0 | 12.0 | 12.5 | −0.5 | −0.5 |
| Pet Food | 17.0 | 21.0 | 22.0 | −5.0 | −1.0 |
| Analgesic | 3.0 | 3.0 | 2.0 | 1.0 | 1.0 |
| Cereal | 8.0 | 4.3 | 4.2 | 3.8 | 0.1 |
| Cereal | 6.0 | 5.0 | 4.4 | 1.6 | 0.6 |
| Shampoo | 15.6 | 15.6 | 15.6 | 0.0 | 0.0 |
| Juice Drink | 4.9 | 4.9 | 5.0 | −0.1 | −0.1 |
| Frozen Food | 2.0 | 2.0 | 2.2 | −0.2 | −0.2 |
| Cereal | 9.0 | 7.9 | 7.2 | 1.8 | 0.7 |
| Detergent | 8.5 | 8.5 | 8.0 | 0.5 | 0.5 |
| Cleaner | 8.4 | 5.5 | 6.3 | 2.1 | −0.8 |
| Shampoo | 0.8 | 2.3 | 2.5 | −1.7 | −0.2 |
| Shampoo | 7.1 | 7.9 | 7.6 | −0.5 | 0.3 |
| Dog Food | 2.9 | 2.9 | 2.7 | 0.2 | 0.2 |
| Cleaner | 16.5 | 14.7 | 12.9 | 3.6 | 1.8 |
| Shampoo | 1.1 | 0.6 | 0.6 | 0.5 | 0.0 |
| Frozen Food | 2.6 | 2.0 | 2.2 | 0.4 | −0.2 |
| Lotion | 27.1 | 27.1 | 28.7 | −1.6 | −1.6 |
| Food | 5.6 | 5.0 | 1.5 | 4.1 | 3.5 |
| Shampoo | 5.2 | 2.8 | 1.6 | 3.6 | 1.2 |
| Average | 7.9 | 7.5 | 7.3 | 0.6 | 0.2 |
| Average Absolute Deviation | — | — | — | 1.5 | 0.6 |
| Standard Deviation of Differences | — | — | — | 2.0 | 1.0 |

Source: Urban, G.L. and Hauser, J.R., *Design and Marketing of New Products* (Englewood Cliffs, N.J.: Prentice-Hall, 1980), p. 403. Used by permission. Part of this table appeared as Table 5, 'Predicted and Observed Market Shares for One Pretest Market Model' in A.J. Silk and G.L. Urban, 'Pretest Market Evaluation of New Packaged Goods: A Model and Measurement Methodology', *Journal of Marketing Research*, vol. 15, no. 2 (1978) pp. 171-91. The permission of the American Marketing Association to reproduce that table is gratefully acknowledged.

ASSESSOR, along with such other pretest predictive devices as COMP and the sophisticated laboratory simulation methods made available by such marketing research organisations as Yankelovich, Skelly and White, Inc.[37] reduce uncertainty in one or more of four ways. They provide (i) estimates of market share and (ii) help eliminate obviously disastrous products; (iii) ASSESSOR and COMP allow various marketing mix combinations to be assessed and (iv) incorporate useful attitudinal measurement techniques.[38]

An alternative model, NEWPROD, which is described by Assmus,[39] also illustrates the managerial need to forecast the financial implications of continued commitment to a new product venture and the restricted means available to do so. Assmus sets out four criteria by which forecasting models may be judged: (i) they should be capable of application at an early stage of the new product development process in order that the costs of development and testing can be reduced or eliminated and so that data can be accumulated which provide comparisons with subsequent test marketing results; (ii) they should incorporate measures derived from managerially controllable factors such as advertising levels — a requirement which is especially pertinent in view of the (independent) Project NewProd findings with regard to controllable factors; (iii) they should use existing data, i.e. information gained in previous new product introductions; and (iv) they should produce trustworthy predictions. NEWPROD is claimed to fulfil these requirements. It forecasts, on the basis of pre-test market data, market share at that future time when the product has been on the national market for one year by following the progress of prospective purchasers who are at the various stages in the ATR process which were discussed in Chapters 6 and 7; aware, triers and repeats (see Figure 10.1). Initially all potential consumers are unaware of the new item; they may become aware (measured as the ability to recall the brand name when required to specify brands in a given product class) in one of three ways: through advertising, sampling or couponing. The model, which is only superficially described by Assmuss, is based upon six measures: weekly advertising expenditure, the number of samples distributed each week, the number of coupons similarly distributed, the *awareness rate* (i.e. the rate at which individuals move from unawareness to the advertising aware category), the *trial rate* (that at which persons move from the advertising aware to the purchase-trier category) and the *repeat rate* (that at which they move from being purchase-triers to repeaters). At any stage, buying may cease, temporarily or permanently. The results for the prediction of new consumer brands' market shares are quite encouraging, though they relate to continuous products and do not take account of the vicissitudes of the marketplace which may impede diffusion beyond the time period to which the forecasts relate.

Figure 10.1: Essentials of the NEWPROD Model

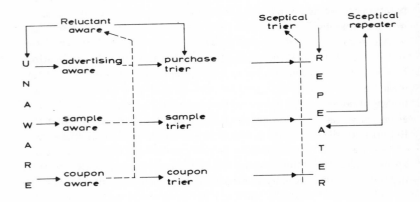

Source: Derived from Assmuss, 'NEWPROD: The Design and Implementation of a New Product Model', p. 18.

Indeed, although all of the available models which predict a new product's test market share are subject to a range of criticisms,[40] their most problematic feature (in the present context) derives from their limited applicability; while they perform well, or at least predictably, for continuous products, they are of little value in forecasting the fate of products which require radical modification of buyers' purchase and/or consumption behaviours. (ASSESSOR, for instance, proceeds by comparing consumer reactions to the new brand with those to established members of the identical product class while NEWPROD makes a virtue of its reliance upon past data.) For many new products, they are sufficient because so many new products are of a continuous nature; hence their development in the context of fast-moving consumer goods. But it must be borne in mind that, even in this limited sphere, they can predict outcomes only on a probabilistic basis. Wherever they are viable, they provide a useful means of making the next decision in the sequential process of innovation development and thus assist managerial judgement in the problem of project commitment and the allocation of resources among competing projects. But, at present, while they represent notable advances, at best they do no more than act as another means of recognising obvious failures which do not deserve the expenditure of test market resources.

## Test-Market Forecasting

Skilful use of pretest marketing forecasting models which have proved reliable on previous occasions may well obviate test marketing but where it does not the possibility now exists of gaining from test marketing an idea of the new product's potential in the national marketplace which was, until recently, unavailable to managers. Again this involves the use of quantitative productive models and again progress to date has generally been made in continuous, consumer products rather than durables, industrial goods or services. A variety of predictive models exists to trace the progression of consumers through awareness, trial and repeat buying[41] and to assess at each stage the probability that the buyer will proceed to the next. Models differ in their data sources – some, such as TRACKER, using surveys while others, such as NEWS, employ diary-panel responses – and thus in their levels of cost and complexity. They differ too in their coverage of all three stages in the buying process, their commercial acceptance, quality of modelling, diagnostic capabilities and the extent to which they have been tested across product boundaries.[42] The need for commercial secrecy sometimes precludes the authors of models from identifying the product groups actually tested except in the broadest terms, though we already know that the models in question are capable of relating only to relatively continuous, fast-moving or packaged consumer goods which, in Howard's terms (see Chapter 2), require only routinised response behaviour on the part of customers. (Navasimham and Sen,[43] and Dodson[44] provide recent critical reviews and comparisons of the available models.) There exist also diffusion models which track and predict the post-launch progress of new products on the basis of diffusion theory and empirical research into the nature and correlates of customer innovativeness.[45]

## Predictive Models: Summing up

Much has been said already from which the value of quantitative sales prediction models may be gauged but the following summary points may help crystallise their capacity to inform and guide the new product development process. First it must be said that with the advent of such models the management of innovation has entered a new era. Information about the probable success of new products can now be obtained a little earlier and a lot less expensively; test markets costing millions of pounds or dollars can now be substituted by limited experimentation and consumer research which entail a tenth of this expenditure. Furthermore, the information gained appears reliable, at least as far as it is possible to judge from the sometimes veiled details that have been published. However, certain caveats must be entered. Sound information is still available only rather late in the development process when many costs have been incurred and when many of the organisational barriers to project abandonment have been erected. The models are highly limited with respect to scope; they apply to incrementally-different brands of packaged consumer products which involve minimal, if any, decision-making on the part of the consumer. Important as these products are to the national economy and to the fortunes of individual companies and whole industries, the need to extend and improve predictive modelling in the cases of consumer durables, services and industrial goods is obvious. Urban and Hauser[46] forecast the development of models for these categories within a few years, but there is far to go. The models which have thus far been developed for consumer product forecasting show signs of being highly-situation-specific in their applications. Engel and Blackwell[47] sum up as follows:

> To date there has been little application of a model developed by one individual or group to data or problems faced by other individuals or groups. That is the ultimate test of a model's generality. This type of testing is occurring . . . but the situations involved are often proprietary business applications, which do not lend themselves to widespread publication of the results. Perhaps, also, if the results were more conclusive, publication would be more widespread.

Quantitative sales forecasting models should be the subject of cautious celebration rather than defeatism. They cannot, of course, remove the necessity for managerial judgement: the go/no go; test market/no test market decisions must still be made and the increase in information may complicate rather than simplify certain decisions. Perhaps this accounts for another problem faced by these models, especially those which deal with the pretest marketing stage of new product development — that of reluctant managerial acceptance. Industrial product and service innovations are frequently not amenable to market testing or test marketing as are consumer products. But even where tried and tested forecasting and market testing techniques do exist — and that certainly includes many consumer innovations — new products are still launched in large numbers without adequate prior assessment of the probability of their being successful in the marketplace.

## Conclusion

Corporate innovation is a process rather than an act because of the uncertainties which surround the decisions and behaviours of those who are responsible for it, uncertainties which are inherent in marketing-oriented management itself since they derive from the vicissitudes of a competitive and dynamic environment in which customers have the capacity to choose. Managerial commitment to any given project naturally increases as the new product in question clears successive hurdles; but it is also apt to increase as the emerging innovation becomes more familiar, has more resources devoted to it and appears to be a winner simply because so much managerial effort, time and talent have been devoted to it. Cooper[48] argues strongly against the uncritical accumulation of organisational commitment in this way: in the case studies he presents, even technical and marketing testing and development were sequential (and consequential) rather than parallel operations. Because effective innovation represents a competent managerial response to the fact of limited knowledge,

> the process is a stagewise one, rather than a one shot effort. It is discrete rather than continuous. Each step has a clearly discernible start and finish. Activities or stages are defined by what information is required. The stage begins with this definition and ends when the information has been obtained. Each activity itself is essentially an information gathering activity: identifying customers' needs; determining if the product is technically feasible, and if so, how; learning about market demand and price sensitivities; discovering how much the product will cost to manufacture; etc.
>
> It is important that each activity remain distinct so as to be able to provide specific information to move on to the next step. But equally important is the fact that each activity is intimately linked with the preceding step whose findings justified the continuation of the project. The result is a flow or network of information acquisition activities. Each one is discrete and identifiable, and each is hinged on the outcomes of previous activities.

But the quality of managerial decision-making with respect to innovation depends vitally upon the *quality* of the information obtained at each stage. Robertson and Fox[49] review several empirical studies which indicate that textbook prescriptions are infrequently followed in industry because managers are suspicious of the alleged usefulness of the mathematical procedures that are advocated, given the quality and quantity of the informational inputs they demand.[50] They report from their own direct investigations of innovation in practice[51] that 'none of the managers whom we observed appeared to make use of well-known decision-making tools such as "trees" or "matrices". Their decisions seemed to be made in sets as experience and knowledge built up and was modified or reversed in the light of further experience or knowledge from meeting to meeting.' Their account confirms Cooper's idea of 'stagewise' decision-making in which projects may receive a 'go' or 'no go' or 'hold' decision as the information suggests.

Neither the view that innovative decision-making is an entirely logical affair nor that which portrays it as the result of intuition and hunch is supported by the evidence. New product development in actual companies includes both quasi-rational, quantified information-based decisions and those which are apparently based upon intuition but which reflect experience and qualitative assessment of marketing opportunities and corporate skills. Those managers who are operationally involved in successive stages of the new product development process are, moreover, quite capable of editing, ignoring, forgetting or de-emphasising information for deliberate intra-organisational political reasons or just because they are human employees rather than the computer-like information processors depicted in so many models of managerial decision-making.

Furthermore, the 'stagewise' portrayal of new product development lays stress upon the fact that as soon as management obtains sufficient, high quality information upon which to base one decision, another decision becomes inevitable. The managerial dilemma posed continually by this 'hierarchy of decisions' is nowhere more apparent than in the case of test marketing. The purposes of test marketing (to obtain an idea of national sales levels; to test the marketing mix element by element but, especially, as a whole, to obtain information which otherwise would not be available; and so on) have been ubiquitously known for decades. So have its demerits (that competitors are warned and informed; that time is at a premium; that there is difficulty in interpreting the results and, particularly, in making the decision to stop test marketing and begin the national launch; and that test marketing is often inappropriate to industrial goods companies and superfluous in the case of those firms which pursue a reactive strategy). The consequent thrust of research has been towards improving the former and reducing the effects of the latter, especially in terms of increasing the effectiveness of grossing up test market results to give national projects.[52] And, as this chapter has shown, considerable advance has been made in quantitative modelling which promises to extend significantly the quality of managerial decision-making and reduce the various costs of test marketing. Yet, as soon as the decision to go national has been made, the need for information relating to the launch of the product looms large. Many new products are of relevance to the market only if they are launched at the appropriate time, i.e. when competition and demand are such that the product will be well-received. Bucknell[53] speaks of the 'product timing window' through which the new product must pass in order to have a successful impact upon the market beyond. An innovation might come on-stream at just the time at which demand is itself becoming strong. In the early 1970s, the US Department of Transportation required that certain motor car components should be flame-retardent. Monsanto had foreseen the potential of flame-resistent materials twenty years earlier and its product, *Phosgard*, 'cleared the ready window in 1974'. Another possibility is that, although marketing managers perceive correctly customers' requirements at the earliest phase of the product development process, those requirements have shifted drastically by the time the new product is introduced to the market: this is exactly what happened in the 1950s as Ford's Edsel motor car progressed from concept to product. The final possibility is that the company monitors its selected target market only to discover that the signs of sufficient demand are becoming weaker. Monsanto's device to reduce the hydrocarbon emissions from cars was not developed beyond the prototype stage when it was realised that motorists would not fit the product unless legally required to do so and no relevant legislation appeared to be forthcoming.[54] A stepwise development process, in which the market is constantly monitored, is again indicated, though once again, the solution of one problem leads inexorably to the identification of others as the need to decide upon the most suitable strategy for propelling the new product into the growth phase of its product life cycle and beyond as quickly as possible, becomes immediately apparent.

The depiction of the new product development process as an (ideally) orderly means of obtaining the information upon which sequential decisions are based should not, however, lead to the underestimation of the complexity of new product strategy; nor should the step-wise portrayal of corporate innovation imply that this is a simple linear process in which all events are serially-organised. The operational production and

## Figure 10.2: Critical Path Design for the Introduction of an Electric Typewriter

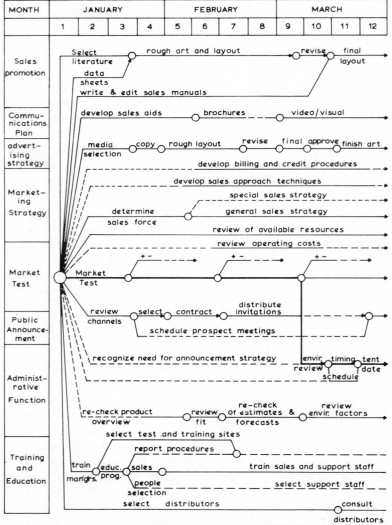

+ positive test market results indicate continuation of plan

− negative test market results indicate termination of plan

x test begun prior to announcement plan start: initial test results positive

xx if objectives change, notify functional managers for possible revision of plan

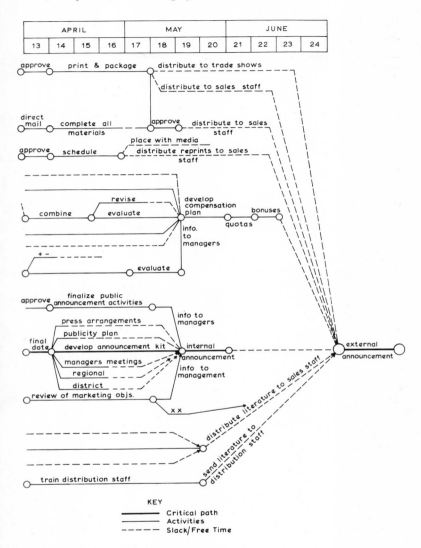

| APRIL | | | | MAY | | | | JUNE | | | |
|---|---|---|---|---|---|---|---|---|---|---|---|
| 13 | 14 | 15 | 16 | 17 | 18 | 19 | 20 | 21 | 22 | 23 | 24 |

KEY
——— Critical path
——— Activities
- - - - - Slack/Free Time

Source: Reprinted by permission of the publisher from 'Critical Path Method for Introducing an Industrial Product' by G.R. Dundas and K.A. Krentler, *Industrial Marketing Management*, vol. 11 (1982), p. 129. Copyright 1982 by Elsevier Science Publishing Co. Inc. The authors' permission to reprint is also acknowledged.

marketing of innovative products are exceedingly involved and usually require extensive planning, organisation and co-ordination. Figure 10.2 indicates, in critical path analytical form, the operations involved in bringing just one product, a new electric typewriter, to the market.

## Notes

1. An interesting discussion of this problem is found in Baker and McTavish, *Product Policy and Management*, pp. 119-25.

2. Von Hippel, E. and Finkelstein, S.N., *Product Designs which Encourage – or Discourage – Related Innovation by Users: An Analysis of Innovation in Automated Clinical Chemistry Analyses* (Cambridge, Massachusetts: Sloan School of Management, Massachusetts Institute of Technology Working Paper No. 1011-78, 1978).

3. Rogers, E., Eveland, J. and Klepper, C., *The Diffusion and Adoption of GBF/DIME Among Regional and Local Governments*, Stanford, CA.: Institute for Communications Research, Stanford University. Working Paper; cited by von Hippel and Finkelstein, *Product Design*.

4. White, P.D. and Cundiff, E.W., 'Assessing the Quality of Industrial Products', *Journal of Marketing*, vol. 42, no. 1 (1978), pp. 80-6; McGuinness, N.W. and Little, B., 'The Influence of Product Characteristics on the Export Performance of New Industrial Products', *Journal of Marketing*, vol. 45, no. 2 (1981), pp. 110-22.

5. Banting, 'Unsuccessful Innovation in the Industrial Market', *Journal of Marketing*, vol. 42, no. 1 (1978), pp. 99-100.

6. Urban and Hauser, *Design and Marketing of New Products* (Englewood Cliffs, NJ: Prentice-Hall, 1980), pp. 155-66.

7. McGuiness and Little, 'The Influence of Product Characteristics', pp. 120-2.

8. Pessemier, 'Managing Product Innovation', p. 334.

9. Nystrom, H., 'Company Strategies for Research and Development' in Baker (ed.), *Industrial Innovation*, pp. 417-40; the quoted material is from p. 417.

10. Ibid. The following discussion of Nystrom's work is based upon this source.

11. E.g. Burns, T. and Stalker, G.M., *The Management of Innovation* (2nd edition, London: Tavistock, 1966). For a recent discussion and evaluation, see Child, J., *Organisations* (London: Harper and Row, 1977), Chapter 1.

12. The issue of communications at the R&D stage is discussed by Tushman, M.L., 'Managing Communication Networks in R&D Laboratories', *Sloan Management Review*, vol. 20 (1979), pp. 37-49. Other factors which impinge upon productivity and communications behaviour are tangential to the theme of this book but are nevertheless important to the management of innovation. Thus the career structures, aspirations, perspectives and professions ethos of the corporate R&D scientist or engineer receive attention from Twiss, B., *Managing Technological Innovation* (London: Longman, 1980); see especially pp. 178-9. A somewhat different view is presented by Ritti, R., 'Work Goals of Scientists and Engineers', *Industrial Relations*, vol. 7 (1968), pp. 118-31.

13. Nystrom, 'Company Strategies', p. 422.

14. Ibid., p. 428.

15. I have deliberately not discussed Nystrom's analysis with respect to successful innovation in detail because of the difficulty of finding a convincing explanation of all of the results. The generalisation of this sentence seems valid

but there are some apparent inconsistencies from firm to firm and variable to variable which make further empirical investigation essential. See Commentary on Nystrom's paper by Eric Haeffner in Baker (ed.), *Industrial Innovation*, pp. 441-3.

16. Drucker, P.F., *Managing for Results* (London: Pan, 1967), p. 132.

17. Reekie, D., 'A Fresh Look at the Marketing:R&D Interface' in *Innovation in Marketing* (University of Strathclyde: Department of Marketing, 1973).

18. While detailed description of the procedures is not possible in the current work, they are discussed in numerous texts which the newcomer might wish to consult. See, for instance, Foxall, *Strategic Marketing Management*, Chapter 4. For succinct and useful accounts by practitioners, see: White, *Consumer Product Development*, pp. 84-8; Kraushar, *New Products and Diversification*, pp. 135-8; and Collins, M., 'Product Testing' in Aucamp, J. (ed.), *The Effective Use of Market Research* (London: Staples, 1971), pp. 144-60.

19. Kraushar, *New Products and Diversification*, p. 136.

20. Midgley, *Innovation and New Product Marketing*, pp. 228-35.

21. E.g. Rehorn, 'Product Tested — What Then?', *European Research*, vol. 2, no. 3 (1974).

22. Baker and McTavish, *Product Policy and Management*, p. 145.

23. I have dealt with the development of advertising and its testing elsewhere in some detail — see Foxall, *Strategic Marketing Management*, pp. 111-28. The development of brand strategy is admirably discussed in a number of texts, e.g. Bureau, J., *Brand Management* (London: Macmillan, 1981). On the subject of brand names and the considerations involved therewith, see Kraushar, *New Products and Diversification*, Chapter 11, and Collins, L., 'A Name to Conjure With', *European Journal of Marketing*, vol. 11, no. 5 (1977), pp. 340-63.

24. Cooper, R.G., 'Introducing Successful New Industrial Products', *European Journal of Marketing*, vol. 10, no. 6 (1976), pp. 299-329.

25. Sands, 'Test Marketing: Can it be Defended?', p. 8.

26. Urban and Hauser, *Design and Marketing*, p. 419.

27. Cadbury, N.D., 'When, Where and How to Test Market', *Harvard Business Review*, vol. 53, no. 3 (1975), pp. 96-105.

28. Nuttall, G., 'Pouring Money into the Wash', *Marketing* (29 July 1982), p. 22.

29. Tidsall, P., 'Chocolate Soldiers Clash', *Marketing* (29 July 1982), p. 34.

30. Tauber, E.M., 'Forecasting Sales Prior to Test Market', *Journal of Marketing*, vol. 41, no. 1 (1977), pp. 82-3.

31. Ibid., pp. 83-4.

32. Ibid.

33. E.g. ASSESSOR: Silk, A.J. and Urban, G.L., 'Pre-test Market Evaluation of New Packaged Goods: A Model and Measurement Methodology', *Journal of Marketing Research*, vol. 15, no. 2 (1978), pp. 171-91; LTM: Goldberg, R., 'Basic Description of the Estimating Process for the Laboratory Test Market' (New York: Yankelovich, Skelly and White, 1973); COMP: Burger, P.C., Gundee, H. and Lavide, R., 'COMP: A Comprehensive System for the Evaluation of New Products' in Wind, Y., Mahajan, V. and Cardozo, R.N. (eds), *New-Product Forecasting* (Lexington, Mass.: Lexington Books, 1981), pp. 269-83.

34. Silk and Urban, 'Pre-test Market Evaluation of New Packaged Goods'.

35. Ibid.

36. Urban and Hauser, *Design and Marketing of New Products*, p. 403.

37. Goldberg, R., 'Basic Description of the Estimating Process for the Laboratory Test Market'.

38. See, for a valuable assessment of available pre-test forecasting models: Robinson, P.J., 'Comparison of Pre-Test-Market New-Product Forecasting Models' in Wind, Mahajan and Cardozo, *New-Product Forecasting*, pp. 181-204.

39. Assmus, G., 'NEWPROD: The Design and Implementation of a New Product Model', *Journal of Marketing*, vol. 39, no. 1 (1975), pp. 16-23.

40. Levine, J., 'Pre-Test-Market Research of New Packaged-Goods Products – A User Orientation' in Wind, Mahajan and Cardozo, pp. 285-90.

41. E.g. Fourt, L.A. and Woodlock, J.W., 'Early Prediction of Market Success for New Grocery Products', *Journal of Marketing*, vol. 25, no. 4 (1960), pp. 31-8; Parfitt, J.H. and Collins, B.J.K., 'Use of Consumer Panels for Brand Share Prediction', *Journal of Marketing Research*, vol. 5, no. 2 (1968), pp. 131-45; Massy, W.F., 'Forecasting the Demand for New Convenience Products' (STEAM), *Journal of Marketing Research*, vol. 6, no. 4 (1969), pp. 405-12; Urban, G.L., 'SPRINTER Mod III: A Model for the Analysis of New Frequently Purchased Consumer Products', *Operations Research*, vol. 18, no. 4 (1970), pp. 805-54; Eskin, G.J., 'Dynamic Forecasts of New Product Demand Using a Depth of Repeat Model', *Journal of Marketing Research*, vol. 10, no. 2 (1973), pp. 115-29; BBDO International Inc., 'How to Predict New Product Success' (NEWS) (Unpublished, n.d.); Blattberg, R. and Golanty, J., 'TRACKER: An Early Test-Market Forecasting and Diagnostic Model for New Product Planning', *Journal of Marketing Research*, vol. 15, no. 2 (1978), pp. 192-202.

42. Narasimhan, C. and Sen, S.K., 'Test-Market Models for New-Product Introduction' in Wind, Mahajan and Cardozo, *New-Product Forecasting*, pp. 293-321.

43. Ibid.

44. Dodson, J.A., 'Application and Utilisation of Test-Market-Based New-Product Forecasting Models' in Wind, Mahajan and Cardozo, *New-Product Forecasting*, pp. 411-21.

45. E.g. Mahajan, V. and Muller, E., 'Innovation Diffusion and New-Product Growth Models in Marketing', *Journal of Marketing*, vol. 43, no. 4 (1979), pp. 55-68; Bass, F.M., 'A New-Product Growth Model for Consumer Durables', *Management Science*, vol. 15, no. 1 (1969), pp. 215-27; Midgley, D.F., 'A Simple Mathematical Theory of Innovative Behaviour', *Journal of Consumer Research*, vol. 3, no. 1 (1976), pp. 31-41; Roa, V.R., 'New-Product Sales Forecasting Using the Hendry System' in Wind, Mahajan and Cardozo, *New-Product Forecasting*, pp. 499-527; Lawrence, K.D. and Lauton, W.H., 'Applications of Diffusion Models: Some Empirical Results' in Wind, Mahajan and Cardozo, *New-Product Forecasting*, pp. 529-41.

46. Urban and Hauser, *Design and Marketing of New Products*, pp. 408-11.

47. Engel and Blackwell, *Consumer Behaviour*, p. 409.

48. Cooper, 'Introducing Successful New Industrial Products', pp. 326-9.

49. Robertson, A. and Fox, M., 'A Study in "Real Time" of the Innovation Process in Two Science-based Companies' in Baker (ed.), *Industrial Innovation*, p. 309.

50. E.g. McTavish, R., *A Study of Selected Problems of the Evolutionary Cycle of Highly Technical New Capital Goods* (Glasgow: University of Strathclyde, unpublished Ph.D. Thesis, 1974). See also the reports of Project SAPPHO cited in Chapter 4.

51. Robertson and Fox, 'A Study in "Real Time"', p. 310.

52. Buttle, F., 'Test Marketing: Go National or Go Broke?', *Management Decision*, vol. 14, no. 1 (1976), pp. 25-34.

53. Bucknell, R.W., 'The Product Timing "Window"', *Industrial Marketing* (May 1982), pp. 62-4.

54. Ibid., p. 64.

# PART FOUR

# CONCLUSION

# 11 MARKETING, INNOVATION AND STRATEGY

## Corporate Strategy and Strategic Marketing

Economic innovation is valued in most societies as a means of securing a more productive industry and the material wellbeing which derives from it. But macroeconomic prescriptions for innovation-led economic growth have tended to ignore those facets of new product development which are bound up with the strategic and marketing-oriented competences which determine the performance and effectiveness of companies. Theoretical assumptions which relate innovation and growth, like prescriptions for state intervention in the innovative process, are generally based upon a definition of innovation which casts it as invariably discontinuous. But innovation is a process which includes continuous as well as discontinuous product development. Effective innovation occurs, moreover, as a function of corporate managements' perceptions of and responses to their strategic needs for innovation. Consideration of how best to stimulate innovation by extra-industrial means should await the empirical determination of the circumstances under which managers value innovation, their purposes in doing so, and the steps they take to ensure success.

This book has sought to draw attention to the need to understand more comprehensively and more deeply the strategic and marketing contexts in which innovation occurs. Clearly, innovation *per se* is not enough. The requirement, at both micro-and macro-economic levels, is for *effective* innovation. How far can governments and their agents assist in the delivery of effective innovation? A strong case has been made by several recent writers[1] for governments to support technical and managerial innovation and, where their economic activities impinge upon industry — as for instance in the procurement of hospital supplies — to pursue policies which enhance the scope for innovation throughout the supplying industries and thus indirectly improve the economic performance of other purchasers. Indeed, British governments would do well to reflect upon the more effective use which competitor nations make of their technological universities, and governments in general might well pursue more enlightened procurement policies. But more direct action cannot be so easily prescribed. When four or five of every six man-days devoted to R&D earn no return and when so many companies' managers see no commercial need to be innovative because they cannot or will not become more marketing-oriented or because innovation − of the more radical kind − is not for them a rational strategy, who can lay down specific guidelines for intervention by outsiders?

Effective innovation − the conceptualisation, creation, introduction and nurture of new products in ways which contribute to the attainment of corporate objectives − cannot be separated from the strategic positions and needs of actual companies. Unless managerial vision and alertness are exceptional, the incentive and rationale for innovation may well be reduced as those objectives are fulfilled. The capacity of successful companies to revise objectives and to adapt to the changing phases of the industrial innovative process appears to be in limited supply. Even when corporate goals are not being met or are, in the face of success, revised upwards, innovation is but one possible strategic response: acquisition or market penetration may present legitimate alternatives in specific circumstances. Before the broader concerns of macro-economic policy in relation to the stimulation of innovation can be realistically pursued, it is necessary to understand further the nature of corporate and marketing strategies and the corporate response to the industrial process of innovation described by, among others, Abernathy and Utterback. The remainder of this chapter reviews these closely related themes in the light of recent research and advances in thought. Its main purpose, however, is to indicate areas for further research which will extend further our understanding of corporate strategy. In particular, it is necessary to examine closely the relationships of innovation, strategy, marketing and entrepreneurship assumed in earlier chapters.

Corporate and marketing strategies are conceptually distinct areas of business management. The former is the responsibility of those top or general managers who are concerned for the long-term planning of the entire enterprise. Ansoff[2] speaks appropriately of 'the realisation that a firm needs a well-defined scope and growth direction, that objectives alone do not meet this need, and that additional decision rules are required if the firm is to have orderly and profitable growth. Such decision rules and guidelines have been broadly defined as *strategy* or, sometimes, as *the concept of the firm's business*.' The terms 'strategic marketing' and 'marketing strategy' refer to the fact that marketing management, which is a subset of the company's overall managerial activity, is a means to ends which are ultimately derived from the long-range plans and policies of the organisation. Marketing strategy is involved with matching profitably corporate offerings with buyer behaviour by means of the creation and exploitation of specific marketing mixes aimed at particular target markets.[3] Marketing strategy and marketing management are, therefore, consequences of the definition of the company's business by corporate policies and strategies; they do not, of themselves, determine what the firm's business is, what its purposes are, and how it shall seek to fulfil them. Marketing strategy is formulated and executed within the framework of corporate policies and chosen strategies constructed by top or general management. Effective management of corporate strategy naturally requires consultation with marketing (and other functional) managers and the participation of the marketing director. But corporate and marketing strategies remain harmonious yet conceptually separate.

They have, nevertheless, been frequently confused in the management literatures. Many marketing writers were, until recently, content to assume that the company which had adopted and implemented the 'marketing concept' had done as much as needed to be done about corporate policy and strategy. The bias is not all in the same direction, however. While business strategy analysts have come to ask the sorts of questions (with respect to the definition of markets and market segmentation) that have been central to marketing for decades, they have still not come fully to terms with the need for customer-orientation to pervade the operations of the whole enterprise. This tendency of managerial authors specialising in one area of business behaviour to make simplifying assumptions about another is perfectly understandable: to speak of the strategic behaviour of managers, to attempt to analyse and order it by establishing its regularities, and to try to 'explain' it is to impose layers of abstracted thought on observed reality. Actual behaviour is seldom as orderly, regular and predictable as science tries to make it; though general and marketing managers have numerous separate functions and responsibilities, their work and roles have much in common. Especially in the pro-active, marketing-oriented, innovative company, their objectives and strategic concerns are interactive, though their temporal horizons may differ significantly. It is usually possible to improve upon the earliest theoretical formulations produced in any area of scientific endeavour; indeed few theories are so sophisticated as to raise fewer problems than the number of solutions they offer. Moreover, because of the constraining assumptions they employ, theories apply to rather specific aspects of behaviour. Analysts of managerial action have, for instance, frequently found that orthodox microeconomics does not answer their needs because it was never intended to explicate such features of human behaviour as intrafirm decision-making. The incapacity of economic theory to cope with organisational complexity was one of the mainsprings of the development of behavioural theories of the firm.[4] These have also been limited in the scope of their applicability by the simplifying assumptions they make and their failure to deal adequately with *marketing* strategy and its place within the overall business organisation.

Anderson[5] proposes a general theory of the firm which is intended to overcome both (i) the blinkered approach to the organisational decision-making and managerial behaviour which is so often the result of a partisan perspective caused by the theorist's overconcern with the functional area of the firm that is his specialism, and (ii) the tendency to ignore major functional areas such as marketing which often characterises 'general' theories of corporate management. The essence of Anderson's approach is the observation that any given functional subsystem features strongly in the firm (acquires power, influences corporate strategy, appears prominent, and so on) to the extent that it contributes to the company's ability to negotiate successfully with its environment. Especially during periods in which environmental changes make new demands, affecting the way in which the firm obtains the resources and public responses it needs (labour, capital, customer patronage, governmental support, etc.), the particular function whose members have the skills to achieve acceptable exchanges between the firm and those groups which control the needed resources and responses comes to the fore. When production-orientation characterised many companies, the functional areas of production and finance were able to negotiate the exchange of the key resources required by companies and thus became prominent. As the external environment changed, compelling companies to adopt new orientations (salesorientation, followed by marketing-orientation), so different functions become powerful since they were needed to negotiate effective exchanges for the now essential resources. Thus the expansion of trade unions' power made resource demands upon the firm (for labour) which brought the personnel and industrial relations functions to the fore; the growth of competition, discretionary income, consumer sophistication and consumerism led subsequently to the development and acceptance of marketing-oriented management and, with it, the emergence to prominence of the marketing function. Nowadays, recession, customer power and state intervention in industry have increased the importance to the firm of having effective purchasing, legal and public relations functions. Thereby the prominence of the emergent function is assured. External coalitions thus impinge upon the organisation to achieve their own ends but those companies which are capable of making the appropriate response experience new jockeying for power among their internal constituencies: that functional area or constituency which contributes most to achievement of the desired position *vis-à-vis* the environmental coalition receives the greatest increase in status and power. While it remains in competition with other functional areas, its goals are the most likely to become the objectives of the entire organisation.[6] In this scenario, the promulgation of the marketing concept by the members of the marketing function appears less an altruistic or relatively disinterested activity of marketing managers who perceive that marketing-oriented management is an essential prerequisite of commercial success and more a political attempt by a single function to accumulate and/or consolidate its hold upon power and resources. Within the bargaining process which surrounds the development of corporate strategic plans, 'marketing considerations may not have a significant impact . . . unless marketers adopt a strong advocacy position within the firm'.[7] Marketing strategy consists, therefore, not simply in the identification of opportunities, market targeting and the production and delivery of marketing mixes which exploit those opportunities (topics recognised by any marketing text) but the negotiation with top management and the firm's other functional constituencies for leeway to pursue the opportunities selected. 'The conditional perspective suggests that marketing must take an active role in promoting its strategic options by demonstrating the survival value of a consumer orientation to the other internal coalitions . . . In the final analysis, the constituency model of the firm suggests that marketing's role in strategic planning must be that of a strong advocate for the marketing concept.'[8]

## Marketing-orientation and Innovative Strategy

Anderson's perspective on the firm is a prelude to a more useful theory rather than a theory in itself but it poses, nonetheless, interesting conceptual and practical problems which bear upon the relationship of marketing, innovation and strategy and which provide foci for further research into the new product development process. He and other authors have drawn attention to the tendency of many British and American companies to concentrate upon incremental product changes and short-term opportunities for profit rather than upon the development of more discontinuous innovations upon which long term corporate survival depends. Such companies may, according to these writers, appear to be marketing-oriented as a result of superficial observation of their emphasis upon customer research, attention to the minutiae of consumers' wants as manifest in continual minor product modification and improvement and use of such techniques as portfolio planning. Piercy[9] argues along similar lines that marketing managers are evincing 'cost and profit myopia', a condition whose symptoms include an obsession with short-term profit, risk-aversive defensive policies and the premature or unnecessary elimination of products which do not fulfil arbitrary, full-cost criteria of performance. The similarity of this view to the constituency approach to the theory of the firm is apparent from the following normative account of the role of marketing in the business organisation:

> The central point is that marketing does create profit, but not by cost accounting, penny pinching and bean counting. Marketing determines the potential for profit by managing demand and achieving sales volume targets. . . If marketing is seen as a department, then it should carry out specialised, differentiated tasks. Its role must be recognised as the management of the *demand* side of the business equation, leaving other specialist departments to fulfil their responsibilities. Of course, volume should not be pursued to the exclusion of all else, but marketing should concentrate on the management of volume, within the policies established by general management.[10]

Marketing should, however, lose the direct responsibility for profit with which it is so frequently invested.

Although the constituency-based view of marketing is persuasively argued, it raises at once some practical concerns. The analysis upon which the thesis rests might be accurate but might point to the necessity of *de-emphasising* short-term financial criteria in marketing rather than reorganising entire companies; the appropriate prescription may involve a change of degree rather than kind. Marketing is intimately concerned with price as an integral component of the marketing mix and thereby with revenue considerations: has it been shown that an entirely new place for marketing has to be found? Furthermore, volume can easily become obsessive and short-term an aim as profit and smacks of the sales-management orientation to business that dominated many managements from the 1920s to the 1950s and which relied heavily upon selling and promotional techniques to move the goods at all costs. Even if marketing were to be relieved of short-term financial responsibilities, suitable economic criteria would have still to be applied to it in order that its operations might be properly monitored and controlled. These issues provide plenty of scope for empirical analysis directed towards the rigorous testing of the constituency thesis.

There are, however, two more fundamental questions for the management and organisation of marketing, innovation and strategy which are raised by this line of thought. First, it is interesting that advocates of constituency-type approaches recommend that the changes they see as necessary should be brought about by the adoption of novel attitudes, behaviours and organisational forms *within the company*. 'The real difficulty,' writes Anderson,[11] 'lies in designing an internal performance measurement and reward system that balances the need for short run profitability against long-term survival.' Whereas many managers mistake their short-term obsession with consumer research and highly-continuous innovation with marketing-orientation, he argues that 'The marketing concept is essentially a state of mind or world view that recognises that firms survive to the extent that they meet the real needs of their customer coalitions' and it by communicating this to members of other functional areas that the marketing function will enhance its status and power in the firm. Similarly, Piercy believes that managers, through a process of self-appraisal, organisational evaluation and internal changes, can themselves transform the nature of marketing within their companies. These perceptions of the source and location of the prescribed changes is especially interesting given that it arises — notably in the former case, though by implication in the latter — out of consideration of the controlling role of the environment in the structure, organisation and behaviour of the firm. The constituency approach, it will be recalled, proposes that external coalitions of people and interests impinge upon the firm and bring certain of its internal coalitions to the fore: it is reasonable to assume, therefore, that in the absence of the external, contextual or environmental factors, internal change is unlikely to be seen as necessary or to occur spontaneously. Respective change within the company (such as a reorientation of managerial attitudes towards consumer wants) is, of course, a vital component of progress but, according to the central assumption of the constituency model, there must first be the requisite environmental conditions (e.g. strong consumerist pressures) to compel alert perceptive managers to react accordingly (e.g. by adopting a more consumer-oriented approach). Where external conditions are already such as to make the achievement of specific objectives contingent upon the adoption of appropriate attitudes, behavioural and organisational structures, the constituency theorists' advocacy of these internal changes may be relevant; where the contextual factors are not faced by a particular firm, such advocacy is likely to be both irrelevant and misunderstood.

The second fundamental issue raised by the constituency model is connected with the first but requires a rather different approach. It derives from the view that 'market-driven firms', those which react incrementally to any perceived change or unexploited opportunity in consumer behaviour which can be met by using existing technology, are not marketing-oriented. Anderson asserts that 'The real marketing concept divorces strategic thinking from an emphasis on contemporary technology and encourages investment in research and development with long-term payoffs.' The adoption and implementation of the marketing concept may well lead to such investment but to claim that it must do so, indeed that investment in technology for the long-term is a *sine qua non* of marketing-oriented management, comes close to production-orientation and technological determinism. It contradicts two statements made in the preceding chapters of this book. First, Chapter 8 noted Langrish's statement that effective innovation depends upon the coincidence of the development of technological means to fulfil customers' needs in a comparatively advantageous way. In other words, both market demand patterns and the technical means of supplying demand profitably must occur simultaneously in order for successful, customer-oriented innovation to occur. Companies which supply continuous innovations (e.g. producers of supermarket products) may be working at the frontiers of their technology and their only means of achieving comparative advantage may be through incremental innovation. Such firms are as innovative as they need to be, as customer-oriented as the market demands. Secondly, Chapter 4 pointed out that marketing-oriented management is itself a *response* to prevailing market conditions, notably competitive endeavours and the availability to potential buyers of discretionary income. All productive units, be they located in socialist, centrally planned or relatively open, decentralised economies, must carry out the functions of marketing, the assembly and delivery of the four P's. Marketing-orientation management is not universally-encountered, however, because it is a style of managerial response to the execution of the basic functions of marketing within specific environmental circumstances — those which result from a relatively high degree of customer sovereignty.[12] As such, marketing-orientation is the latest in a series of business perspectives: production-orientation, sales-management-orientation and marketing-orientation have provided a sequence of managerial styles, each suited to and appropriate for a given set of environmental conditions. Thus, *production-orientation* is a valid and predictable response to conditions of scarcity, where demand exceeds supply either throughout an economy or in a discrete product-market; consumers' discretionary income is likely under such circumstances to be small. Although it is common to find that production-orientation is strongly criticised in the marketing literature, it *may* be a legitimate response to prevailing conditions. While it deserves censure when it represents no more than the marketing myopia described by Levitt,[13] it is a predictable response among those companies which are temporarily sheltered from the vicissitudes of the marketplace, by, for example, patent rights, monopoly positions or similarly myopic competitors. As Baker[14] points out, ' . . . the much-despised production orientation with its emphasis upon manufacturing and volume of output may be the most appropriate to conditions of chronic under-supply' or, it may be added, to *any* conditions which do not compel a more consumer-oriented marketing outlook

Similarly, *sales-oriented management* is the requisite response to rather more affluent circumstances, in which there are fewer constraints on production and an understanding that high levels of sales volume are likely to contribute effectively to the attainment of corporate financial objectives. *Marketing-orientation* is itself no more than an appropriate response to a given market structure: high levels of intraindustrial competition, the capacity for supply to exceed demand and consumer affluence as manifested in a large measure of discretionary spending. The adoption and implementation of the marketing concept are by no means the altruistic acts implied by some marketing textbooks: they derive from the recognition that, under appropriate conditions, a particular form of attention to customer requirements is essential if the goals of the producer are to be achieved. Decentralised economies evince marketing-orientation as their characteristic managerial mode simply because they provide the structural conditions which compel this managerial mode. Such conditions do not characterise centralised economic systems and nor does customer-oriented marketing. But, even within privatised, decentralised economies the conditions which make marketing-orientation an appropriate response are far from universally encountered. This observation, fundamental as it is to the study of marketing, raises a number of issues in connection with delineation of the legitimate domain of marketing-oriented management. If some companies within the latter type of economy remain strategically reactive rather than proactive, it is because they do not face external conditions and coalitions which *compel* them to be more marketing-oriented. They are as customer-oriented as they need to be and, as long as market and other external circumstances do not force them to change, they may remain relatively reactive but effective in terms of the types of innovation required of them. The strategies of innovation they evince are entirely appropriate given the environments in which they operate. Naturally, if these environments become more competitive, if customers become more demanding, their survival and continued success will be contingent upon their accommo-dating strategically to altered conditions. But it would not be appro-priate to change the internal structure before the environment demands such change. Constituency theory appears to treat all companies as though they were proactive, existing in environments which made any other response untenable. As Chapter 3 pointed out, many firms are compelled to be more reactive: their characteristic pattern of internal strength and external opportunities makes such a response inevitable. The constituency model provides a useful way forward in explaining the nature of relationships between corporate strategy and strategic marketing; but the conclusions drawn by its authors with respect to the mainsprings and consequences of internal change appear to contradict the environmental emphasis of much of their analysis.

## *Innovation and Strategy: Directions for Research*

The constituency model of the firm presents many opportunities for theoretical and empirical research. Some of these were mentioned briefly above. Obviously the theory itself, as it develops, must be constructed in such a way as to enable its explanations and predictions to be put to empirical test and this will involve a more satisfactory treatment of the connection between managerial behaviour and organisational structure on the one hand and the external environment upon which they are contingent on the other. The next section of this chapter, which is concerned with innovation and organisation, returns to this theme. In the meantime, two research needs which are cognate to the preceding chapters deserve mention.

First, there is the need for positive (as opposed to normative) study of new product strategy. Most textbook accounts of strategy formula-tion depict it as a rational, sequential matter, based upon compre-hensive exploration for and of information and evaluation thereof on the basis of clear-cut criteria. Chapter 6 pointed out that this is rarely if ever descriptive of buyers' decision-making: nor is it of managerial decision-making. So formalised a depiction of managerial decision-making as the familiar: (i) goal clarification, (ii) determination of all means to attaining goals, (iii) examination and evaluation of all consequences of using these means, and (iv) selection of the most appropriate means of achieving the specified goals, may have limited theoretical uses but is of little value as a guide to actual managerial practice.[15] Lindblom's account of strategic decision-making as 'the science of muddling through' was reviewed in that chapter but it may be worth summarising here, by quotation, his thoughts on this area of managerial behaviour:

> Conventional rational decision making is . . . in fact not just difficult, it is strictly speaking, impossible. And, if it could be made practical, it would, for complex problems, reach decisions too late to be useful. For complex choices, it is never literally possible to follow the four prescriptions of conventional rationality. For a complex problem it is never possible to be clear about all the values affected by a decision, including their relative weights, never possible in fact to ascertain *all* possible means of achieving the objective, never possible exhaustively to trace through the chain of consequences that are attached to each possible means of achieving the objective . . .
> The conventionally scientific model of decision-making tells how to go about making a completely analysed decision. A strategic model would tell how to go about making an incompletely analysed decision. Since, for complex problems, decisions cannot be completely analysed, the latter model, if it can be developed, gives guidance where the first does not . . . To reduce the policy alternatives down to a manageable number, an extremely common practice is to restrict consideration to those policies that are only incrementally different from existing policies in effect.[16]

Students of marketing strategy are frequently aware that the conventional notion of decision-making is inadequate for their purposes but, as we have seen, the development of an alternative has been slow. Research is required which makes clear the consequences of strategic decision-making as it is actually practised upon marketing generally and corporate innovation in particular.

Secondly, the role of buying in the entrepreneurial and innovative processes requires research attention. Chapter 3 introduced this theme. Turnbull and Cunningham[17] point out that

A closer need exists for purchasing strategies to be more fully integrated into corporate plans. By doing so, a company can derive the
maximum cost benefits from its purchasing decision and can also
achieve greater security of supplies. . . . [Yet] what is rarely discussed is the contribution of purchasing to the achievement of
company performance and profit objectives.

This is true both in industry and among academic researchers, and
points to an evident area of research which should have important consequences for our understanding both of the creation and adoption of
innovative goods and services.

## Organisation for Innovation

The orientation of this book towards viewing the new product development process primarily as a means of reducing uncertainty has pre-
cluded detailed consideration of the organisation of that intra-corporate
process. The possibilities for organising new product development have,
in any case, been the subject of comprehensive discussion and debate in
numerous textbooks and articles.[18] The major problem centres on the
question of who should be responsible for innovation and there are
arguments for and against product managers, new specialist product
managers, new product committees, venture teams, and so on.[19] Discussion of organisation for innovation within the firm has also included
consideration of the nature and role of leadership,[20] and the problems
of communication both within R&D departments[21] and between R&D
and marketing personnel.[22] These issues are far from unimportant, but
no book on corporate innovation can cover all the themes of this vast
subject, and they have not been central to the issues that have been
examined.

What has been identified as crucially important within the present
context, however, is the design and use of organisations which are
appropriate to the generation of innovation at different stages of the
industry-wide process of innovation described in Chapter 2. The emergence of a new technology and the effective marketing of the discontinuous innovations which derive from it usually involves a flexible,
relatively unstructured form of organisation, though it is, to be
accurate, usually associated with little formal organisation at all. Once
the dominant product design emerges, however, and further innovation
is of a more continuous kind, more formalised production and market-

ing procedures become necessary and more stable and predictable organisational structures become apparent. Whereas at the beginning of the industrial innovative process, there was no scope for companies to employ an essentially reactive strategy, at the post-dominant-design stage, such a strategy is more appropriate for companies whose resource base allows them to be relatively imitative or specialised. The problem with industries which have reached this point is to ensure that the more radical innovation of which foreign competitors facing different technological, product-market, and cultural conditions – are capable, are forthcoming at home. The macroeconomic need is to encourage companies in such industries to adopt more proactive strategies and to build the appropriate form of organisation to go with it; the chief problem occurs at the micro level of analysis where managements may not perceive the need to pursue a more proactive policy.

Several approaches to the study of organisational behaviour are available,[23] but that framework of analysis which appears most suitable for the study of organisations' adaption to their environments and which, therefore, harmonises well with the approach to strategy and organisation discussed above, is a form of contingency theory. Greenwood and Hinings[24] describe this as 'a theory that rests on the assumption that organisational characteristics have to be shaped to meet situational circumstances. The theory implies that the extent to which an organisation secures a "goodness of fit" between situational circumstances and structural characteristics will determine the level of organisational performance.' And they quote Child[25] who writes that contingency theory 'regards the design of an effective organisation as necessarily having to be adapted to cope with the "contingencies" which derive from the circumstances of environment, technology, scale, resources and other factors in the situation in which an organisation is operating'. The importance of this approach in the discussion of the industrial innovative process is that it signals the abandonment of the search for the 'one right' form of organisational structure for effective innovation. The quest for the unique, universally-applicable structure of organisation and management goes back at least as far as such management thinkers as Taylor, Urwick and Fayol. It is still apparent in the debate over who should be responsible for new product development, though contingency theory stresses that 'different approaches to organisational design are conducive to high performance, depending on whether the environment in which the organisation is operating is variable and complex in nature, or stable and simple' . . .[26]

Two pioneers of the contingency approach, Burns and Stalker[27] argued persuasively on the basis of their empirical work that the appropriate form of management organisation and behaviour for a company operating in a variable and complex environment was relatively 'organic', while that suited to an organisation whose environment was stable and simple was relatively 'mechanistic'. ('Appropriate' and 'suited' refer to the capacity of the organisational form to facilitate the achievement of the economic goals of the firm.) Companies whose products, markets and technological bases are highly dynamic are more likely to perform satisfactorily or better if they are organised in such a way as to encourage the formation of flexible, task-oriented work groups, flexible communications, the absence of formal rules and to attract highly-qualified personnel; pharmaceutical companies, for instance, are likely to benefit from this style of 'organic' organisation. Companies whose products, markets and technologies are relatively stable, however, are more likely to achieve their performance objectives if they are organised more hierarchically, with essentially vertical communications' systems; a plant which manufactures standard industrial components for a distribution company might benefit from such a 'mechanistic' form of organisation. Burns and Stalker and other analysts of organisational structure and behaviour who adopt a broadly-based contingency approach have investigated the relationships of a number of environmental (e.g. competitive dynamics of the market), corporate (e.g. size, policy) and technological (e.g. mass vs. batch production) variables and organisational structure in order to establish the general assumption of contingency noted above.[28] The relatively mechanistic organisation is, moreover, particularly appropriate in the case of businesses which are pursuing essentially reactive strategies in stable or at least well-known environments, perhaps towards the end of the industrial innovative process; the firm which is pursuing a proactive strategy in a dynamic and uncertain environment, notably during the early phases of the innovative process (up until the emergence of a dominant product design) requires an organisational structure which conforms much more closely to the organic ideal type. The requirement for both types of company is not simply for more marketing-oriented managerial attitudes and intentions − though these may help − but for the most suitable organisational design to operationalise this orientation in the circumstances in which the firm finds itself.[29]

While this prescription is easy to make, however, the realisation of appropriate organisation in practice is notoriously difficult. In particular, it has proved difficult for companies which have adopted the organisational forms suitable for product development at the late stages of the industry innovative process to engage in the radical innovative activities necessary for the long-term survival of themselves, their industries and, ultimately, the economies in which they operate. It is true, as noted earlier in this chapter that an effective reactive company which is well-accommodated to supplying the wants of the market it serves (e.g. the second-but-better type) may be as customer-oriented as it need be; but if a whole industry comes to be dominated by comparatively reactive organisations (from the purely imitative to the responsive), the very lack of proactive organisations in the industry must spell its eventual decline. But companies which have adjusted organisationally and strategically to the demands of the late stages of the innovative process have usually acquired an internally-oriented, bureaucratic or mechanistic structure which precludes proactive management. Even when managers appreciate the need for discontinuous new products, the organisations they administer prevent the instigation of a more proactive strategic orientation. A noteworthy attempt at overcoming this organisational lethargy is 'venture management' which seeks to exploit the advantages for radical innovation of the organic type of structure. Venture management has been employed in some organisations with success[30] but its overall success rate is no higher than that for new product development as a whole.[31] The role of the individual entrepreneur or 'product champion'[32] is easily overlooked in discussions of the appropriate *organisation* of new product development. Furthermore, the need to see the entrepreneurial process as involving buyers and users as well as producers and marketers (which was discussed in Chapter 4) must be borne in mind. The overall problem is that to which contingency theory addresses itself: the determination of the most suitable form of organisation for the accomplishment of acceptable performance in the objective task, given the circumstances of environment, technology and strategy in which the firm operates. Organic organisation is not appropriate to all kinds of innovation. Table 11.1 suggests the degree of organisational change and flexibility that should accompany various types of continuous and discontinuous innovation. Contingency theory provides a valuable perspective on organisational form and effectiveness which is frequently overlooked in marketing where the anxiety to prescribe panaceas for managerial action tends to predominate over the need to provide situation-specific remedies. The contingency approach is more complex than the above discussion suggests but there are signs that it is having a growing impact upon marketing thought and analysis.[33] But there remain two urgent research needs. The first concerns the requirements that specialists in

Table 11.1: Innovation and Organisation

| | Scale of innovation | Appropriate organisational change |
|---|---|---|
| Type 1 | Present product<br>Present technology<br>Present market | This is a product improvement and can be easily accommodated within the existing organisation. |
| Type 2 | New product<br>Present technology<br>Present market | Can again be developed within the existing organisation with the formation of a new project team in the R&D department. |
| Type 3 | Present product<br>Present technology<br>New market | Again, existing organisation more or less maintained. Marketing must learn the idiosyncracies of new customers and perhaps a new sales team will be formed. |
| Type 4 | New product<br>Present technology<br>New market | In this case, a new product group might be established, staffed primarily by R&D and marketing personnel. Manufacturing can still be done in company's existing department. Conventional firms might simply form new R&D project and sales teams. |
| Type 5 | New product<br>New technology<br>Present market | Again, a new product group might be established but staffed primarily by R&D and manufacturing personnel. Group may utilise the firm's existing marketing and sales department. |
| Type 6 | New product<br>New technology<br>New market | Represents a new business to the company. A completely new business organisation (new venture company) might be established or a new division formed within the existing organisation. |

Source: Rothwell, R., 'From Invention to New Business via the New Venture Approach', *Management Decision*, vol. 13, no. 1 (1975), p. 17. Used by permission of MCB Publications Ltd.

organisational behaviour clarify the relationship between environmental and other contextual variables on the one hand and organisational structure on the other. The correlations of these variables obtained thus far suggest a far from determinative relationship. The simplistic context → structure → behaviour → performance model is clearly in need of refinement. As Child[34] points out, more than one organisational form may be appropriate for a given environment and strategic management is, in any case, required to perceive the need for changes in organisational structure to fit the environment and can, in some cases, select, act upon and modify the environment in which the firm performs. The second need is for research within the marketing discipline to determine the extent of the usefulness of this approach to the development of strategically-appropriate innovations. The importance of this research is apparent from the fact that the extent to which marketing managers are able to exert influence upon the development of effective innovations will depend upon their capacity to demonstrate that the concept of marketing-oriented management is more than the professional ideology of an interested intrafirm coalition.

## Final Summary and Conclusions

Business strategy is concerned with the unknowable.[35] Part Three of this book considered the new product development process as a means of reducing uncertainty. It is clear that to study new product development is to study diversity: the tendency of marketing analysts to put forward what they claim to be the unique solution to the problem of corporate innovative strategy is shown by such study to be founded upon rather simplistic reasoning. Any generalisation about corporate innovation requires qualification. The very term 'innovation' is capable of many meanings and whether a company seeks relatively continuous or relatively discontinuous innovations is contingent upon the strategic adjustment its managers are able to make to its environment. This environment includes its customers and competitors; their needs and behaviours reflect, in turn, the stage the generic product has reached in its life cycle and thus the phase of the industrial innovative process. Strategies vary — partly in response to this cycle and process — from extremely reactive to aggressively proactive and any of the strategic modes introduced in Chapter 3 (with the exception of those which are entirely imitative) may represent an appropriate customer-oriented accommodation to the market place. But that market place is dynamic, subject to the changing demands of buyers and to entrepreneurial attempts to fulfil those demands; the changing market place thus necessitates a strategic vigilance and managerial willingness to adapt to or perhaps modify the environment in order to retain the marketing-oriented strategy upon which survival and effectiveness depend. It is easy enough to specify these requirements of management but difficult to prescribe the role or determine the efficiency of the marketing strategy which would fulfil them. Indeed, marketing management remains the area of corporate innovation in which uncertainty and risk are most emphatically encountered, while marketing-oriented management, some decades after the phrase became widespread, is still an enigmatic element in business strategy.

Marketing is by no means generally recognised as the area in which most of the risk of product development is found. Rather, any additional resources are usually allocated to technical research and development because that is the area in which risks are perceived. However, on the basis of their empirical investigations of industrial innovation, Mansfield *et al.*[36] have concluded that the technical risks of innovation are overestimated both in analysis and policy-making. 'This conclusion,' they write, 'has several implications, one being that some of the models that are used to characterise private research and development in the civilian sector — models that suppose that the bulk of this work is very risky, far out work aimed at really major innovations — are misconceived and perhaps misleading.' Not only are the greatest costs of new product development incurred by the procedures concerned with commercialisation, the highest levels of risk are also encountered in new product marketing. Cooper's most recent analysis of his survey data on corporate innovation[37] confirm the results of the research reviewed in Chapter 4. In particular, he writes that

> no direct link was found between R&D spending and the effectiveness of firms' new product programmes. Success, failure and 'kill' rates were not at all tied to R&D inputs. While R&D spending did result in more sales by new products, the relationship was not linear, certainly until a threshold level of spending was attained. Moreover, while more R&D obviously leads to more new product sales, it did so in an inefficient manner: there were rapidly diminishing returns to R&D spending.[38]

The reduction of commercial risk requires that new developmental work be concentrated upon projects which promise continuous products. Companies other than those which habitually pursue highly proactive strategies, are likely to embrace innovative opportunities which resemble those whose exploitation has previously resulted in effective new products. Observation of corporate innovation indicates that 'the single largest producer of new product risk is a lack of synergy between the new business and the old; and if risk reduction is the objective, the firm is wise to seek compatible projects in terms of financial, managerial, marketing and technical resources'.[39] High technology and discontinuous projects and those designed for dynamic markets are an anathema to all but a few companies since they lack the resources to develop and use strategies which can cope with the uncontrollable environments which surround such projects. As Part Two illustrated, buyer behaviour is situation-specific and many companies have not come to terms with accommodating their internal innovative processes to its unpredictability. This again represents a reason for pursuing cautious continuous product developments in most cases.

Part Three emphasised that the earliest decisions of the new product development process must be made in the general absence of useful information. Screening and business analyses are essentially negative procedures (Chapter 9). Even after the firm has made a commitment to a project, usable information becomes available, if at all, only late in the process when decisions with respect to the investment of major resources have been made (Chapter 10). Even that information is far from comprehensive and its value in forecasting is limited. It relates in any case to the most continuous of products, fast-moving consumer goods. Innovative successes need to be sufficiently lucrative to compensate for the several failures experienced for every effective new product. The formal, systematic procedures used by some firms to achieve higher than average success rates have not yet been shown to be generalisable. But to draw these conclusions is to be realistic rather than pessimistic: strategy, as has been stated, is about the unknowable; it involves decision-making under conditions of partial ignorance rather than knowledge which permits optimisation. Even the research reviewed in Chapter 4 in connection with identifying the components of marketing-oriented innovation has been strongly criticised,[40] while low market share (see Chapter 3) is not necessarily a barrier to high profitability — a fact which complicates portfolio planning considerably.[41] Strategic analysts should celebrate uncertainty as central to their interests rather than show surprise that it is so widespread. What is important is that marketing research has advanced rapidly during the last decade and shows signs of continuing to do so. Thus, it is unreasonable to ignore the complexities and uncertainties which characterise corporate innovation but reasonable to be hopeful.

## Innovating the Future

A major purpose of this book has been to make a case for greater understanding of the complexities of the new product development process in the firm. A greater appreciation of the actual nature of this process is essential for at least two reasons. Innovation is a social value of immense proportions: it is widely believed that economic progress and wellbeing depend uniquely upon the creation and exploitation of new industrial products and processes. So strong is this value that the contribution of innovation to social, economic and physical outcomes which are not valued, e.g. pollution, is frequently ignored. Innovation is in such demand that the intervention of governments in the industrial system in order to promote the emergence of more new products and processes is now a part of the manifesto, policy and practice of all major political parties. The assumption behind this acceptance of central intervention is that governments can see and do what managers and investors cannot: the way to a more successful and enjoyable material future. Although there are different emphases to be found among those who advocate state intervention in industry for the purpose of expediting innovation, they have one thing in common. By and large, they share this with advocates of non-intervention. It is a failure to appreciate the nature of innovation at the level of the firm and, sometimes, at the level of the industry.

A greater understanding of the nature of innovation is required also by marketing managers and marketing academics. The former are often too close to the problems and excitement of the new product development process to assess the outcomes of their actions. High new product failure rates are not the responsibility of marketing managers alone but more effective innovation cannot be achieved unless marketing managers first stand back and examine the process of which they are a part in order to return to it and improve it. Marketing academics have sought to do this for them, producing prescriptions and techniques which promise to be universally applicable, textbooks which describe the 'one right or best way' of approaching new product development, and courses which teach the value of 'marketing-oriented management' and the 'principles of marketing' without critically assessing why the marketing conept might be valid and the circumstances in which both the marketing philosophy of business and marketing principles might apply. To do so would be to limit marketing as a discipline but to establish the sphere of applicability of marketing knowledge and principles would represent a considerable gain for the discipline and for marketing practice. The achievement of this requires a rather different approach to the teaching and researching of marketing phenomena from that fostered by the majority of institutions of higher education whose charter, academic product and technology encourage a production-oriented approach to business education. Indeed, it may well be that the innovative development of marketing itself requires quite different organisational forms from those encountered in the typical university or polytechnic: the mechanistic structure may have advantages for the more mature subjects whose purpose and paradigm are more straightforward and predictable but emerging disciplines undoubtedly require the freedom and flexibility engendered by a more organic structure.[42]

A second major purpose of this book has been to make clear the nature of innovation and the process which produces it. Those who value innovation, including politicians, macroeconomic commentators, managers and their customers, tend usually to think in terms of the creation of discontinuities. In one respect, they may be correct for new products and processes often require discontinuous changes in technology or production systems. These production-related discontinuities have important consequences for the efficiency and profitability of companies and perhaps for the achievement of macroeconomic objectives such as employment and price stability. These outcomes and their causes are obviously important. But the innovations which deliver the most valuable consequences both for companies and economies are those which are discontinuous in market- and marketing-related terms, those which are disruptive of customer behaviour. Major innovations in this respect are comparatively rare, however. Most companies, most of the time, are involved in continuous new product development. The new product development process as a means of reducing uncertainty is unable to deliver the informational goods sufficiently early to encourage many managements to risk the production and commercialisation of more discontinuous items. There must clearly be greater concentration upon the need to carry out the function of continuous innovation more effectively but the direct intervention of government in this appears unlikely to improve matters. It is the managers whose interests lie in improved innovative performance who must be encouraged to develop the entrepreneurial alertness required for this task, for it is unlikely that governments can be expected to develop and make practical use of such alertness at the level of the firm where it is required or exceed new product managers in their ability to forecast the market performance of new products. Furthermore, much can be accomplished by way of improving the management of innovation by means of more appropriate training of managers and technologists. The knowledge upon which improvement of the innovative process depends can be taught; much of it is available but is only now emerging within the research and training programmes of business schools. Take, for instance, the emerging importance of the buyer's role in industrial innovation. Neglect of demand-pull has been identified as a major contributor to the failure of the Advanced Passenger Train, while attention to this factor was an important component in the success of the more continuous High-Speed Train developed by the same organisation.[43]

Similarly, British and West German machine tool manufacturers differ not only in innovative performance but in terms of the quality and quantity of their relationships with machine tool purchase and in terms of the role of the latter in the product development process.[44] Evidently managers have either too little time to investigate such matters or too little recognition of the need to do so and there exists a clear opportunity for business schools to undertake on a larger scale the necessary research and training. Government's role, if any, in the process could, accordingly, be directed towards the encouragement of such research and training. The more discontinuous the desired innovation, the more probable it is that new organisational forms and structures will be necessary to produce it. As the traditional university structure may be inappropriate for the kind of management research and education now required by our industrial system, so traditional industry may present unsuitable organisation contexts for the development of discontinuous innovation. It is possible, however, that higher education and industry may solve their organisational problems symbiotically. The British Government's reduction in its expenditure on higher education which has had major consequences for such university institutions as Aston, Bradford, Salford and the University of Manchester Institute of Science and Techology is, from the point of view of those who value industrial innovation, wrongheaded. But, if this move results in the establishment of genuinely technological universities,[45] the result may be a collaboration between industry and education which makes possible a more organically-organised approach to idea generation, product testing and the commercialisation of new products.

The tendency of so many companies to pursue continuous innovation, however, is understandable in view of what has been said about general corporate strategy. Strategy is, in part, a function of the market environment in which the company operates and that context is not entirely controllable by managements. Moreover, the resource base of the firm, which similarly influences its dominant strategic mode, cannot be changed dramatically in the short run. Reactive or proactive strategies represent, therefore, appropriate corporate accommodations to the internal and external demands made upon the company. It is inappropriate to expect a firm whose appropriate strategy is relatively reactive and which accordingly produces relatively continuous new products to switch to the proactive pursuit of discontinuous innovation in the absence of changed environmental conditions even if managerial awareness of the need to innovate is revamped. Marketing-orientation itself cannot be expected to emerge in the absence of a more demanding competitive environment as well as the development by managers of more effective strategies for putting that orientation into effect. More fundamentally, there may well emerge a need for marketing managers and academics to see the marketing concept as a professional ideology rather than a universal truth and to seek its replacement by a more suitable philosophy of the required match between a company and its environment. Advances in the contribution of marketing thought and management to the achievement of more effective innovation — and, thereby, in the status of marketing within the company of the future — will depend increasingly upon the development of a more satisfactory understanding of how marketing is related to strategy, to entrepreneurship, to organisation and to innovative customer behaviour. One approach is through recognition and analysis of the situational determinants of appropiate managerial responses and the reduction in emphasis on the search for general marketing principles. Another is to re-evaluate the suitability of managerial techniques based upon the search for 'optimal' solutions to problems and to concentrate upon the nature of the uncertain decision environments of executives. At present, as a philosophy of business or even of the marketing function, the 'marketing concept' promises far more than its adherents can deliver. To that extent, *all* marketing is, and looks like remaining, *test* marketing.

## Notes

1. See Chapter 2.
2. Ansoff, H.I., *Corporate Strategy* (London: Penguin, 1968), p. 90.
3. Kevin, R.A. and Peterson, R.A. *Strategic Marketing Problems* (Boston, Mass: Alleyn and Bacon, 1978) p. 3.
4. E.g. Cyert, R.M. and March, J.G., *A Behavioural Theory of the Firm* (Englewood Cliffs, N.J.: Prentice-Hall, 1963); Pfeffer, J. and Salancik, G.R., *The External Control of Organisations* (New York: Harper and Row, 1978).
5. Anderson, P.F., 'Marketing, Strategic Planning and the Theory of the Firm', *Journal of Marketing*, vol. 46, no. 2 (1982), pp. 15-26.
6. The idea that a function's status varies with its capacity to help the organisation visibly to cope with external coalitions derives from: Hickson, D.J., Hinings, C.R., Lee, C.A., Schneck, R.E. and Pennings, J.M., 'A Strategic Contingencies' Theory of Intra-organisational Power', *Administrative Science Quarterly*, vol. 16, no. 2 (1971), pp. 216-29. See also: Slancik, G.R. and Pfeffer, J., 'Who Gets Power — And How They Hold on to It: A Strategic-Contingency Model of Power', *Organisational Dynamics* (Winter, 1977).
7. Anderson, 'Marketing, Strategic Planning and the Theory of the Firm', p. 23.

8. Ibid., p. 24.

9. Piercy, N., 'Cost and Profit Myopia in Marketing: Strengthen Your Marketing Department by Reducing its Profit Responsibility', *Quarterly Review of Marketing*, vol. 7, no. 4 (1982), pp. 1-12.

10. Piercy, N., 'Marketers' New Myopia', *Marketing* (20 May 1982), p. 37.

11. Anderson, 'Marketing, Strategic Planning and the Theory of the Firm', p. 24.

12. The following is based upon Foxall, G.R., 'Marketing's Domain', *European Journal of Marketing*, vol. 18 (forthcoming, 1984).

13. Levitt, T., 'Marketing Myopia', *Harvard Business Review*, vol. 38, no. 4 (1960), pp. 45-56.

14. Baker, M.J. (ed.), *Marketing: Theory and Practice* (London: Macmillan, 1976), pp. 4-9.

15. Lindblom, C.E., *Strategies for Decision Making* (Urbana, Illinois: Department of Political Science, University of Illinois, 1971), p. 4.

16. Ibid., pp. 6, 9.

17. Turnbull, P.W. and Cunningham, M.T., *International Marketing and Purchasing* (London: Macmillan, 1981) pp. 58-9.

18. E.g. Kotler, P., *Marketing Management* (Englewood Cliffs, N.J.: Prentice-Hall, 1980), pp. 313-5; Thomas, M.J., 'Product Managers: Catalysts for Innovation', *The Business Graduate*, vol. 12, no. 1 (1982) pp. 40-2; Tregoe, B.B. and Bentley, B., 'The New Strategic Manager: The Key to Innovation', *The Business Graduate*, vol. 12 (1982), pp. 33-6.

19. Among the analytical approaches see: Fast, N., 'Key Managerial Factors in New Venture Departments', *Industrial Marketing Management*, vol. 8, no. 3 (1979); Roberts, E.G., 'New Ventures for Corporate Growth', *Harvard Business Review*, vol. 58, no. 4 (1980); von Hippel, E., 'Successful and failing Internal Corporate Ventures: An Empircial Analysis', *Industrial Marketing Management*, vol. 6, no. 3 (1977). On the subject of ensuring the continuing of innovative organisation, see Jelinek, M., *Institutionalising Innovation* (New York: Praeger, 1979).

20. Robertson and Fox, 'A Study in "Real Time" of the Innovation Process in Two Science-based Companies', pp. 318-19.

21. Epton, S.R. 'Ten Years of R&D Management – Some Major Themes: The Role of Communciaton in R&D', *R&D Management*, vol. 11, no. 4 (1981), pp. 165-70.

22. Millman, A.F., 'Understanding Barriers to Product Innovation at the R&D/Marketing Interface', *European Journal of Marketing*, vol. 16, no. 5 (1982), pp. 22-34.

23. See, for instance: Lockett, M. and Spear, R. (eds.), *Organisations as Systems* (Milton Keynes: Open University Press, 1980).

24. Greenwood, R. and Hinings, C.R., 'Contingency Theories and Public Bureaucracies' in Pugh, D.R. and Hinings, C.R. (eds.), *Organisational Structure: Extensions and Replications* (Farnborough: Teakfield, 1976), p. 87.

25. Child, J., 'Strategies of Control and Organisational Behaviour', *Administrative Science Quarterly*, vol. 18, no. 1 (1973), pp. 1-17.

26. Bowey, A.M., 'Approaches to Organisation Theory', *Social Science Information*, vol. 11, no. 6 (1972), pp. 108-28.

27. Burns, T. and Stalker, G.M., *The Management of Innovation* (London: Tavistock, 1966).

28. See, among many others, Aiken, M. and Hage, J., 'The Organic Organisation and Innovation', *Sociology*, vol. 5, no. 1 (1971) pp. 63-82; Lawrence, P.R. and Lorsch, J.W., *Organisation and Environment* (Homewood, Illinois: Irwin, 1969); Woodward, J., *Industrial Organisation: Theory and Practice* (London: OUP, 1965).

29. 'Organic' organisation *per se* is not sufficient for all types of radical innovation. Hull and Hage suggest that it is appropriate for small-scale, high technology innovation: large scale, high technology firms require a modified structure. See Hull, F. and Hage, J., 'Organising for Innovation: Beyond Burns and Stalker's Organic Type', *Sociology*, vol. 16, no. 4 (1982), pp. 564-77.

30. Sweeting, R., 'Internal Venture Management: Analytical Aspects', *Journal of General Management*, vol. 7, no. 1 (1981), pp. 34-45. For an interesting account of a venture which failed, see Jones, W.H. and Oakley, M.H., 'A Case Study in Venture Management', *OMEGA*, vol. 7, no. 1 (1979), pp. 9-13.

31. Sweeting, 'Internal Venture Management', p. 34.

32. Rothwell, R., 'From Invention to New Business via the New Venture Approach', *Management Decision*, vol. 13, no. 1 (1975), pp. 10-21; 'Intracorporate Entrepreneurs', *Management Decision*, vol. 13, no. 3 (1975), pp. 142-54.

33. Weitz, B. and Anderson, E., 'Organising the Marketing Function' in Enis, B.E. and Roering, K.J. (eds.), *Review of Marketing 1981* (Chicago: American Marketing Association, 1981), pp. 134-42.

34. Child, J., 'Organisational Structure, Environment and Performance: The Role of Strategic Choice', *Sociology*, vol. 6, no. 1 (1972), pp. 1-22.

35. See especially Quinn, J.B., 'Managing Strategies Incrementally', *OMEGA*, vol. 10, no. 6 (1982), pp. 613-27.

36. Mansfield, F., *et al.*, *Research and Innovation in the Modern Corporation* (London: Macmillan, 1971), concluding chapter.

37. Cooper, R.G., 'New Product Success in Industrial Firms', *Industrial Marketing Management*, vol. 11, no. 3 (1982), pp. 215-23.

38. Ibid., p. 222.

39. Cooper, R.G., 'The Components of Risk in New Product Development: Project NewProd', *R&D Management*, vol. 11, no. 2 (1981), p. 49.

40. Mowery, D. and Rosenberg, N., 'The Influence of Market Demand upon Innovation: A Critical Review of Some Recent Empirical Studies', *Research Policy*, vol. 8, no. 2 (1979), pp. 702-53.

41. The various circumstances include: profitable low market share businesses in low growth markets; whose products change little over time; whose products are standardised and provide few if any extra services; whose products are industrial components or supplies that are infrequently purchased. See Woo, C.Y. and Cooper, A.C., 'The Surprising Case for Low Market Share', *Harvard Business Review*, vol. 60, no. 6 (1982), pp. 106-13. Cf. Allessio, H., 'Market-share Madness', *Journal of Business Strategy*, vol. 3, no. 2, (1982), pp. 76-9.

42. Foxall, G.R. and Driver, J.C., 'The Ends of Marketing Education', *Quarterly Review of Marketing*, vol. 8, no. 1 (1982). pp. 1-21.

43. Taylor, C.T., 'Railway Innovation and Uncertainty', *R&D Management*, vol. 12, no. 1 (1982), pp. 37-47.

44. Parkinson, S.T., 'The Role of the Buyer in Successful New Product Development', *R&D Management*, vol. 12, no. 3 (1982), pp. 123-31.

45. Ashworth, J., 'Reshaping Higher Education in Britain', *Journal of the Royal Society of Arts*, vol. 130, no. 5315, (1982), pp. 713-29.

# SUGGESTIONS FOR FURTHER READING

## Part One: Effective Innovation

The issues involved in the contributions made by industrial innovation to economic growth and material well-being and in the question of government intervention in the innovative process are thoroughly discussed in:

Carter, C. (ed.), *Industrial Policy and Innovation* (London: Heinemann, 1981);

Pavitt, K. (ed.), *Technical Innovation and British Economic Performance* (London: Macmillan, 1980); and

Rothwell, R. and Zegveld, W., *Industrial Innovation and Public Policy* (London: Frances Pinter, 1981).

Several useful papers on the process of innovation are collected in:

Tushman, M.L. and Moore, W.L. (eds.), *Readings in the Management of Innovation* (London: Pitman, 1982), Section I: 'Innovation Over Time'.

The subjects of Corporate strategy, entrepreneurship and marketing-oriented management are covered and their relationships explored in:

Henderson, B.D., *Henderson on Corporate Strategy* (Cambridge, Mass.: Abt Books, 1979);

Jain, S.C., *Marketing Planning and Strategy* (Cincinnati, Ohio: Southwestern, 1981), Parts One, Three and Four;

Lorange, P., *Corporate Planning* (Englewood Cliffs, N.J.: Prentice-Hall, 1980);

Minkes, A.L. and Foxall, G.R., 'Entrepreneurship, Strategy and Organisation', *Strategic Management Journal*, vol. 1, no. 4 (1980), pp. 295-301.

Minkes, A.L. and Foxall, G.R., 'The Bounds of Entrepreneurship: Interorganisational Relationships in the Process of Industrial Innovation', *Managerial and Decision Economics*, vol. 3, no. 1 (1982), pp. 41-7;

Rothwell, R., 'Policies in Industry' in Pavitt (ed.), *Technical Innovation and British Economic Performance*, pp. 299-309; and

272

Tushman and Moore (eds.), *Readings in the Management of Innovation*, Section III: 'Setting Strategy and Direction for Innovation'.

## Part Two: Innovative Buying

A critical approach to the study of consumer behaviour is contained in:
Foxall, G.R., *Consumer Choice* (London: Macmillan, 1983).

A useful summary of recent work by the 'invisible college of diffusion researchers' is provided in:
Rogers, E.M., 'New Product Adoption and Diffusion', *Journal of Consumer Research*, vol. 2, no. 4 (1976), pp. 290-301;

and a very wide range of themes and researches is addressed in:
Baker, M.J. (ed.), *Industrial Innovation* (London: Macmillan, 1979).

## Part Three: Corporate Innovation

Valuable accounts of the new product development process written by marketing practitioners are available in:
Kraushar, P.M., *New Products and Diversification* (London: Business Books, 1977); and
White, R., *Consumer Product Development* (London: Penguin, 1976).

The later stages of new product development receive excellent coverage in:
Twiss, B.C., *Managing Technological Innovation* (London: Longman, 1980).

See also
Sahal, D. (ed.), *Research Development and Technological Innovation* (Lexington, Mass.: Lexington Books, 1980).

Recent texts include:
Pessemier, E.A., *Product Management: Strategy and Organisation* (New York: Wiley, 1977) and
Wind, Y., *Product Policy: Concepts, Methods and Strategy* (Reading, Mass.: Addison-Wesley, 1981).

On the strategic management of innovation, see:
Midgley, D.F., *Innovation and Competitive Marketing Strategy* (London: Croom Helm, 1983).

and on demand/sales forecasting, see:
Wind, Y., Mahajan, V. and Cardozo, R.N. (eds.), *New-Product Forecasting* (Lexington, Mass.: Lexington Books, 1981).

For a general account of new product management which is particularly strong on quantitative analysis, see:
Urban, G.L. and Hauser, J.R., *Design and Marketing of New Products* (Englewood Cliffs, NJ: Prentice-Hall, 1980).

## Part Four: Conclusions

Strategic and organisational issues in which marketing plays a central role are discussed., from varying theoretical and practical standpoints in:
Jelinek, M., *Institutionalising Innovation* (New York: Praeger, 1979); and
Pfeffer, J. and Salancik, G.R., *The External Control of Organisations (New York: Harper and Row, 1978).*

Wider aspects of marketing, innovation and strategy are discussed in:
Baker, M.J. (ed.), *Industrial Innovation* (London: Macmillan, 1979);
Kirzner, I.M. *et al., The Prime Mover of Progress: The Entrepreneur in Capitalism and Socialism* (London: Institute of Economic Affairs, 1980); and
Tushman and Moore (eds.), *Readings in the Management of Innovation.*

Two books which have appeared since the present work went to press deserve close attention. They are:
Baker, M.J., *Market Development* (London: Penguin, 1983) and
Rogers, E.M., *Diffusion of Innovations*, Third Edition (N.Y.: The Free Press, 1983)

# INDEX